THE
TURKS AND CAICOS
GUIDE

A
Cruising Guide
to
The Turks and Caicos Islands
SECOND EDITION

by

Stephen J. Pavlidis

Seaworthy Publications, Inc.
Port Washington, Wisconsin

Published in the USA by Seaworthy Publications, Inc., 215 S. Park St., Suite #1, Port Washington, WI 53074
Phone: 262-268-9250, Fax: 262-268-9208
E-mail: publisher@seaworthy.com
Web pages: www.seaworthy.com

CAUTION: The charts in this publication are intended as supplements for NOAA, DMA, or British Admiralty charts and no warranties are either expressed or implied as to the usability of the information contained herein. The author and publisher take no responsibility for their misuse.

A publication like this is actually the result of a blending of many people's talents, knowledge and experiences. I would like to take this opportunity to thank the following for their help in this effort: Milt and Judy Baker; Capt. Lee Bakewell of the S/V *Winterlude* for his help with programming; Dean Bernal; *Caicos Marina and Shipyard* and manager David Taylor; Judd Clarence; Titus H. DeBoer of the *Bamboo Gallery*; Andy Lowe and Star Droshine of the S/V *Moria*, for their help with the diving sections and areas around Provo; Captain Bob Gascoine of the M/V *Aquanaut,* whose years of experience in these waters made my job that much easier; Ralph Higgs of the *Tourist Board*; a special thanks goes to Carol Hochberg-Holker of the S/V *Alcyone*, for her dedicated editing; Captain Willis Jennings of South Caicos; Chuck and Alexis Kehn of S/V *Caicos Sol* and *Tropic Sol*; *Leeward Marina* and Dockmasters Dwayne and Denver Pratt; Josiah Marvel, Providenciales historian and proponent of the Grand Turk Landfall Theory; Captain David Matthews of the S/V *Tao* whose twenty-plus years of experience here are now available for all to benefit from; Beryl Nelson of *TACRA*; D.J. Piltingsrud; Nicolas Popov of *Island Expeditions School at Sea*; *Scooter Bob's*; Pierre Seymour, Deputy Chief Conservation Officer of the *DECR* in Provo; Jack and Pat Tyler of the S/V *Whoosh*; and Lenny Williams of *Lenny's Photo*. If there is anybody that I have neglected to mention here, rest assured that it is an oversight and I sincerely apologize.

Front cover art: Waves breaking at Mudjin Harbour, Middle Caicos by Dwight Outten.
Back cover art: Locally built fishing sloop on Middle Caicos by Phillip Outten.

Other books by Stephen J. Pavlidis:
A Cruising Guide to the Exuma Cays Land and Sea Park; ISBN 0-9638306
The Exuma Guide 2nd Edition, A Cruising Guide to the Exuma Cays; ISBN 0-9639566-7-1
On and Off the Beaten Path, The Central and Southern Bahamas Guide; ISBN 0-9639566-9-8
The Abaco Guide; ISBN 1-892399-02-4

Library of Congress Cataloging-in-Publication Data

Pavlidis, Stephen J.
The Turks and Caicos guide : a cruising guide to the Turks and Caicos islands / by
Stephen J. Pavlidis.-- 2nd ed.
p. cm.
Includes bibliographical references and index.
ISBN 1-892399-11-3 (alk. paper)
1. Boats and boating--Turks and Caicos Islands--Guidebooks. 2. Boats and
boating--Dominican Republic--Guidebooks. 3. Turks and Caicos Islands--Guidebooks. 4.
Dominican Republic--Guidebooks. I. Title.

GV776.29.T94 P38 2002
917.296'104--dc21

2002070757

THE
TURKS AND CAICOS GUIDE

A Cruising Guide to the Turks and Caicos Islands
SECOND EDITION

Part I

THE CAICOS ISLANDS

Includes
Providenciales, The Caicos Cays, West Caicos, French Cay, North Caicos, Middle Caicos, East Caicos, South Caicos, the Ambergris Cays, and Routes Across the Caicos Bank

Part II

THE TURKS ISLANDS

Includes
Grand Turk, North Creek Anchorage, Hawksnest Anchorage, Salt Cay, and Great Sand Cay

Part III

THE DOMINICAN REPUBLIC

Includes
Luperón and Puerto Plata

by
Stephen J. Pavlidis

Thornless Escape-A Prescription

by
Captain David Matthews, S/V *TAO*

When you've done Stocking Island, up the hill and told your lies at Chat and Chill, checked Peace and Plenty, Two T's in turn, now put Chicken Harbour to the stern.

Northeast Breakers to starboard side, West Plana's fine after this wild ride, barrel sponges, big guys, stories told, best SCUBA in the western world.

Dreaded cold front's on the way, wind's gone south, it's time to say, "Conception Island here we come, your eastern side will be some fun."

Behold a miracle, the sea got smooth, get this wagon in the groove. On to Mayaguana's northwest side, west wind coming, nowhere to hide.

Feeling smug's a wee bit catching wind a' howling, but seas not matching, raise a glass, boats set to go all waiting for Herb's weather window.

Wind and current, the choppy situation, acknowledge Caicos Passage's reputation. But we're smokin' now and doing fine, ticking miles off the ole rhumb line.

Frontal passage does its thing, back of the front has a certain ring. Reefed main and spitfire is our dream, just love that breeze abaft the beam.

Following sea and sails are light, Surf Sellar's cut and hang a right. Customs' coming out and hooks are down, passage complete with nary a frown.

Now we're out where the big boys play, making easting it's safe to say, it sure beats slogging it under power, rum-time soon passing Bird Rock tower.

Marine sunrise, hot water we've got, Tiki Hut breakfast hits the spot. IGA shopping and e-mail that works, welcome to Provo, toast of the Turks!

Shore-leave over, diesel to the top, ready now for the next wee hop. Attwood thirty seems slow to close, motorsailing madness, wind on the nose.

DEDICATION

Andy Lowe,

Star Droshine,

and

Chief

Contents

Part I

Part II

Part III

APPENDICES

Hurricane Tracking Chart and Locator

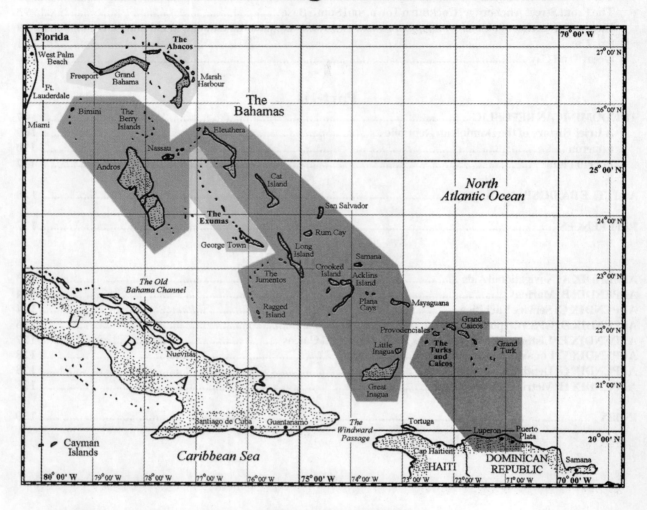

This chart shows the regions covered in the following guides by Steve Pavlidis:

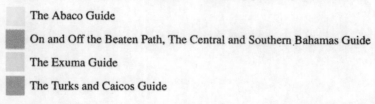

The Abaco Guide

On and Off the Beaten Path, The Central and Southern Bahamas Guide

The Exuma Guide

The Turks and Caicos Guide

The colored boxes above correspond to the outlined regions on the chart. This shows both the area covered by each guide as well as the location of the region covered by each guide in relation to the area as a whole. Using lat/lon information you may be able to plot your location in relation to an approaching hurricane or tropical depression.

INTRODUCTION

There is an ancient bit of wisdom that has been passed down over the centuries about slowing down the maddening pace of one's travels through life long enough to appreciate what life has placed along your path. More commonly called stopping to smell the roses, this sage advice is often a way of life aboard some cruising boats, not all, just some and therein lies a sadness. All too often voyagers rush from one port to another seeing little of what lies between, save sea and sky. Most cruisers will tell you that it is the voyage itself that is important; your ultimate destination will still be there and you will arrive there eventually, at worst, a bit more fulfilled for savoring each and every tiny destination along your route.

The Turks and Caicos Islands are a perfect example of those tiny destinations. Like the lady who is always a bridesmaid and never a bride, the Turks and Caicos Islands are, more often than not, used as a stopover, a place to refuel and get some sleep, perhaps even wait out some weather, for those boaters sailing between the U.S. and the Caribbean. Some older publications have given the Turks and Caicos Islands, and especially Providenciales (usually just called Provo), the thumbs down in some regards for reasons I cannot fathom. Perhaps the authors of these publications were not treated well. Perhaps they had a bad attitude about the Turks and Caicos Islands and could not view the area objectively. That, my friends, is a sin for the author of a cruising guide. We must be objective, impartial. We have a tremendous responsibility that cannot be taken lightly. We must show off the best of the areas we visit, and yet, we cannot blindly ignore the worst. But if we have been treated badly at one time or another, we must hope that it was just a bad day. We must return a few days or weeks later, and see if things have changed. One must spend a lot of time in an area to notice trends, to get the feel for the way of life. Our written word is very often taken for "Bible truth" concerning the areas we write about. That is why I get so angry when I hear cruisers say that "So and so doesn't have anything good to say about Provo!" or "What's his name said that you can't do this or you can't do that there so why stop?" I know immediately that these people did not spend enough time in the Turks and Caicos Islands, that they did not stop to smell the roses, to savor each and every nuance of their aroma, going from flower to flower like a bee in search of droplets of tasty, sweet nectar. Instead they hastily grabbed the bunch and suffered a thorn. One must learn how to handle the thorns and to delight in the fragrant bouquet presented by the delicate petals.

With the help of this book you will learn how to handle the thorns. You will learn that there are several all weather anchorages, even a few good hurricane holes. Boats heading to the Caribbean will learn that you can provision in Provo for less than in Nassau or George Town with some prices being almost equivalent to those in the U.S. You will learn that there are quite a few National Parks where fishing is prohibited, the result is fantastic diving rich in marine life. Fishermen will come to know the Pinnacles and some of the other hot spots for piscatorial action. More important, you will come to understand that there is more to the Turks and Caicos Islands than simply being a rest stop on the superhighway to and from the Caribbean. The Turks and Caicos Islands can be a destination in themselves.

Stephen J. Pavlidis
S/V *IV Play*

A BRIEF HISTORY OF THE TURKS AND CAICOS ISLANDS

The Coat of Arms of the Turks and Caicos.

The Bahamas Platform, of which the Turks and Caicos are a part, was formed approximately 11-25 million years ago during the era known as the Miocene. The platform was created by the shifting of the Earth's plates that created rising land masses in certain areas in a process known as plate tectonics. During the Pleistocene Era, about two million years ago and during the glacial ages, the rise and fall of the sea level segregated the islands of this archipelago. The cays themselves are basically limestone that was laid down as windblown deposits during the Tertiary, approximately 1 to 2 million years ago. Most of the current aspect of The Turks and Caicos Islands has been produced in geologically recent times by coral formation during the four glacial and interglacial epochs. The Cays themselves are generally flat with few hills over a hundred feet high. The external limestone is worn razor sharp by the action of wind and wave and several of the cays are honeycombed with caves and cave holes.

The first inhabitants of the Turks and Caicos Islands of which there is any record of were the Tainos. The Tainos were in fact Arawakan in origin and originated in South America where their descendants are still to be found in parts of Venezuela and the Guianas. They colonized the Caribbean in dugout canoes, a specimen of which in Jamaica was 96' long with an 8' beam and may have carried as many as 150 rowers.

The relatively peaceful Tainos, although they were brave warriors, were forced to keep on the move by the presence of the far fiercer Caribs. The Caribs were a cannabilistic group whose chief purpose seemed to be murdering the Arawakan men and enslaving their women. They would castrate the young Tainos and fatten them up with rich diets and prevent them from engaging in any form of labor to ensure tender flesh. The Carib religion promised a paradise for the courageous warrior wherein the Arawaks he killed would serve him as slaves while assuring the coward that he would be doomed to a hell wherein he would eternally serve a Taino master. A handful of Caribs survive to this day in Dominica though even less is known of their early culture than the Arawakans.

In their search for peace, the Tainos pushed their canoes northward into the Caribbean, reaching Hispaniola around 200 A.D. and then settling in Cuba and Jamaica over the next two hundred years. They reached the Turks and Caicos and The Bahamas sometime around 700-900 A.D. in the last wave of their migration. Here they became known as *luddu-cairi* or *lukokayo,* meaning *island people*. We know them today as the Lucayans.

The Caribs were never far behind the Lucayans. By the time Columbus reached the New World, the Caribs had conquered the Lesser Antilles and were raiding Puerto Rico and Hispaniola. Columbus noted scars on the bodies of some of the Lucayans and through sign language was told that people on neighboring islands wanted to capture them and that they had defended themselves.

The Lucayans built circular, conical houses of wood and thatch and survived on conch, fish, native game and plants. They were basket makers and were adept at manufacturing polished stone implements. Lucayan pottery is called palmettoware and was tempered with bits of conch shell to improve the quality. Lucayan pottery has turned up at several archeological sites throughout the Caicos Islands starting with the de Booy digs of 1912. Unfortunately, most of these early finds were removed from the country or simply turned up missing. With the exception of some small gold decorations, the Lucayans had no knowledge of the use of metal. They slept in hammocks, a habit Spanish seamen soon picked up. There seems to have been some commerce between the Lucayans on Middle Caicos and their Taino cousins in Cuba and Hispaniola.

The Lucayans were a handsome people, almost oriental in appearance, with broad faces and foreheads flattened in infancy by tying them to boards. This practice was designed to add distinction to their appearance as well as hardening the bone as protection against blows. Mayans and Egyptians shared this unique custom at one time, as did an Indian tribe in Montana called the Flatheads. Lucayans wore their coarse hair in bangs in the front and long in the back. For the most part they wore no clothing, although they painted their faces and sometimes their entire bodies with red, black and white pigments.

They decorated themselves with tattoos, necklaces, bracelets, bones, and feathers. Their chiefs, or *caciques*, were allowed to practice polygamy and served as chief, judge, and priest in their culture. The Lucayans had a class structure and the caciques enjoyed all the benefits afforded to their position. The cacique's canoe was the only one that was painted; when traveling by land, they were borne on litters while their children were carried on the shoulders of their servants. After death, the cacique was buried along with sufficient supplies for the journey to *Coyaba* along with one or two of his favorite wives.

The Lucayans were lovers of peace and simple pleasures with a gentle and generous nature, sharing anything they had with Columbus and his men. Next to singing and dancing, the Lucayans loved *batos*, an organized ball game similar to volleyball and soccer. The remains of a Lucayan ball court were found on the island of Middle Caicos. Ball courts have been found in Puerto Rico and points farther south but never this far north.

Though they had no written language, their spoken language was described as "soft and not less liquid than Latin." Some 20 Lucayan words and their derivatives survive to this day. Avocado, barbecue, canoe, Carib, cannibal, cassava, cay, guava, hammock, hurricane, iguana, maize, manatee, pirogue, potato, and tobacco all are Lucayan in origin.

It was the Lucayans who taught Columbus' crew their custom of smoking the *cohiba* plant in their strange y-shaped pipes called *tobacco*. The tubes of the "Y" were inserted in their nostrils and the smoke inhaled until the smoker fell into a stupor. The Spaniards quickly picked up this habit although they did not inhale to the point of intoxication. Although Columbus never reported seeing the Lucayans smoke, he described a leaf that he found a Lucayan carrying in his canoe as being highly valued by the Lucayans.

The Spaniards originally thought the Lucayans had no religion, leading Columbus to believe that they would readily become Christians. They actually had a highly developed religion with two supreme beings, a male and a female, and a belief in an afterlife. They also believed in numerous spirit beings called *zemis* who lived in sacred trees, carved images, and in the relics of the dead. The zemis had to be appeased with great festivals in their honor. To induce visions of the future, the Lucayans ground into a powder a potent narcotic called *yopo* that they then snorted up the nostrils. A similar drug is still in use by Amerindians in Venezuela to this day (I'll give you three guesses as to what drug it is!). A Lucayan chief, while under the influence of *yopo*, foresaw the destruction of his civilization by ". . . strange blonde men in winged canoes."

The discovery of the New World by Columbus (who had red hair) in 1492, sounded the death knell for the Lucayan civilization. Columbus brought back seven Lucayan captives in chains, but two escaped en-route, some say on Providenciales. One returned to Europe with Columbus and was baptized at the Cathedral of Barcelona with the King and Queen of Spain standing as godparents. He took the name of Diego Colón and returned with Columbus to the New World in the fall of 1493, where he served as Columbus' interpreter.

It was not long before King Ferdinand of Spain authorized raiding parties to the "useless islands." The Spaniards made some 500 journeys to the islands of The Bahamas and the Turks and Caicos to enslave the Lucayans for their mines and plantations in Cuba and Hispaniola. By 1513, within one generation, no Lucayans were estimated to be left in the Turks and Caicos Islands. The Spanish historian Herrera tells us that when Ponce de León arrived in Grand Turk in late 1512, he could only find one Lucayan to assist him in his search for the Fountain of Youth on Bimini. Maps of that period show Grand Turk called "Del Viejo" or "Old Man." By contrast, in 1517 there were an estimated 20,000-40,000 Lucayans in The Bahamas and their price fluctuated at about 4 gold pesos each. The asking price skyrocketed to 150 gold pesos each for these excellent divers when rich pearl beds were discovered off Venezuela and Trinidad. The Spaniards played upon an Arawak superstition and enticed many Lucayans to board ships with promises of returning them to South America, their ancient homeland and the place where their souls would go when they died, Coyaba. Many Lucayans did not go willingly, choosing instead to fight the heavily armed Spaniards. Others, even mothers with small children, committed suicide by drinking the juice of the cassava plant to avoid a life of wretchedness at the hands of the cruel Spaniards. The rest died of starvation and ill treatment while in bondage and only a very few lived to old age. By the early 1520's, this peaceful, innocent civilization, that had lived only to satisfy nature without all the trappings of laws and governments, was obliterated from the face of the earth and sadly reduced to a footnote in history.

After the time of the Lucayans, the Turks and Caicos had few visitors save a few Spanish ships stopping in the Turks Islands for salt. The first Englishman to make mention of the island group was Captain John Hawkins of Plymouth, a privateer who passed by the Caicos group in 1564 in search of salt. The islands re-entered history in the middle of the 17th Century when salt rakers from Bermuda decided to use three of the Turks Islands for an entrepreneurial venture. In the 1640's they created salt ponds on Salt Cay, Grand Turk, and South Caicos, and their endeavor was successful enough to create the basis for the local economy for the next two centuries. Even today, some consider the fine, white Turk's Island salt the preferred preservative and seasoning. From about 1678 onwards, Bermudian salt rakers of British descent were populating the islands, at first only in the dry season, and later on, living on the islands full time. They immediately set out to destroy all the trees, seeking to increase salt production.

At first the salt rakers collected salt for their own use, but as their commodity increased in value it became the backbone of the Bermudian economy for over 100 years. Settlers on these islands during this time lived primarily on their salt production, fishing, and wrecking. While The Bahamas severed its ties with Bermuda in 1663, the salt rakers in the Turks and Caicos continued to maintain a link with the island. Several petitions were submitted to Parliament to annex these islands to Bermuda but all were turned down.

As Spanish shipping activity increased in the New World, the era of privateering began. Spanish ships laden with the riches of the New World would pass through the waters of the Turks and Caicos and The Bahamas on their way back to Spain making wrecking very profitable in these waters. It was said that if a crewman were lucky enough to survive the wreck, it was uncertain as to whether he would survive the wreckers. If the Spanish knew of the location of their wrecks they would send crews to salvage the valuables. Bahamian and Turks Island wreckers would drive off the intruders and loot what they had salvaged. As Captains became wise to the ways of the wreckers, wrecks became fewer and fewer, the privateers had to find other uses for their talents. This was not difficult, the era of the buccaneers was in full swing.

The original buccaneers (*boucaniers*), the forerunners of the pirates, were based just south of the Turks and Caicos Islands in northern Hispaniola. They were a wild group of men from France, Holland, and England, indentured servants, seafarers, and adventurers. They wore colorful, picturesque garb and hunted the semi-wild cattle and pigs on the island, descendents of escapees from Spanish farms. They roasted the meat over fires called *boucans* and would sell this smoked meat product, along with hides and tallow, to passing ships. Hispaniola soon became the location of a huge illicit meat and hides trade. The boucaniers quickly learned to live less off hunting and to rely more on their commerce with Spanish ships, first in canoes, then "acquiring" ships, and finally in small flotillas.

From 1629 to 1641, English buccaneers were organized as a company, using the island of Providence off the Nicaraguan coast as a base. The 1630's were a prosperous era for the Providence based buccaneers. Their prosperity ended abruptly in 1641, when the Spanish invaded the island and massacred every settler they could find. The few who escaped shifted their base of operations to Tortuga, an island off the northern coast of Hispaniola just south of the Turks and Caicos Islands. Recruits from every European trading nation began to pour in. By the middle 1600's the buccaneers formed armed bands who were accustomed to hardship, had strong codes of honor that they chose to live by, and were extremely well led. For over 75 years these buccaneers were the scourge of the Spanish fleet. In the 1640's a buccaneer from Normandy who called himself Pierre Le Grand, often called the "Father of Piracy in the West Indies," boldly captured a Spanish galleon in the passage between Tortuga and the Caicos Bank while her crew slept. He is believed to be the only pirate to have ever taken a galleon. After Le Grand, and 28 men divvied up their spoils, they sailed away and retired from the sea. Le Grand was said to have lived happily to a ripe old age.

Most prominent of the buccaneers were Edward Mansfield and the legendary Sir Henry Morgan. In 1664, Mansfield and Morgan set up a base in Nassau and were received quite favorably. Nassau came to be quite the haven for the wandering buccaneers. Mansfield's early and untimely death created confusion in the leadership of the buccaneers and Morgan set them off on a course of plunder and profit. The years between 1671 and 1686 were a time of buccaneer ascendancy as the buccaneers gained major European finance against the Spanish Empire. After the capture of Jamaica in 1655, Port Royal, just outside of Kingston, became the headquarters for English buccaneers and remained so for 20 years. Under Sir Thomas Modyford and Sir Henry Morgan their achievements reached a climax. The Treaty of Madrid with Spain in 1670, the death of Sir Henry Morgan in 1688, and finally the destruction by earthquake of Port Royal in 1692 dispersed these Jamaican-based buccaneers.

There is no fine line as to when the buccaneers became pirates. Webster's dictionary offers little difference between the two. History suggests that the code of honor of the early buccaneers was forgotten and the bands degenerated into piracy. The buccaneers had articles called *chasseparties* that allocated duties, rewards, and compensations. In all things, their brotherhood was expected to observe a rigid code of honor called *la coutume de la côte*, which roughly translated means, *the custom of the coast*. Despite their code and the chasseparties, the English and French buccaneers were always quarrelling. The number of English buccaneers at Tortuga having to rely on French protection increased year by year. The Jamaica and Carolina legislatures passed severe acts against them and the buccaneers became less and less particular about their prey. By 1685 their own people were even calling them pirates. Whatever unity there was between the British and French buccaneers dissolved when their two countries went to war after William of Orange ascended the English Throne in 1689. This struggle was to last 126 years with only one long break. Loyal English were no longer welcome in Hispaniola and when the Anglo-French fighting reached the Caribbean in 1691, the last of the English pirates left the safety of Tortuga and settled in areas of The Bahamas and the Turks and Caicos. Most of their activity was centered in the Nassau area but roaming pirates are said to have consistently used areas such as Parrot Cay, French Cay, and Grand Turk as bases from which to stage raids. By 1713, there were an estimated 1,000 active pirates operating in the waters of The Bahamas and the Turks and Caicos. One interesting theory about how the Turks Islands received their name suggests that in the 16th and 17th centuries, under the leadership of the two Barbarosa brothers, a band of Barbary pirates operated out of these waters. Originating in Constantinople, the brothers eventually settled on an uninhabited salt island that the Spanish later referred to as Grand Turk.

Some of the most notorious pirates to be found in the pages of history have been reported as lurking in Turks and Caicos waters over the years. Mary Read and Anne Bonney, the "lady" pirates who sailed with Calico Jack Rackham, Stede Bonnet the Gentleman Pirate, Benjamin Hornigold, Charles Vane, Captain Kidd, L'Olonnois, and Edward Teach who was much better known as Blackbeard. If any one pirate could embody the spirit of the era and of piracy itself, none would be better suited for it than Blackbeard. From 1713 until 1716, he teamed up with Benjamin Hornigold and was based in Nassau along with Captains Jennings, Burgess, and White. Blackbeard's independent pirate career lasted only two short years, from 1716, when he acquired his first ship, the *Queen Anne's Revenge*, until his death in the Carolinas in 1718.

Jean-David Rau, who named himself L'Olonnois after his birthplace in les Sables D'Olonne in Brittany, was one of the old guard, one of the last of the original *boucaniers* of Tortuga, and one of the most ruthless psychopathic pirates in history. He is said to have used French Cay, just south of Providenciales, as a hideout to wait on Spanish vessels heading northward through the Windward Passage. Recently the gentleman who started that rumor has withdrawn his original statement though it is possible that L'Olonnois actually might have stayed there. Such a reputation did he create for himself that Spanish sailors would rather die fighting or drowning than to fall into his hands. If a captive would not tell L'Olonnois what he wished to know, L'Olonnois would often cut him to pieces and pull out his tongue. He had been known to hack a man to pieces one slice at a time, first a finger, then a hand, then an arm, until there was nothing left to remove, or the poor fellow died. He also practiced *"woolding,"* that is, tying a piece of rope around a man's head and twisting it tighter and tighter with a stick until his eyes popped out. L'Olonnois was the scourge of Central and South America from the Yucatan to Venezuela. His most famous torment involved a Spanish crew that remained silent. L'Olonnois ripped open one man's chest and began to gnaw on his still beating heart telling the rest of his hostages "I will serve you alike if you do not show me another way." L'Olonnois met a fitting end. After an engagement with a Spanish flotilla that nearly decimated his band of buccaneers, he and some of his crew took to land working their way into the jungles of the Central and Southern America. Here cannibals made a meal of him and all but five of his surviving crew.

A stranger piratical trio than Calico Jack Rackham, Anne Bonney, and Mary Read would be hard to find. Anne Bonney and her penniless sailor husband moved to Nassau seeking employment. There she meet Calico Jack Rackham who soon swept her off her feet. She eloped with Rackham, heading off to sea in men's clothes. Calico Jack put her ashore with friends in Jamaica when she became pregnant until such time as she gave birth and could rejoin him. She later accompanied Rackham on all his later exploits. Mary Read, raised as a boy by her grandmother, joined an army unit as a cadet and fought bravely. She fell in love and eventually married another soldier, who at first did not realize that she was a woman. After her husband died she again dressed up as a man and went on board a vessel bound for the West Indies. She soon joined up with a band of privateers under Woodes Rogers on the island of Providence. Mary Read claimed she detested the life of the pirate; however, when some of the crew mutinied and returned to their former lifestyle, with them went Mary Read. She wound up on board Calico Jack's ship and no one had guessed she was a woman. And then along came Anne Bonney. Bonney thought Read was a rather handsome fellow and became enamored of her, forcing her to reveal her secret. Jealous Calico Jack, noticed the partiality Bonney was showing to Read and threatened to shoot him/her. Once again her secret was revealed. Mary Read later fell in love with another crewmember and revealed herself to him. When her lover fell into a disagreement with another crewmember and the two were to duel ashore in two hours, Read found out and engaged the crewmember in an argument and promptly killed him.

In 1719, Calico Jack was finally captured and removed from his ship. During the battle Anne Bonney, Mary Read, and one other crewmember were the last fighters on deck, the rest of the crew fleeing below. Mary Read tried in vain to rouse the crew, finally killing one and wounding another before the lady buccaneers were captured. Rackham, who at this point was estranged from his mate, had taken to enjoying a bush hallucinogen and was removed from his below decks hiding place in a stupor. In court, when asked how they pled, Mary Read and Anne Bonney promptly announced, "My Lord, we plead our bellies!" Both women were pregnant and English law at the time forbade hanging a mother-to-be, no matter how serious her crime. Mary Read later became ill and died in prison, thereby cheating the hangman. Anne Bonney, through the intercession of some notable Jamaican planters, escaped the noose and was never executed. Calico Jack, while awaiting execution, was allowed a brief visit from Anne Bonney. Instead of consoling Rackham, she only told him that she was sorry to see him here and that if he had fought like a man he would not have to die like a dog. Anne Bonney wound up in Virginia, married with children. Parrot Cay is said to be a corruption of Pirate Cay and one of Rackham, Bonney's, and Read's favorite hideouts. Legend also had it that in 1850, the English Captain Delaney recovered over $130,000 in pirate loot from Sand Cay.

When Woodes Rogers began to break up the pirate presence in The Bahamas, fewer and fewer brethren of the coast visited the nearby Turks and Caicos Islands. Some privateering and wrecking continued through the remainder of the 18th and into the 19th centuries. Details of this era are sketchy at best, but it is known that in 1725 Grand Turk was seasonally occupied by upwards of 1,000 laborers raking salt, fishing for turtles, and wrecking.

Spain occupied the Turks Islands in 1710, even as the salt rakers prospered. France claimed the Turks and Caicos Islands in 1753, and erected wooden columns on them bearing her coat of arms. The crew of a British vessel from Charleston, Carolina, destroyed these columns the following year. France later occupied Grand Turk and Salt Cay from 1778 to 1783 as the salt rakers continued their flourishing enterprise. During the American Revolution, Bermudian Salt Rakers ignored the British blockade and shipped salt to Washington's armies.

In 1766, in spite of the Bermudian's objections, the Bahamas Government extended its jurisdiction to the Turks and Caicos Islands, while on the North American continent a rebellion was brewing. The Stamp Act of 1765 was the beginning of the end of British rule in the colonies. The American Revolution was getting underway and it was as much a revolt as it was a civil war. An estimated 20% of the population of the colonies was fiercely loyal to the Crown and hostile to the American cause.

Known as Tories, the Loyalists favored reconciliation with the Crown. Many stood to lose jobs, commerce, or prestige if the upstart rebels were victorious. Many Loyalists suffered greatly at the hands of the Patriots. Some were socially ostracized and their business boycotted; others who refused to sign loyalty oaths to the rebellion were accused of treason and often had all their land and possessions confiscated. Still more were tarred and feathered in the name of Patriotism. Many Loyalists were sent to the notorious Simsburg Copper Mines in Connecticut. They worked in holes 150' below the surface and so many died there that the mine was known as the "Catacombs of Loyalty." The Patriots became even more hostile and vengeful after the defeat of Cornwallis at Yorktown in 1781. Many Loyalists sought refuge in eastern Florida, as Florida was not involved in the American Revolution.

In 1783, just before the end of the American Revolution, a French contingent seized the Turks Islands. They successfully repelled a counter attack by the Captain of the *H.M.S. Albermarle*, the young Horatio Nelson. The French had little influence on the islands and the Treaty Of Versailles finally restored control of the islands to Great Britain. The Treaty of Versailles on January 20, 1783 restored The Bahamas and the Turks and Caicos to England and gave Florida to Spain. The Loyalists in Florida felt cheated that Florida was being traded for The Bahamas and were irate at having to move again. No longer feeling safe in the colonies, the Loyalists looked elsewhere for safe haven.

Most of the Loyalists that arrived in the Turks and Caicos had holdings in the South Carolina and Georgia area. Probably the best known of these Loyalists was Wade Stubbs, who emigrated from Gasworth in England's County Cheshire to East Florida, near St. Augustine between 1775 and 1778. When the Loyalists fled the mainland, the Crown granted 72 of them approximately 18,000 acres on North and Middle Caicos. Stubbs received 860 acres, the second largest of the 332 grants given, fashioned from the 10,090 acres on North Caicos. He initially called his plantation "Bellefield." In 1790, Wade Stubbs convinced his brother Thomas to leave Cheshire and join him. Thomas built a plantation called Cheshire Hall on Blue Caicos, what is today known as Providenciales.

Thomas Stubbs started out growing Anguilla or long staple Sea Island cotton. Anguilla cotton grew to the size of small, bushy trees and produced a high quality cotton. Many of these plants still survive today in the bush on North and Middle Caicos. For several years the plantations flourished and were producing large yields; land values soared from £9,450 for a tract to over £70,000 per tract. Soon yields began getting smaller and smaller. The problems in production came from removing the sticky seeds from the cotton bolls, the chenille bugs that devoured the sweet leaves, and the fact that cotton quickly strips the soil of nutrients mandating long fallow periods of manuring to maintain yields. Eli Whitney's cotton gin solved the first problem in 1793, but the other two problems caused the downfall of the cotton business in the Turks and Caicos Islands. Also, a devastating hurricane in 1813 added to the abandonment of the plantations. Thomas Stubbs' Cheshire Hall cotton plantation was hit harder than most by the chenille bug and fertilization problems, and in 1810 he sold Cheshire Hall.

In 1791, Wade Stubbs was named a Justice of the Peace and as the years went by, added to his holdings of land and slaves, he was quite the Loyalist success story. He had purchased plantations from other Loyalists who were deserting them and had so much land that he could leave vast tracts of land to fallow as yields fell. He purchased the Haulover Plantation on Middle Caicos after the original owners left. Cotton on that estate was still being raised within the memory of people still living today. Stubbs success was in part due to the fact that he raised enough stock to supply his fields with manure. So successful and important was this cotton trade that after the independence of Haiti in 1799, the British government built Fort George on a small cay just southwest of North Caicos to protect the cotton industry.

In 1800, 14 of Wade Stubbs' slaves stole one of his sloops and escaped. After 1806, Stubbs referred to Bellefield as Wade's Green, a name indicating his affection for the land and his prosperity. Wade Stubbs died in 1822, and was buried in a stone crypt behind St. Thomas' Church on Grand Turk. At the time of his death Wade Stubbs owned over 3,000 acres on North Caicos, 5,000 acres on Providenciales, and even more land on Middle Caicos, including Haulover. He had 384 slaves, all but 8 of whom were in the Caicos Islands. Some of his estate went to his nephew Henshell Stubbs, a Grand Turk salt producer, but most went to his namesake cousin, another Wade Stubbs, who continued living at Wade's Green until about 1850. After emancipation in 1833, the Stubbs slaves, some farming and some working in salt in the Turks, were freed and the plantations came to disrepair and disuse. In 1882, the government of the Turks and Caicos Islands purchased 1,800 acres of Wade's Green for division into 25-acre parcels to encourage farming. In 1885, the Stubbs house was refurbished as a combination courthouse, jail, and quarters for a magistrate who was posted there to stimulate the faltering settlement.

Between the years of 1827 and 1847, a salt tax was producing a quarter of the revenue of The Bahamas and Turks islanders were indignant. None of the money they paid in taxes was going to help their islands, and the price of salt dropped considerably though the Salt Tax stayed the same. Though they were represented in Nassau, the distance and travel time involved limited the time a representative actually sat in Assembly. Although a mailboat reached Long Cay once a month and Grand Turk only four times a year, the only Bahamians they ever saw were tax collectors. Several boats bound for Jamaica passed through on a regular basis however, and the Turks islanders grew to feel more kinship with Kingston than with Nassau.

After continuing complaints to the Crown, an investigation was in order. The Governor of The Bahamas, George B. Matthew, made a perilous 18-day voyage from Nassau to Grand Turk which convinced him of the difficulties in transportation, communication, and life in general on these harsh islands. Separation was recommended. In 1848, the Turks and Caicos Islands were granted a separate charter providing for internal self-government subject to the Governor of Jamaica, a more pleasing proposition for the Turks islanders than continuing Bahamian rule.

The next few years were marked by prosperity in the salt business and the new government seemed to be working well. Then, in the evening of September 30, 1866, a devastating hurricane hit Grand Turk. By morning 63 were dead, over 750 homes destroyed, and more than a million bushels of salt were washed away. The country and its economy were literally left in ruins and the salt market became depressed in the ensuing years. In 1872, the islanders petitioned Queen Victoria to annex the Turks and Caicos Islands to Jamaica, which she did in 1873.

Over the following years the Turks and Caicos islanders continued to run their own affairs to a large extent. Unfortunately, Jamaican rule became no more popular than the preceding Bahamian rule. In reality, little was gained in the islands by their bond to Jamaica. When Jamaica became independent in 1962, the people of the Turks and Caicos Islands overwhelmingly wished to become a British Crown Colony. They got their wish. Also in 1962, John Glenn, after his famous space flight, first set foot back on planet Earth at Grand Turk.

Today the islands enjoy autonomous internal rule although the Governor is appointed by the Queen. Since undergoing massive economic development from 1967, the Turks and Caicos Islands have emerged as a world-class tourism destination and a major offshore financial center.

In 1976, the first constitution was granted to the islands creating a ministerial form of government. The present constitution did not come into being until March 4, 1988. The Turks and Caicos Islands are a parliamentary democracy implementing the traditional Westminster model. The government consists of a governor, appointed by the Crown, who acts as the Queen's representative and is responsible for internal security, external affairs, defense, and certain judicial matters. The Legislative Council (LegCo) consists of 13 elected members serving four-year terms, three appointed members, a Speaker who is selected from outside or from the elected or appointed members who are not Executive Council (ExCo) members. The Executive Council, which is responsible for the day-to-day business of government, consists of the Governor, Attorney General, Chief Secretary, Financial Secretary, and the Chief Minister and his cabinet of four appointed ministers selected from the elected members of the Legislative Council. The Turks and Caicos Islands have a well-developed judicial system administered by a magistrate and by the resident Chief Justice of the Supreme Court. Presently there are four political parties: The People's National Party (PNP), the People's Democratic Movement (PDM), the Turks and Caicos United Party (TCUP), and the National Democratic Alliance (NDA).

In recent decades many Turks and Caicos islanders left their homes to find work in The Bahamas leaving huge gaps in the work force at home which are quite often filled by workers from Haiti and the Dominican Republic. With the huge tourism boom on Providenciales, this is slowly changing, as more and more native sons and daughters are finding adequate employment in their homeland. The tourism boom is increasing steadily with each passing year; one can only foresee prosperous times ahead for the Turks and Caicos islanders.

Participants in the Provo Regatta.

Photos Courtesy of Nicolas Popov

THE BASICS

ANCHORING

Just as important as getting your vessel moving and keeping her heading along your chosen courseline quickly and efficiently is the fine art of keeping your vessel from moving. One benefit of cruising the Turks and Caicos Islands is the abundance of dive boat moorings. Any skipper approaching a landfall such as West Caicos, or the northern shore of Providenciales, can pick up a white-ball dive mooring overnight. These moorings are rated for vessels to 60' and must be vacated the next day so that the local dive boats can use them. For the most part, these are very safe moorings that are constantly checked and maintained by the dive boat operators. If you have any doubts contact one of the dive operations listed in this guide on VHF ch. 68. Do not pick up any moorings off Long Cay in the Caicos Islands and Sand Cay in the Turks, they are for smaller vessels.

Anchor choice is basically a personal preference. Some skippers prefer CQRs, while others swear by a Bruce or a Danforth. Of the "Big Three," you will find that a Danforth holds as well or better than a CQR or Bruce in sandy bottoms while the CQR or Bruce is preferred when anchoring in rocky bottoms. Whatever your choice of anchor, you must deploy your anchor correctly and with sufficient scope to hold you when the tide changes, if a front approaches, or if a squall should blow through at 2:00am (which seems to be the time they choose to blow through). Your anchor should have a length of chain (at least 15') shackled to your anchor to keep your rode from chafing against coral or rocks and to create a catenary curve that helps absorb shock loads while lowering the angle of pull on your anchor. Too high an angle may cause your anchor to pull up and out of the bottom. Some cruisers prefer all chain rodes with a nylon snubber to absorb the shock loads. This is an excellent arrangement, but a windlass may be needed unless you prefer the workout involved with hauling in the chain and anchor every time you move.

In many of the lee side anchorages in the Turks and Caicos you will find that you can lie quite comfortably to only one anchor. When setting your anchor, do not just drop it and let your rode run out, piling itself on top of your anchor. Lower your anchor to the bottom and deploy the rode as you fall back with the current or wind until you have a 7:1 scope out. When calculating the amount of scope required, be sure to allow for high tide as well as the height of your anchor roller or fairlead above the water. Without being precise, you can figure on a 2'-3½' tidal rise in The Turks and Caicos although occasionally you may find a 4' rise such as during spring tides, a little more during a full moon and a little less at new moon. When you have secured your rode, back down with the engine at about ½ throttle to set the anchor. If you have not succeeded in securing your anchor, try again. To check the set it is best to dive on your anchor(s) or at the very least, look at their set through a glass bottom bucket from your dinghy. You may find that you will have to set them by hand, especially in rocky areas.

Many of the anchorages in this book are swept by swift tidal currents, sometimes up to 2.5 knots. To avoid bumping into your neighbor in the middle of the night or putting your vessel on the rocks or a beach, two anchors, such as in a Bahamian moor, are required. Although one anchor may be fine if you have the swinging room, when the tide changes it may pull out and fail to reset. Sometimes these anchorages can be crowded and while you may swing wide on your one anchor and not find yourself endangered by the rocks or the beach, you and your neighbor may go bump in the night because his two anchors have kept him in one spot. If unsure, the best thing to do is follow the lead of those boats that are there before you. Conversely, if you arrive at an anchorage and everyone is on one anchor and you choose to set two, do so outside the swing radius of the other boats. If you are riding on one anchor and find that you are lying to the wind but that the swell is rolling you, position another anchor at an angle off the stern so as to align your bow into the swell making for a more comfortable night. A better idea is to set a bridle: run a line from your anchor rode at least half your waterline length from your bow and lead it back to a winch through a block near your stern. You can then winch in the line to change the angle your boat lies to the swells.

To set a Bahamian moor you must first decide where you wish for your vessel to settle. You will lay out two anchors, one up-current and one down-current of that spot, which will keep you swinging in a small circle. Head into the current to where you will drop your first anchor and set it properly. Let out as much rode as you need, setting your anchor on the way by snubbing it, until you are at the spot where you are to drop your down-current anchor. If the wind has pushed you to one side or the other of the tidal stream, you will have to power up to the position where you will set your second anchor. Lower your second anchor and pull your vessel back up-current on your first rode, paying out the rode for the second anchor and snubbing it as you maneuver back up-current to your chosen spot. You may want to dive on your anchors to check their set. Keeping your rodes tight will keep you swinging in a tighter circle. Check your anchor rodes daily as they will twist together and make it extremely difficult to undo them in an emergency. You can also set your up-current anchor and settle back to where you wish to lie, and then dinghy your second anchor out down-current. The only problem with this is that you must make sure your down-current anchor has set well before the tide changes.

In some tight anchorages you will be unable to set your anchors 180° apart. An alternative is to set them 90° apart in a "Y" configuration perpendicular to the wind. A skipper with a large swing radius in very tight quarters is apt to find out what his neighbors think of his anchoring technique as soon as the wind shifts. Responsible anchoring cannot be overstressed.

Always set an anchor light. Some cruisers feel this is unimportant in some of the more isolated anchorages. What they probably do not understand is that many locals run these islands at all hours of the night, even on moonless nights, and an anchor light protects your vessel as well as theirs.

It is important to note that the lee-side anchorages, can get rolly at times. The Atlantic Ocean surge seeks out any way it can to round the tips of these islands to cause you seemingly no end of discomfort and there is not much you can do about it, except possibly use a second anchor or bridle arrangement to keep your bow or stern into the swell. Anchorages on the eastern shores of the Turks and Caicos Islands are all daytime anchorages only, due to the prevailing winds and should be used only in settled or westerly weather.

Never anchor in coral, even with your dinghy anchor. An anchor can do a great deal of damage to a very fragile ecosystem that will take years to recover if it is to recover at all. Besides, sand holds so much better.

In summer months and on into the early fall, or when there is no wind, you may wish to anchor a good distance from shore to keep away from the relentless biting insects. Cays with a lot of vegetation or mangroves will have a higher concentration of biting insects.

Proper anchoring etiquette should by practiced at all times. For instance, if the anchorage is wide and roomy and only one boat is at anchor, don't anchor right on top of them; give your neighbor a little breathing room and some solitude. You would probably appreciate the same consideration should the situation be reversed. All too often cruisers exhibit a herding instinct where they seek the comfort of other nearby cruisers, anchoring much too close at times. Many boaters, after a long, hard day in rough seas or bad weather, anxiously await the peace and tranquillity of a calm anchorage. The last thing they want is noise and wake. If you have a dog aboard that loves to bark, be considerate of your neighbors who don't wish to hear him. They do have that right. Jet skis can be a lot of fun, but only when you're astride one. Many cruisers have little tolerance for the incessant buzzing back and forth of high-speed jet skis. It is a good show of manners to slowly leave the anchorage and go to where you can have your high-speed fun and games and not disturb anyone. If at all possible, try not to run your generators at sunset or after dark. At sunset, many cruisers are sitting in their cockpits enjoying cocktails and watching the sun go down and don't want a generator disturbing their soft conversations. Many powerboats use a lot of electricity by running all sorts of lights at night. Some will leave on huge floodlights for one reason or another with no idea of the amount of glare and light it produces in nearby cockpits to other boaters. This is not an incrimination of all powerboaters, only the careless few. The vast majority of powerboaters are very considerate and professional and do not approve of their noisy, blinding, cousins. Courtesy shown is usually courtesy returned.

CHARTERING

There are quite a few companies and individuals running charters in the Turks and Caicos Islands, mostly based in *Leeward Marina*. There are several day-sailing charter boats that offer snorkeling, diving, and sunset sails. Captain Dave Matthews' 50' trimaran *TAO* (946-4783) has been cruising these waters for over twenty years and specializes in day and term charters. For day sailing try *Sail Provo* (946-4783), *Beluga* (946-4396), and the trimaran *Minx* (946-5512).

Students wishing to do research in the Turks and Caicos, should contact Nicolas and Dragan Popov of *Island Expeditions School at Sea* at P.O. Box CB11934, Love Beach #4C, Nassau, N.P., The Bahamas, 242-327-8659. *Island Expeditions* has several sailing trips each year through the Exumas, the southern Bahamas, and the Turks and Caicos on the way to the Silver Banks as part of a humpback whale study program.

CHARTS

The best charts that you can buy for the Turks and Caicos Islands, besides the ones in this publication, are *TC-001* and *TC-002*, by Captain Bob Gascoine, (*Wavey Line Productions*). Bob, the dean of Turks Islands divers, has done a remarkable job and created some truly accurate and reliable charts that also show all the major dive sites along the shores of the Turks and Caicos Islands. His charts go into a little more detail than I endeavour in the area of the Caicos Bank where he shows the *Damn Fool Channel* route, a small boat or shallow draft route through an incredibly beautiful area that I do not cover for the simple reason that the vast majority of cruising boats are restricted from entry by their draft. Captain Gascoine also has a new chart out for Hispaniola.

CLOTHING

If you are heading to the Turks and Caicos you will enter a tropical climate where the theme for clothing is light. You will most likely live in shorts and T-shirts (if that much). Long pants and sturdy, comfortable shoes are preferred when hiking, for protection from the bush and the rugged terrain. Long sleeved shirts (or old cotton pajamas) and wide brimmed hats are important in keeping the sun off you. Polarized sunglasses (essential for piloting) and suntan lotion (suntan oil tends to leave a long lasting greasy smear all over everything) should be included in your gear. In winter months it is advisable to bring something warm to wear, especially in the evenings. Long pants and sweaters are usually adequate and a light jacket would be a good idea, some frontal passages will occasionally drop the temperature to 60° F.

In the Turks and Caicos Islands, as in The Bahamas, beachwear is not acceptable in town. Men should wear shirts and women should not wear bathing suits except when on the beach, at a pool, or a beach side bar.

CURRENCY

The legally acceptable currency of the Turks and Caicos is the American dollar. The treasury also issues a Turks and Caicos crown and quarter. If you are arriving in the Turks and Caicos from The Bahamas you will want to cash in your Bahamian money in The Bahamas prior to your arrival at Provo. The banks in the Turks and Caicos will not accept Bahamian money and you'll be stuck with it unless you find a cruiser heading north. Traveler's checks are accepted almost everywhere and many places, including some grocery stores, take major credit cards. If you are coming from someplace without a sales tax such as The Bahamas, restaurant and grocery bills will take some getting used to as the Turks and Caicos charges an 8% sales tax on food items. There are no company or personal income taxes in the Turks and Caicos Islands. The government's budget is derived from the 10%-30% customs duty on incoming goods.

CUSTOMS AND IMMIGRATION
Turks and Caicos Ports of Entry

Providenciales: Sapodilla Bay (South Dock), *Turtle Cove Marina, Leeward Marina, Caicos Marina and Shipyard*

South Caicos: in Cockburn Harbour at *Sea View Marina* or at the government dock

North Caicos: airstrip

Grand Turk: at the new freighter dock at South Base

All vessels entering the waters of the Turks and Caicos must clear in with *Customs and Immigration* officials at the nearest port of entry listed above. Failure to report within 24 hours may subject you to a penalty and make you liable for confiscation and forfeiture of your vessel. When approaching your selected port of entry be sure to fly your yellow "Q" flag. Only the captain of the vessel may go ashore to arrange clearance and no other shore contact is permitted until pratique is granted. During normal working hours, 9:00am to 4:00pm, Monday through Friday, the fee for clearing Customs is $5.00. If arriving outside these hours or on holidays you may expect to pay overtime charges, usually a $15.00 boarding fee and $6.00 overtime; $8.00 overtime on Sundays and holidays. North Americans need proof of citizenship, a passport (not required) or voter registration card, and a photo ID. If you are flying in and returning by way of a boat in transit you need some proof that you are able to leave the country. It is suggested that you purchase a round trip ticket and leave the return reservation open. When you return aboard your boat you may then cash in your unused ticket or use it for a future flight. Check with the airline when buying your ticket as to their policy in this matter. As soon as the captain has cleared *Customs*, you must take down your yellow "Q" flag and replace it with the British courtesy flag. Canadian citizens need a valid passport or some proof of identity such as a birth certificate along with a photo ID and a return ticket if arriving by air and a visa is not required. Australian, New Zealand, EU, and Japanese citizens need a valid passport and a return ticket, but no visa is required. Citizens of countries not listed above should check with the embassy or consulate in their home country for details on entry requirements.

If you plan to stay in the Turks and Caicos for seven days or less, no cruising permit is required. If you intend to stay more than seven days you must get a cruising permit from *Customs* at no charge. You must also report to *Immigration* to secure a Visa for your stay. Visas are granted for periods not to exceed 30 days and can be renewed twice. After 90 days in the Turks and Caicos you must leave and return to be eligible for another 90 days. Some yachts simply head to the DR for a week or so to reprovision at Puerto Plata and then return.

Most vessels heading across the banks and venturing south to the DR or Puerto Rico leave Provo and head to Ambergris Cay and then Sand Cay. As long as you do not stop at any other inhabited islands in the Turks and Caicos Islands, you may proceed straight across the banks and stage your trip from Sand Cay. When clearing out of Sapodilla Bay, you can clear out in the afternoon and not actually leave until the next morning, as long as you are gone before *Customs* opens. This enables you to have an early morning start to get to Ambergris before dark. There are no fees to clear out unless you choose to do so outside of normal working hours. The same rates for overtime are charged as for clearing in. If you or your guests are flying out, be advised that the airport departure tax is U.S.$15.00 for visitors over the age of 12.

Firearms, including those charged with compressed air, must be declared and brought in to *Customs* with you when you clear. Unless you have prior approval in writing from the Commissioner of Police, *Customs* will impound them and store them for you at the police station until your departure. Spearguns are also illegal and must be brought in to *Customs* when you clear. All pets must be declared and have a recent bill of health from a certified veterinarian. Pets must also have a recent rabies shot. The importation of controlled drugs and pornography is illegal in the Turks and Caicos Islands.

Anyone over the age of 17 may bring certain items duty free including personal effects such as wearing apparel, ship's stores, 1 liter of alcohol or 2 liters of wine, 200 cigarettes, 100 cigarillos, 50 cigars or 12.5 grams of pipe tobacco. Fifty grams of perfume or .25 liters of toilet water are also permitted. Dutiable goods, up to a value of $200.00 and purchased outside the Turks and Caicos, may be brought in by visitors as gifts and must be declared when clearing in. Persons arriving in the islands with the intention of working are allowed to bring in personal effects duty free, providing they intend to remain in the islands not less than 12 months. Duties on imported goods run in the neighborhood of 10%-33% depending on the particular item. In the spring of 1998, the government of the Turks and Caicos dropped all duties on computer products so you might not have to pay duty for parts shipped into the country. For more information you may telephone the Collector of Customs on Grand Turk at 655-946-2993/4, their fax number is 655-946-2887.

American flag vessels are not required to obtain clearance when departing U.S. ports. If you are clearing back into the United States you must, upon entry, call the *U.S. Customs Service* to clear in. You are required to go to a nearby telephone immediately upon arrival and dock nearby. You can dial 1-800-432-1216, 1-800-458-4239, or 1-800-451-0393 to get a *U.S. Customs* agent on the line to arrange clearance. When you have *Customs* on the phone you will need to give them your vessel's name and registration number, the owner's name, the captain's name and date of birth, all passenger names and dates of birth, a list of all foreign ports visited and the duration of your stay there, a list of guns aboard, the total value of all purchases, and your *U.S. Customs* User Fee Decal number, if one has been issued, and whether you have anything to declare (total of all purchases, fresh fruit, vegetables, or meat). If you do not have a decal you may be directed to the nearest *U.S. Customs* station to purchase one within 48 hours. Decals may be purchased prior to departing on your voyage by ordering an application (Customs Form #339) and submitting the completed application with a $25.00 fee (money order or check drawn on a U.S. bank) to *U.S. Customs Service*, National Finance Center, P.O. Box 198151, Atlanta, Georgia 30384.

Each resident of the United States, including minors, may take home duty-free purchases, up to U.S.$600.00 if they have been outside the U.S. for more than 48 hours and have not taken this exemption in 30 days. This includes up to 2 liters of liquor per person over 21, provided that one liter is manufactured in the Turks and Caicos or a member of the Caribbean Basin Initiative (CBI). A family may pool their exemptions. Articles of up to $1,000.00 in excess of the duty-free $600.00 allowance are assessed at a flat rate of 10%. For example, a family of four may bring back up to $2,400.00 worth of duty-free goods. If they were to bring back $6,400.00 worth of goods, they would have to pay a duty of $400.00 on the $4,000.00 above the duty-free allowance. This flat rate may only be used once every 30 days. If the returning U.S. resident is not entitled to the duty-free allowance because of the 30 day or 48 hour restrictions, they may still bring back $25.00 worth of personal or household items. This exemption may not be pooled. Importation of fruits, plants, meats, poultry, and diary products is generally prohibited. More than $10,000.00 in U.S. or foreign coin, currency, traveler's checks, money orders, and negotiable instruments or investment securities in bearer form must be reported to *Customs*. Importation of tortoise or turtle shell goods is prohibited.

Any number of gifts may be sent to the U.S. from the Turks and Caicos and the recipient will pay no duty provided that the gift is worth U.S.$50.00 or less. If the value is over U.S.$50.00, duty and tax is charged on the full value. The following regulations must be complied with: Only U.S.$50.00 worth of gifts may be received by the U.S. addressee in one day. The value of the gifts must be clearly written on the package as well as the words "Unsolicited Gift." No alcoholic beverages or tobacco may be sent. Perfume with value of more than U.S.$5.00 may not be sent. Persons in the U.S. are not allowed to send money to the Turks and Caicos for gifts to be shipped to them duty-free; the gifts must be unsolicited. Persons may not mail a gift addressed to themselves. For more information, contact the *U.S. Customs Service* before you leave or call them in Nassau at 242-327-7126.

Canadian residents may take advantage of three categories of duty-free exemption. If you have been out of Canada for 24 hours, you may make a verbal declaration to claim a CDN$20.00 duty-free allowance any number of times per year. This exemption does not include alcohol or tobacco. If you have been out of the country for 48 hours, any number of times per year, a written declaration must be made and you may claim a CDN$100.00 allowance. This allowance can include up to 200 cigarettes, 50 cigars, or 2 lbs. of tobacco, and 1.1 liters of alcohol per person. If you have been out of Canada for over seven days, you may make a written declaration and claim a CDN$300.00 exemption including the above mentioned amounts of tobacco and alcohol. After a trip abroad for 48 hours or more you are entitled to a special 20% duty rate on goods valued up to CDN$300.00 over and above the CDN$100.00 and CDN$300.00 personal exemption. For importation of tobacco the claimant must be 16 years of age. For alcohol, the claimant must have attained the legal age prescribed by the laws of the provincial or territorial authority at the point of entry.

Unsolicited gifts may be sent to Canada duty-free as long as they are valued under CDN$400.00 and do not contain alcoholic beverages, tobacco products, or advertising matter. If the value is above CDN$400.00 the recipient must pay regular duty and tax on the excess amount.

The following items may be imported into the Turks and Caicos Islands without incurring customs duty: 200 cigarettes or 50 cigars or 225 grams of tobacco; and 1.136 liters of spirits or wine. There are no restrictions on the import of cameras, film, or sports equipment except spear guns. Firearms without a permit are prohibited. Some boat parts for vessels in transit can be shipped in without duty while duty on other parts duty may range from 10% to 33%. Before shipping in a part, check with *Customs* and have them look it up in their book so you'll know well ahead of time what, if any, the duty will be.

DINGHY SAFETY

Most cruisers spent a considerable amount of time in their dinghies exploring the waters and islands in the vicinity of their anchorage. It is not unknown for a dinghy engine to fail or a skipper to run out of gas miles away from the mother vessel. For this reason I urge boaters to carry some simple survival gear in their dinghies and to check their gas every time they get in their dink to go anywhere. First, I would recommend a handheld VHF radio for obvious reasons. If there are any other boats around this may be your best chance for getting some assistance. A good anchor and plenty of line is also high on the list. I do not mean one of those small three pound anchors with thirty feet of line that is only used on the beach to keep your dinghy from drifting to Cuba. It may pay to sacrifice the onboard room and use a substantial anchor with a couple of feet of chain and at least 100' of line. Just as you would go oversize on your mother vessel do the same with your dinghy. If you are being blown away from land a good anchor and plenty of line gives you a good chance of staying put where someone may find you. Next, a dinghy should have a supply of flares. In The Bahamas I learned a trick from the locals there who often carry a large coffee can with a rag soaked in oil lying in the bottom. If they get in trouble lighting the rag will produce an abundant amount of smoke which can be seen from a quite a distance. A dinghy should be equipped with survival water, a bottle or small packages of water manufactured by DATREX. It would be a good idea to throw in a few MRE's (Meal Ready to Eat). These are the modern, tastier version of the K-rations which our armed forces survived on for years. Each MRE also contains vital survival components such as matches and toilet paper. Another handy item that does not take up much room is a foil survival blanket. They really work and take up as much space as a couple of packs of cigarettes.

Please don't laugh at these suggestions. I have seen people forced to spend a night or two in a dinghy and these few items would have made their experience much more pleasant, if not entirely unnecessary. I have run out of gas and used flares to attract some local attention even though one of my boat mates was ready to dive in and swim for the nearest island to fetch some help. Now, I never leave in my dinghy without my little survival bag stashed away in the dink. It doesn't take much effort to prepare a small bag for your dinghy, and it will be worth its weight in gold should you need it.

DIVING

From shallow water reef dives to deep water wall drop-offs, the diving in The Turks and Caicos is as good as it gets anywhere and much better than most places. You don't need scuba equipment to enjoy the undersea delights that are available, many reefs lie in less than 30' and are easily accessible to those with snorkels, dinghies, and curiosity.

Providenciales is a hotbed of diving activity with more than a half-dozen different diving shops offering dive trips, charters, and complete instructions. Here you can dive with *Dive Provo*, *Art Pickering's Turtle Divers*, *Flamingo Divers*, *Beaches Resort*, *Club Med*, and *Caicos Adventures*. For those wishing a longer-term dive, the liveaboard dive boat *Turks and Caicos Aggressor* is based at *Turtle Cove Marina*, while Peter Hughes' *Sea Dancer* is based out of the *Caicos Marina and Shipyard*. *Sea Dancer* can be contacted in the U.S. at *800-9DANCER*. In the waters between Grace Bay and Pine Cay you'll find wonderful spur & groove coral reefs, which consist of central reefs with arm-like lateral extensions and grooves. The spur and groove coral generally runs perpendicular to the wall, which runs parallel to the shoreline. West Caicos is known for its many great dives just off its dramatic limestone cliffs. In Sapodilla Bay you'll find the 65' M/V *Island Diver* offering snorkel and SCUBA trips. For more on *Island Diver* and their *Ocean Outback* services, see the section on Sapodilla Bay at Providenciales. The new guys on the block are *Big Blue Diving* operating out of Leeward Going Through. These energetic and enthusiastic young men are making a big impact on eco-diving in the area and well worth checking out. They are so new that I didn't have their phone number at press time but you can always dial information in Provo or check at *Leeward Marina* for the owners.

Grand Turk represents a wealth of tremendous experiences for the diver. Less than a quarter of a mile off shore and starting in just 25'-45' of water, a coral wall runs the full length of the island, with profiles ranging from steeply sloping terrain to interesting coral undercuts and perfectly vertical drop-offs. The sponge growth and fish populations are spectacular and distinctively different from the other Turks and Caicos sites. You can expect manta rays in the summer, turtles year-round and humpback whales in the winter, this a primary corridor for the migrating humpback whales from December through April.

Some of the world's best wall diving can be found within 300 yards of the western shore of Grand Turk. Here coral cliffs drop from 30' below the surface to over 7,000' deep. Mooring buoys protect the delicate coral structure and there are several dive operations working these waters. In Grand Turk try *Blue Water Divers*, *Sea Eye Divers*, or *Oasis Divers*, all located on Front Street in Cockburn Town.

Although the waters in The Turks and Caicos are crystal clear and the obstructions plainly visible in the ambient light, divers must take proper precautions when diving in areas of current. Experienced divers are well aware of this, but it must be stated for novices and snorkelers. Tidal fluctuations can produce strong currents that must be taken into account when diving. Waves breaking over and around inshore reefs can create strong surges that can push or pull you into some very sharp coral. For safety's sake, only experienced divers should penetrate wrecks and caves.

Most of the dive sites in the Turks and Caicos have moorings installed by the *National Parks Committee* and maintained by the many dive boats that use them. Please do your part to protect these fragile coral eco-systems and don't anchor on the reefs; anchor nearby in sand, it holds better anyway.

While summer waters run about 82°-84°F at the surface, it is certainly warm enough for swimsuits though most divers welcome protection in the form of a light cover-up. In the winter, water temperatures of 74°-78°F would suggest the use of a wetsuit. Dive computers are an advantage owing to the multi-level nature of the diving in the Turks and Caicos.

A must for divers in the Turks and Caicos Islands is the *Diving, Snorkeling, & Visitors Guide to the Turks and Caicos Islands* by Captain Bob Gascoine. Bob is the dean of all Turks Islands divers and his excellent guide has loads of useful information about the cays as well as about the diving surrounding them.

FISHING

The drop-offs around the Turks and Caicos Islands offer fishing that is as good as it gets anywhere. The annual *Provo International Billfish Tournament*, usually held in mid-summer, results in a great number of billfish including blue marlin and swordfish being weighed-in. In 1996 for example, a 599 lb. blue marlin was hauled in, the largest ever caught in the Turks and Caicos Islands. Of course you can also find dolphin, wahoo, kings, yellowfin, and bonita in large numbers when trolling offshore. The Caicos Banks are ideal bonefishing grounds and there are several guides around the Provo area to choose from.

There are several different categories of fishing permits. Most visiting skippers only need a regular sportfishing license. Tournaments and charter sportfishing boats have separate categories. If you intend to fish on the Mouchoir

Banks you will need a special permit for that privilege. A regular sportfishing permit costs $15.00 for thirty days and is renewable. They can be purchased at the *DECR*, the *Department of the Environment and Coastal Resources* (sometimes just referred to as *Fisheries*), upstairs from the *Public Treasury* in Provo or at their office on Grand Turk. Licenses can also be picked up at *Turtle Cove Marina* at Sellar's Pond on Provo, and at *J & B Tours* at *Leeward Marina,* also on Provo. Remember that you are not allowed to fish within the boundaries of any National Park in the Turks and Caicos Islands, and especially at the drop-off along the reefs bordering Provo.

Fishing permits are only valid for hook and line fishing, the use of spearguns, pole spears, and Hawaiian slings are not permitted in the Turks and Caicos Islands. Every July the Minister must go before the Executive Council to lift the ban on the use of hooks to catch lobsters for the local licensed commercial fishermen. This allows the commercial fellows to use a hook on the end of a pole to snag the lobster and also to have a Hawaiian sling in the water with them for protection (visiting skippers may also have a Hawaiian sling with them in the water for protection but if caught the burden is on you to prove its necessity; fines for violations of Turks and Caicos fishing regulations can go as high as $50,000 and/or 12 months in jail and yes, *Fisheries* does patrol their waters!). Visiting yachtsmen must use some other method of capturing a lobster for dinner, either a tickle stick or a mop. In other words, you must use some method of capturing the lobster without harming him. Some folks use a mop to entangle the lobster's many barbs on his antennas and body and then pull him out of his hole. The closed season for lobster is April 1st through August 31st. The law prohibits taking eggbearing (berried) lobsters and those with a carapace length of less than 3 ¾". The use of SCUBA and hookah rigs for fishing are also not permitted in the Turks and Caicos Islands. Even with a fishing permit, you are only allowed 10 pounds of fish per day for consumption. In other words, you are not allowed to fill your freezer. Skippers holding a valid license may remove one fish from the Turks and Caicos for trophy mounting purposes.

By the way, in the introduction to this book I mention the *Pinnacles* as being a favorite sportfishing destination for local fishermen. The *Pinnacles* are the tips of undersea mountains that lie between West Caicos and Little Inagua. Check your NOAA or DMA charts and you'll see them. Good fishing!

FLIGHTS

Flying in and out of the Turks and Caicos poses little problem. Provo's *Fritz Luddington International Airport* is the hub of flying activity in The Turks and Caicos with daily flights to the U.S. and points beyond. Twice daily service from Miami to Provo is provided by *American Airlines* (800-433-7300) while *Northwest Airlines* (800-447-4747) arrives every Sunday from Detroit. *Lynx Air International* (800-LYNXAIR) flies from Ft. Lauderdale to Provo six days a week and to Grand Turk three times a week. There are also international airports on North Caicos, South Caicos, and on Grand Turk. Domestic air service is supplied by *Sky King* (941-KING), *Interisland Airways* (941-5481), *Turks and Caicos Airways,* and several other local charter companies. *Air Jamaica* has just added the Turks and Caicos Islands to its routes.

GARBAGE

When I first began cruising I had this naive idea that all cruisers lived in a certain symbiosis with nature. My bubble finally burst with the bitter realization that many cruisers were infinitely worse than common litterbugs. So often they have the attitude of "out of sight, out of mind." I sometimes wonder if they believe in supernatural beings, hoping that if they dump their trash somewhere imaginary garbage fairies will come along and take care of the disposal problems for them. One cruiser leaves a few bags of garbage in some secluded (or not so secluded) spot and the next cruiser says "My, what a good spot for a garbage dump. Ethel, bring the garbage, I've found the dump!" This is why you often go ashore on otherwise deserted islands and find bags and piles of bags of garbage. Nothing is worse than entering paradise only to discover some lazy, ignorant, slob of a cruiser (no, I have not been too harsh on this type of person, I can still think of plenty of other adjectives without having to consult a thesaurus) has dumped his or her bags of garbage in the bushes. Please do not add to this problem. Remember that your garbage attracts all kinds of foul creatures such as rats and other ignorant, careless cruisers.

Nobody likes storing bags of smelly garbage aboard, but if you cannot find a settlement nearby to take your garbage for free, you will have to make an allowance in your budget to pay for the local garbage disposal service. If you are nowhere near a garbage facility you should stow your trash aboard, separated into three groups for easier disposal. First cans and bottles (wash them first to remove any smells while being stored), then into another container stow the organic stuff such as food scraps, rinds, and eggshells, and finally paper and plastic trash. Your food scraps can be stored in a large coffee can with a lid and dumped overboard daily on an outgoing tide. The paper and plastic should be burned completely when necessary and the ashes buried deep and not on the beach. Cans and bottles should be punctured or broken and dumped overboard in very deep water at least a few miles offshore. Cut off both ends of the cans and break the bottles overboard as you sink them. If you cannot implement a garbage disposal policy aboard your vessel, stay home, don't come to these beautiful islands. Do not abuse what we all use.

GPS

Even with today's crop of sophisticated Loran receivers, accuracy of this system south of Nassau should be viewed as suspect at best. In the search for reliable positioning, more and more skippers are turning to that electronic marvel called GPS as their main source of navigational data. It is a truly remarkable system offering very accurate positioning around the clock anywhere in the world. Nowadays anyone with $100.00 can become an instant navigator.

The GPS waypoints listed in this guide are for general usage only. I do not intend for you to follow a string of waypoints to an anchorage. Instead, I will bring you to the general area where you can pilot your way in the rest of the way. Do not attempt to maneuver your vessel from waypoint to waypoint without a constant lookout. The GPS is truly a marvel, but I have yet to find one that will locate and steer around a coral head or sandbar. Any skipper who attempts to navigate a tricky channel such as the entrance into Leeward Going Through by using only GPS waypoints deserves whatever ill fortune befalls them. The inherent error in such waypoints due to the Selective Availability (SA) of the system is too great to make such dangerous routes viable. I repeat: use these waypoints only as a guideline, trust your eyes and your depthsounder!

GPS datum used is WGS 72. Skippers with DGPS capability tell me that in the Turks and Caicos Islands they can pick up the San Juan, Puerto Rico, DGPS beacon very strong, while the continental United States beacons tend to fade out in the Southern Bahamas.

Ham Radio

All amateur radio operators will need a Turks and Caicos Reciprocal license (VP5) to operate legally in the waters of the Turks and Caicos. Operators should apply at least six weeks before arrival but can apply upon arrival in Provo. Send a U.S. money order for $21.00 made out to *TACARS*, (Turks and Caicos Amateur Radio Society), and mail it to Jody Milspaugh, P.O. Box 218, Providenciales, Turks and Caicos, BWI. A clear copy of your current license must accompany the money order. If you wish to check on the status of your application via the Internet, Jody's email address is jody@caribsurf.com. Reciprocal licenses may be collected by the operator upon arrival in Providenciales or Jody will send you a copy prior to your departure, your regular license will still need to be picked up in person after your arrival in Provo. You can phone Jody Milspaugh, VP5JM, at 649-946-4436 to arrange for pickup. If you arrive in Provo without a reciprocal, you can call Jody at the above mentioned number and she will arrange to meet you so you may apply for your license. Jody will give you a receipt that will allow you to transmit until your regular license arrives. Jody, who lives on Providenciales, also has a small one-bedroom house that she rents out for hams interested in using it for contest purposes. The house includes an Icom radio, tuner, and antennas.

The Turks and Caicos does not have a third-party agreement with the United States; this means that you cannot make a phone patch from The Turks and Caicos to the U.S. If you head offshore three miles you will be in international waters and can make a phone patch from there without using your VP5; you will be MM2 (Maritime Mobile) once you are three miles out.

The following is a listing of ham nets you may wish to participate in during your Turks and Caicos cruise.

NET NAME	FREQUENCY KHz	TIME
TACARS	3780	0800 ET-Sundays
Waterway Net	7268	0745-0845 ET
Computer Net	7268	0900 ET-Fridays
Tech Net	7268	0900 ET- Sundays
CW Net-slow	7128	0630 ET-Mon., Wed., and Fri.
CW Net-fast	7128	0630 ET-Tues., Thurs., Sat., and Sun.
Bahamas Weather Net	3696	0720 ET

NET NAME	FREQUENCY KHz	TIME
Bah. Amat. Radio Soc.	3696	0830 ET-Sundays
Intercontinental Net	14300-14316 (changes often)	1100 UTC
Maritime Mobile Net	14300-14316 (changes often)	After Intercon. until around 0200 UTC
Caribbean Net	7230 (changes often)	1100-1200 UTC
Hurricane Watch Net	14325, 14275, 14175	When needed

HOLIDAYS

The following public holidays are observed in The Turks and Caicos:
New Year's Day - January 1st
Commonwealth Day (March; date varies)
Good Friday
Easter Sunday
Easter Monday
National Hero's Day (May; date varies)
Her Majesty The Queen's Official Birthday (usually the second Sunday)
Emancipation Day - August 1st
National Youth Day (September; date varies)
Columbus Day
International Human Rights Day - October 24th
Christmas Day
Boxing Day - December 26th

Holidays that fall on Sunday are always observed on Monday. Holidays that fall on Saturday are also usually observed on Monday.

Photo Courtesy of Lenny Williams

Police Band parades on the Queen's Birthday.

HURRICANE HOLES

To begin with, there is <u>no such thing</u> as a truly safe hurricane hole, in fact, the term hurricane hole itself is quite misleading. I believe that given a strong enough hurricane, any harbor, hole, or creek can be devastated. Keep this in mind as the places that I am going to recommend offer the best protection and, under most circumstances, give you a better than average chance of surviving a hurricane, but are by no means "safe" in the true meaning of the word. Although you may feel quite safe in your chosen hole, remember that no hurricane hole comes with a guarantee. Many factors will contribute to your survival. The physical location and protection the hole offers is your primary line of defense. But hand in hand with that is the way you secure your vessel, the tidal surge, other vessels around you, and the path and strength of the hurricane. Allow yourself plenty of time to get to your chosen location and to get settled. Only a fool would attempt to race a hurricane. As a side note, let me mention that the Turks and Caicos Islands have only been hit by four hurricanes in the last century.

If you are going to be cruising in the Turks and Caicos from June through November, hurricane season, you'll want to know where the hurricane holes are, what you can expect when you get there, and how far you are away from your first choice at all times. Personally, this skipper prefers a narrow, deep, mangrove lined creek but if one isn't available I'll search for something equally suitable. Some holes are better than others, but like the old adage advises: "*Any port in a storm.*" With that in mind let me offer a few of the places where I would consider seeking shelter in the event of a hurricane. Bear in mind that if you ask ten different skippers what they look for in a hurricane hole, you're likely to get ten different answers. Some of these holes may not meet your requirements. I offer them only for your consideration when seeking safety for your vessel. The final decision is yours and yours alone. For the best information concerning hurricane holes, always check with the locals. They'll know the best spots.

If I was heading south from The Bahamas and a hurricane threatened I would prefer to stay in George Town, Exuma, for shelter. If heading to the Turks and Caicos from the south, I would stay in Luperón, as secure a hurricane shelter as any in the Caribbean.

In the Caicos Islands, Providenciales offers several dredged canals that offer an opportunity to get well inland, hopefully away from any damaging seas though you may still be affected by a storm surge. On the south side of Providenciales, the canals at Discovery Bay (Cooper Jack Bight) are a favorite place for local boaters and are well protected. A 6½' draft can enter here at high water. *South Side Basin Marina*, just inside the entrance to the canals, has emphatically informed me that they do not want boats at their docks during a hurricane and the marina manager will insist on your leaving in the event of a storm. Bear in mind that when anchoring in any of the dredged canals around Provo, that the bottom will likely be poor holding; you'll have to set some of your anchors on shore here.

A small, narrow, shallow canal, leads northward from *Caicos Marina and Shipyard* to some private residences in the *Long Bay Hills* section of Provo and offers excellent protection but draft is limited to 3'-4' at low water; the canal entrance, through a small bascule bridge, prohibits wide multihull vessels.

Just north of *Leeward Marina* in Leeward Going Through is a small canal leading into the Leeward community. The bar at the entrance restricts entry to vessels with drafts of less than 5' at high tide. Leeward Going Through has often been used as a hurricane hole by some skippers and should also be considered as well as the cuts between Pine Cay and Fort George Cay, Ft. George Cay and Dellis Cay, and between Dellis Cay and Parrot Cay. A word of warning about the tides here during hurricanes. When a storm surge approaches from the south across the banks, the water rushes in the southern sides of these cuts at a good clip. One past hurricane raised the water level in Leeward Going Through by over 6'. You can probably imagine the current involved with the movement of that much water, so use extreme care when securing your vessel.

On the northern shore of Providenciales, skippers should consider Sellar's Pond and *Turtle Cove Marina*, a very well protected spot. But check with the marina first for space availability; they might not want to take on any other boats. Just west of Sellar's Pond is small Thompson's Cove, a private dredged community with a sign warning that all unauthorized boats will be removed. Drafts of less than 5' can work their way in here on a high tide. There are several undeveloped lots and if one did not have permission to tie up inside, one would have to hope that the landowners would understand that a life threatening storm chased you inside and you would not leave until the danger passed. As well protected as Thompson Cove is, I would probably make it my last choice.

Shallow draft boats, those with drafts of less than 3', could work themselves into some of the creeks between North Caicos, Middle Caicos, and East Caicos if needed. South Caicos' Cockburn Harbour is excellent in most conditions but it is unsuitable to me as a hurricane shelter.

In the Turks Islands, the only choice for shelter is to round the northern tip of Grand Turk and seek shelter inside North Creek if conditions allow entry (see text in *Part II, The Turks Islands, Grand Turk, The North Creek Anchorage*).

The entrance channel is limited to about 6½' on a normal high tide but once inside the water deepens to over 12' in places. There is quite a bit of north/south fetch to take into consideration, but the holding is excellent in sand and mud.

JoJo the Dolphin

JoJo is a very, very unique Atlantic bottlenose dolphin. Since 1980 JoJo has been plying the waters of the Turks and Caicos Islands centering on the Provo area. This friendly dolphin has become a powerful symbol for nature conservation in the Turks and Caicos Islands.

JoJo is one of the few dolphins around the world who has chosen to voluntarily interact with human beings in his own natural habitat. Much loved by the islanders, the government has proclaimed JoJo a National Treasure and in 1987, appointed a special Warden, Dean Bernal, to protect him. Dean first met JoJo in 1985, when JoJo began following Dean on his long swims out to the reefs off Providenciales. At that time JoJo was already a popular figure along the beachfront but he was known to bite people and he had a dangerous reputation. What most people did not know is that JoJo only bit those who tried to touch him as he cavorted in the shallows. It seems that for some wild dolphins, a human's attempt to touch the mammal is considered a threat and JoJo was simply defending himself.

At that time, Dean was employed as a Dive Instructor on Providenciales and each day after Dean's classes, usually about 5:00 pm, JoJo and Dean would begin their reef swim. They would swim out to the reef where Dean would meet a dive boat to conduct a night dive, and then Dean and JoJo would swim back to shore in the dark. Their nightly dives became a regular part of Dean's daily regimen and the relationship between Dean and JoJo grew stronger steadily. If JoJo showed up before the SCUBA lessons ended, he would playfully pull on Dean's regulator hose trying to drag him away

Photo Courtesy of JoJo Archives

JoJo the Dolphin, with Dean.

from his students. Sometimes he would swim in high-speed circles around the group, effectively reducing the visibility to zero and canceling the instruction. Occasionally he would patiently wait, hovering just over Dean's shoulder, for the lessons to end. One time he herded an 8' shark into the middle of the group to break up the day's class. Knowing that Dean will stay in the water with him for hours when they are with other marine life, JoJo has brought Dean fish, lobsters, turtles, manta rays, whale sharks, an occasional bull and nurse shark, and he has even herded in a baby humpback whale along with its mother. JoJo's playful antics are often aimed at others. Quite often water skiers in the waters off Provo would suddenly find themselves paddling water. JoJo likes to come up underneath the ski and butt it skyward throwing the skier. JoJo once took a diver's $3,000.00 camera and hid it in the reef but playfully returned it 15 minutes later.

Through patient observation since 1987, Dean has compiled an impressive collection of data providing a rare and complete look into a wild dolphin's life in the open ocean. Diaries, data sheets, video and film materials now form a library and a wealth of information on the behavior of dolphins in their natural habitat. Dean has been fortunate to witness and document JoJo's behavior and interaction with whales, sharks, manta rays, other dolphins, numerous other forms of marine life, submarines, people and even terrestrial animals. Over the years, Dean has documented JoJo's growth through puberty, his competing for his position in a pod, his sickness and his well being. Because of Dean's ongoing Dolphin Project, the development of trust in his and JoJo's relationship and Dean's position as a Warden, JoJo's life has been saved on numerous occasions. Dean has been able to treat JoJo's wounds caused by such incidents as entanglement in turtle nets, infections from stingray barbs, confrontations with sharks, and impacts from water ski boats. Dean has contacted *Club Med* about putting guards on their ski boats at a cost of about $200.00. *Club Med* refused and hired a lawyer for $400.00 to fight the case. Doesn't make sense, does it? It shows where *Club Med's* priorities lie. JoJo's first and worst injury came from a jet ski and Dean is fighting the new PWC rental business that just opened in Leeward Going Through.

As JoJo grows older, Dean's research is becoming far more complex. Since JoJo has expanded his 26-square mile home range around Provo to 260 miles (in 1997 JoJo was seen off Grand Turk, thirty miles across the deep Columbus Passage), it makes the research much more challenging, not to mention interesting and rewarding. JoJo is now mating and travelling with other dolphins intermittently, finding new feeding grounds, utilizing new habitats and migratory routes and continuing to expand his experiences of what a young free-roaming, wild dolphin should be living and experiencing. Thanks to the *JoJo Dolphin Project*, the importance of this information from a conservation and animal welfare perspective has given Dean the opportunity to develop his work into a full-time research project. Never before has the chance to learn about the behavior, interaction, health, habitat and needs of a single wild dolphin been so clearly available for study. The information is vital to the conservation of all dolphins because it provides a rare, intimate and relatively complete look at the dolphin's life in the wild.

JoJo is easily recognized. JoJo prefers the waters between Grace Bay and Pine Cay on the northern shore of Providenciales, but may be seen just about anywhere. If a dolphin approaches your vessel, sticking his head out of the water to look at you, or perhaps circling your boat at anchor, the chances are that this is JoJo. If you're diving and a large dolphin approaches you it will likely be JoJo. JoJo has numerous prop marks and scars on his body and fins and this makes him almost unmistakable. JoJo has been known to approach divers very closely, getting as close as a foot or two away to satisfy his curiosity. If you are in the water and JoJo appears, there are several things you need to remember for your protection and his. First, understand that although JoJo is a wild creature, he is capable of expressing his feelings and his personality as well as aggression and anger. Never reach out to touch him, especially around the blowhole at the top of his head; this is his nose and he breathes through it. Do not approach JoJo, remain passive and let him come to you. Don't swim after him, he might perceive it as a threat and act defensively. If provoked he may bite or use his tail to slap you. If JoJo shows any behavior that you are uncomfortable with, do not panic; exit slowly from the water. Dean reminds us not to lie on our backs in the water as JoJo gets unpredictable at this. Actually he gets very amorous (if you follow my drift). He once tried to mate with the SCUBA tank of a female dive instructor I know in Provo.

Today, Dean and JoJo still frolic in the waters of Providenciales. Quite often you'll see JoJo around your boat in places like Leeward Going Through, circling round and round as he sleeps. JoJo's future is uncertain. Everyone hopes that JoJo will remain safe in these islands for many years to come but JoJo has had six life threatening injuries in the last ten years. The *JoJo Dolphin Project* provides for JoJo's care, medical supplies, and research projects. Anyone wishing to contribute to the project can contact Dean Bernal on VHF ch.72, *Sea Base*, or by writing to the *JoJo Dolphin Project*, P.O. Box 153, Providenciales, Turks and Caicos Islands, BWI. You can email Dean at JoJo1@caribsurf.com. For JoJo's website, go to http://ftp.marineweb.com/~tmw/proj/jojo/index.html.

MEDICAL EMERGENCIES

Provo has a few medical centers to fill most any need. On Leeward Highway is the *Menzies Medical Practice and Interisland Medical Services* (946-4242/4321 and 941-5252). Here there are three full-time physicians, plus a dentist, an optometrist, a chiropractor, a psychologist, and a pharmacy. Services include an emergency room and ambulance, general family practice, trauma care, and a pharmacy. Divers will be happy to know that *Menzies* has a hyperbaric chamber on site staffed by trained personnel. *Menzies* offers a Florida lab linkup and obstetric ultrasound. *The Myrtle Rigby Health Clinic* (941-3000) is a Government run facility with a full-time Physician and nursing staff that is also located on Leeward Highway. *Rigby's* offers family practice, X-ray, obstetrics and ultra-sound, lab services, casualty reception, and a maternity unit. The *New Era Medical Centre* (941-5455/3233) is located in Blue Hills and is staffed by one doctor offering family practice, a pharmacy, lab, emergency defibrillation and EKG units, and delivery and post-natal care. *New Era* is open 24 hours and monitors VHF ch. 82.

On North Caicos there are three government clinics at Bottle Creek, Kew, and Sandy Point. There are two resident nurses, three nurse's aides, and a government doctor who visits weekly. Two environmental health officers work weekdays from 8:00am to 4:30pm. In case of emergency call 941-3000 or 946-5422. There is a clinic on South Caicos (946-3216) with a visiting doctor and two full-time nurses. On Middle Caicos there is a government clinic at Conch Bar (946-6985) with a trained nurse. At Lorimars and Bambarra there are community health aids. A doctor visits every two weeks.

On Grand Turk you will find the 20 bed *Grand Turk Hospital* (946-2040/2110) situated on the north side of the island. The hospital is staffed by four physicians and can handle emergency cases, general medicine, surgery, geriatric care, obstetrics, and pediatrics. Also on Grand Turk is the government-run *Downtown Clinic* (946-2328) open from 8:00am to 12:30pm and from 2:00pm to 4:30pm. You will find that all government offices, from post offices to these government-clinics are all closed for lunch from 12:30pm to 2:00pm. Just south of Grand Turk at Salt Cay you will find a government clinic (946-6985) with a full-time nurse and a doctor who visit every two weeks.

National Air Ambulance out of Ft. Lauderdale, Florida (305-359-9900 or 800-327-3710), can transport patients from the Turks and Caicos to the United States. You might also try *AAA Air Ambulance*; call collect to 612-479-8000. If you join *DAN*, the *Divers Alert Network*, for a small yearly fee you are covered under their *Assist America Plan*. This program offers emergency evacuation for any accident or injury, diving related or not, to the nearest facility that can provide you with adequate care. After you have been stabilized to the satisfaction of the attending physician and the *Assist America* doctor, *Assist America* will arrange your transportation back to the United States, under medical supervision if necessary.

If you need a veterinarian and you are near Provo, call *Whichdoctor* on VHF ch. 16, or call 946-4353.

NATIONAL PARKS

One of the largest misrepresentations that visiting cruisers have of the Turks and Caicos concerns its national parks system. I consistently hear misinformed cruisers moaning and groaning to themselves, and others, that they cannot anchor or fish in the Turks and Caicos Islands because of the many national parks. The worst part is that they often impart their lack of knowledge to other cruisers, who may be considering a Turks and Caicos cruise, often ruining their cruise before it even begins.

In 1992, the Government of the Turks and Caicos Islands created a national park system and set aside 33 specific protected areas to protect their scenic environments and habitats, both to preserve and conserve them for future generations as well as make them available for public recreation. The listing includes 11 national parks, 11 nature reserves, 4 sanctuaries and 7 historical sites totaling more than 325 square miles. Two hundred and ten square miles of this total amount are sensitive and ecologically essential wetlands ratified under the Switzerland based *International Ramsar Bureau*. Some of these protected areas include marine replenishment areas as well as breeding grounds for turtles, seabirds and other creatures. All the national parks are under the supervision of the *DECR*.

The Turks and Caicos have five different classifications for their protected areas. At the top of the list is the *UNESCO* (*United Nations Educational, Scientific, and Cultural Organization*) *Heritage Site*. Next is the *National Park* allowing access, recreation, and some development. A *Nature Reserve* allows limited use, recreation, and development. A *Sanctuary* does not allow development and only allows limited access with a permit issued by the *DECR*. A *Historical Site* allows access and limited development. For a complete listing of all protected sites in the Turks and Caicos Islands see *Appendix E: Listing of Protected Areas*. If you are unsure if you are within the boundaries of any protected area, please check this listing.

Vessels under 60' in length may anchor in any national park on any clear sand bottom. Damaging any corals by misuse of your anchoring privileges may result in a fine. Vessels over 60' in length must secure to one of the dive moorings in the areas or get a special permit to anchor. If bad weather is threatening or repairs must be made, vessels over 60' may anchor anywhere except in coral. Water skiing and jet skis are not permitted in any protected area in the Turks and Caicos Islands.

PHONING HOME

Cable and Wireless, Ltd. International, handles all phone and fax communications in the islands. If you see what appears to be a pay phone booth, it is a card booth. There are no pay phones on any of the islands. These phone booths take either *Master Card*, *Visa*, *American Express*, or local *Cable and Wireless* phone cards. Phone cards can be purchased at the *Cable and Wireless* offices on Leeward Highway in Provo and on Front Street in Grand Turk in increments of $10-$25 (add $1 per $10 increment, a $10 card will actually cost you $11 and a $20 card, $22). Phone rates to the U.S. as of 2002 were $2.00 a minute, even getting a wrong number will cost you a minute of your card time, so dial carefully. These fees are exorbitant especially when you consider that the cost in nearby Mayaguana is only $1.00 a minute. *Cable and Wireless* has a monopoly and takes advantage of it. I personally feel they are gouging the consumer, but hopefully this will change. The area code for the Turks and Caicos changed in 1997, and is now 649. Dial 119 for police, hospital, or fire.

PROVISIONING

If you are on a tight budget, it might be best for you to stock up on provisions in the United States or Puerto Plata in the Dominican Republic prior to your Turks and Caicos cruise. Take enough for the length of your cruise and then some.

With few exceptions, prices in The Turks and Caicos are a little higher than American prices but generally lower than Bahamian prices on most goods. Food items are taxed in the Turks and Caicos. Beer and cigarette prices will seem outrageous with cigarette prices some 2-3 times higher than in the States. The Dominican beer *El Presidente* is very good and more reasonably priced than foreign beers. Rum, as one would think, can be very inexpensive while American whiskies and certain scotches are very high. Staples such as rice, beans, flour, and sugar are just slightly higher than U.S. prices. Vegetables can be quite reasonable in season. Meats, soft drinks, and milk all are considerably higher than in America. As you shop the various markets throughout the Turks and Caicos you will find some delightful items that are not sold in the U.S. - foreign butter and meats, for example. The shopping experience will give you the opportunity to purchase and enjoy some new treats. Of course, the prices on fresh fish, conch, and lobster are all open to bargaining with the local fishermen, with the South Caicos fishermen giving you the best deal.

Good drinking water is available throughout the islands from some of the cisterns and wells on various cays. Well water will have a higher salt content than cistern water that is actually rainwater. Always check with the owners before you remove any water. Most stores sell bottled water and you can buy reverse osmosis (watermaker water) in quite a few places; all over Provo in fact.

If you plan to dine out while in the islands, you will find the prices to be comparable to or higher than at home. I have found that it is difficult for two people to have a decent lunch in Provo with a couple of sodas or beers for under $20.00. It is common for dining establishments in the Turks and Caicos to include a 10%-15% gratuity on the check on top of the 8% tax.

RADIO AND TV

The official Government radio station is *Radio Turks and Caicos* (FM) located on Grand Turk and broadcasting on 106 MHz with 7,000 watts of power 24 hours a day. *WIV-FM* Radio on Providenciales broadcasts 24 hours a day on four FM stations with 500 watts of power. Local ads and community announcements are aired seven days a week at various times between 7:00am and 7:00pm. Stereo 92.5 MHz has contemporary easy rock (whatever that is), 90.5 MHz plays country and western music (in the tropics?), 89.9 MHz plays classical music (Aaahhhhh, Bach!), and soft sounds is on 89.3 MHz.

WPRT Radio can be found on the FM band at 88.7 MHz broadcasting with 1,000 watts of power. They provide local programming and community announcements seven days a week and Gospel music on Sundays.

Also found on the FM band at 96.7 MHz with 1,000 watts is VIC FM Radio. This is a religious station broadcasting seven days a week with live programming on Sunday mornings and Wednesday and Sunday evenings.

There are 12 cable channels in Grand Turk and 42 in Provo, with some locally produced programs. However, you can only receive these if you are tied up at a marina that offers a cable service. There are no television broadcasting stations in the Turks and Caicos Islands.

TACRA

TACRA, the *Turks and Caicos Rescue Association*, is modeled after *BASRA*, *the Bahamas Air Sea Rescue Association*, and although operating to a degree, is still in its infancy. Currently there are stations on Grand Turk and one on Providenciales with duty officers on call 24 hours a day with a backup. If an emergency arises, it is still best to call the local police who will call *TACRA*, even if you can get in touch with *TACRA* they will call the police first anyway. *TACRA* on Providenciales is in the process of opening up a base station at *Leeward Marina*. Plans and equipment include a VHF, RDF, HF rig, and a 100' antenna. As soon as *Leeward Marina* accelerates their construction, the antenna tower will go up, hopefully some time in 1999.

TIDES AND CURRENTS

The islands of the Turks and Caicos are affected by the west setting North Equatorial Current on both their northern and southern extremities. After entering the Caribbean the North Equatorial Current splits into two branches, the northern branch flowing northeast of the Turks and Caicos and The Bahamas as the Antilles Current, with an average velocity of approximately ½ knot. To a lesser extent the Antilles Current also flows through the Old Bahama Channel along the northern coast of Cuba and through the islands of the Turks and Caicos themselves. The more southern branch of the North Equatorial Current makes its way around the Caribbean and the Gulf of Mexico and enters the Straits of Florida as the Gulf Stream with an average velocity of approximately 2.5 knots in a northward direction. Once north of The Bahamas, the stronger Gulf Stream merges with the weaker Antilles Current and bears off north and northeastward across the North Atlantic.

Where the shallow banks drop off to deeper ocean waters, the tidal currents flow in and out of the passes and cuts, sometimes reaching 2-4 knots in strength and even more in a few of the more narrow passes. Some cuts may be impassable in adverse wind conditions or in heavy swells that may exist with or without any wind. Even in moderate conditions, onshore winds against an outgoing tide can create very rough conditions.

As a rule of thumb, you can estimate the tidal rise and fall to be about 2'-4' at most times with a mean rise of 2.6'. Neap tides, those after the first and last quarter of the moon, rise approximately ½' less, while tides after new and full moons rise approximately ½' more. During spring tides, when the moon is nearest the Earth, the range is increased by another ½'. Cruising through the Turks and Caicos during spring full moon tides will give you some of the lowest lows and highest highs. It is quite easy to run aground at this time on some of the Banks routes. Boats with drafts of 5' have reportedly run aground in what is normally a 6' depth at low water during this time. To receive tidal information while in the Turks and Caicos see the section *Weather*.

When attempting to predict the state of tide at any time other than at slack tide, you can use the *Rule of Twelfths* for a generally reliable accuracy. To do this, take the amount of tidal fluctuation and divide it into twelfths. For example, if high tide in Nassau is expected to be 3.0' and the low water datum is 0.0', the tidal fluctuation is 3', and each twelfth is 0.25' or 3". To predict the state of tide at different times you can use the *Rule of Twelfths* in the following table. The table is merely to demonstrate a point and uses an imaginary charted high tide of 3'. Always consult your chart tables or listen for tide information broadcasts and calculate accordingly.

TIME OF LOW WATER	TIDE DATUM-0 FEET
1 hour after low, add 1/12	¼ foot above datum - 3"
2 hours after low, add 3/12	¾ foot above datum - 9"
3 hours after low, add 6/12	1½ feet above datum - 18"
4 hours after low, add 9/12 2	¼ foot above datum - 27"
5 hours after low, add 11/12	2¾ feet above datum - 33"
6 hours after low, add 12/12	high water - 3'*

*Caution: *assumes a 3' tidal fluctuation as an example.*

Chart tables give the times and heights of high and low water but not the time of the turning of the tide or slack water. Usually there is little difference between the times of high and low water and the beginning of ebb or flood currents, but in narrow channels, landlocked harbors, or on tidal creeks and rivers, the time of slack water may vary by several hours. In some places you will find that it is not unusual for the currents to continue their direction of flow long after charted predictions say they should change. Strong winds can play havoc on the navigator attempting to predict slack water. The current may often appear in places as a swift flowing river and care must be taken whenever crossing a stretch of strong current to avoid being swept out to sea or onto a bank or rocks. Some of the currents may flow from 2.5 to over 4 knots in places, and in anchorages with a tidal flow, two anchors are a must. Even in moderate conditions, onshore winds against an outgoing tide can create very rough conditions. Some of the passes, cuts, and anchorages shown may be a real test of your ability. If in doubt, stay out. As with cruising anywhere, if you exercise caution you will have a safe and enjoyable cruise in The Turks and Caicos.

Tides in the Turks and Caicos use Hawk's Nest Anchorage at Grand Turk as their datum location. Low tides at this location are usually 14 minutes before Nassau tides and high tides at Grand Turk are 19 minutes before Nassau tides. Both high and low tides run generally. 5' less than Nassau tides. Tides at Provo and Leeward Going Through are approximately one hour later than tides at Grand Turk. Tides on the Caicos Banks are generally northwest on the flood and southwest on the ebb with an average strength of approximately 1 knot.

Printed tide tables can be purchased for $5.00 in Providenciales at the *DECR*, just above the *Public Treasury*, downtown across from *Kentucky Fried Chicken*. They also have an office on Grand Turk.

Tides are sometimes unpredictable around Providenciales. Strong northeast winds will sometimes keep the tides on the southern side of Provo low for days at a time while strong southern winds will give the southern shore higher tides than normal. The tides at Leeward Going Through are erratic at best. While the tides in Provo are generally thought to be about ½ hour after Nassau, this is not the case in Leeward. I have seen tides there occur three hours after Nassau tides and the floods generally tend to flow for a shorter period than the ebbs. I have seen the flood tide only last three hours during strong southeast winds.

VHF

The regulations pertaining to the proper use of VHF in the Turks and Caicos are basically identical to those in the United States. Channel 16 is the designated channel for hailing and distress. Please shift all traffic to a working channel when you have made contact with your party. Most of the local marine interests usually monitor VHF ch. 68, so if you can't find somebody on 16, then try 68 and move off to another channel after making contact.

When you are using your VHF, assume that at least a half-dozen of your neighbors will follow your conversation to another channel. Even if you have a "secret" channel it will not take too long to find you. It is a fact of life that everybody listens in to everybody else.

WEATHER

The Turks & Caicos are cooled by the trade winds, the steady current of air that originates off West Africa and that pushed Columbus' ships to the New World. The consistent breezes of the trade winds protect the islands from excessive heat, contributing to an ideal average temperature of 83°F. Climatic extremes are unheard of here, and about 20"-40" of rainfall leave the skies clear for much of the year.

As a general rule of thumb, the Turks and Caicos Islands are warm and dry. They lie along the path of the northeast trade wind belt which brings somewhat of a cooling effect to the cays. Temperatures usually stay in the neighborhood of 70°F to 85°F. Winter temperatures in the Turks and Caicos rarely fall below 60°F and generally are above 75°F in the daytime. The average year-round temperature in the Turks and Caicos is 83° F. During the summer months the lows are around 75°-78°F while the highs seldom rise above 90°F except in the hottest months of September and October when highs can soar to 95°F. Seawater temperatures normally vary between 74°F in February and 84°F in August. The trade winds also bring rain to these islands, not very much by some standards, but enough it seems. Grand Turk averages 20" per year while the Caicos group averages around 40" per year. These islands are dry with a lot of cactus; they can almost be described as desert-like. The rainiest month is May; the summer months may see a lot of rain depending on the actions of tropical waves and hurricanes. In the winter, rainfall is dependent upon frontal passages.

Humidity is fairly high all year long, especially during the summer months, but there is usually a breeze to lessen the effect. In the summer, winds tend to be light, 10 knots or less from the southeast with more calms, especially at night. In the winter, the prevailing winds are east-southeast and stronger. It is not unusual to get a week of strong winds, 20 knots or better, during the winter months as fronts move through. These fronts tend to move through with regularity during the winter months and become more infrequent as spring approaches. The wind will usually be in the southeast or south before a front and will often be very light to calm. As the front approaches with its telltale bank of dark clouds on the western and northwestern horizon, the winds will steadily pick up and move into the southwest, west, and northwest as the front approaches. Strongest winds are usually from the west and northwest. After the front passes the winds will move into the north and northeast for a day or two before finally settling back into an east/southeast pattern until the next front. Winds just after the front tend to be strong and the temperature a little cooler. Depending on its speed and strength, a front passing off the southeast Florida coast will usually be in Nassau in about 12-24 hours; from there it may arrive in the Exumas within 12-36 hours and the Turks and Caicos about 12-36 hours later.

In the summer the weather pattern is typically scattered showers with the occasional line squall. Although the main concern during June through November is hurricanes, the Turks and Caicos are more often visited by a tropical wave with its strong winds and drenching rains. Tropical waves, sometimes called easterly waves, are low pressure systems that can strengthen and turn into a tropical depression or hurricane. Cruisers visiting The Turks and Caicos during hurricane season are advised to monitor weather broadcasts closely and take timely, appropriate action (also see previous section on *Hurricane Holes*).

Staying in touch with weather broadcasts presents little problem in The Turks and Caicos, even if you don't have SSB or ham radio capabilities. In Grand Turk, *Flagstaff* comes on VHF ch. 16 at 8:00 a.m. local time and informs those who want to hear the latest southwest North Atlantic weather forecast to shift to VHF ch. 13. You can frequently pick up *Flagstaff's* weather transmissions as far away as South Caicos. When *Flagstaff* is off the island Brian Riggs (of the *National Museum*), handles the weather broadcasts using the call *Bluewater*.

WINZ, 940 KHz from Miami, is on the air 24 hours with weather for southern Florida approximately every 10 minutes. Unfortunately, this station is difficult to pick up at night. WGBS, also from Miami at 710 KHz has weather four times an hour 24 hours a day.

If you have ham radio capabilities you can pick up The Bahamas Weather Net every morning at 0720 on 3.696 MHz (sometimes on 7096 MHz), lower sideband. Carolyn Wardle, C6AGG begins with the local weather forecast and tides from the Nassau Met. Office. Next, hams from all over The Bahamas, and sometimes from Provo, check in with their local conditions which Carolyn later forwards to the Nassau Met. Office to assist in their forecasting. If you are interested in the approach of a front you can listen in and hear what conditions hams in the path of the front have experienced. All licensed amateur radio operators with current Bahamian and Turks and Caicos reciprocals are invited to participate. The local conditions in the weather reports follow a specific order, so listen in and give your conditions in the order indicated. If requested, Carolyn will send you some information on the types of clouds and their descriptions along with a log sheet. Be sure to thank Carolyn for her tireless efforts that benefit all mariners, not only those with ham licenses. Thanks Carolyn.

At 0745 on 7.268 MHz you can pick up the Waterway Net. Organized and maintained by the W*aterway Radio and Cruising Club*, this dedicated band of amateur radio operators begin the net with a synopsis of the weather for The Bahamas (with tides), south Florida, the southwest North Atlantic, the Caribbean Sea, and the Gulf of Mexico.

If you have marine SSB capabilities you can pick up BASRA's weather broadcasts every morning at 0700 on 4003 KHz, upper sideband. Later in the day you can pick up the guru of weather forecasters, Herb Hilgenberg, *Southbound II*, from Canada. You can tune in to Herb on 12.359 MHz, upper sideband, at 2000 Zulu. On 4.426, 6.501, 8.764, 13.089, and 17.314 MHz, you can pick up the voice weather broadcasts from NMN four times a day at 0500, 1100, 1700, and 2300 EST.

Starting in the southern Bahamas and continuing on throughout the entire Caribbean, an SSB equipped vessel can pick up David Jones, *Misstine*, who operates from his base in Tortola, BVI. David is on the air each day at 0830 AST (1215-1230 UTC) on 8.104 MHzl. He begins with a 24-48 hour wind and sea summary followed by a synoptic analysis and tropical conditions during hurricane season. After this he repeats the weather for those needing fills and finally he takes check-ins reporting local conditions from sponsoring vessels. During hurricane season David relays the latest tropical storm advisories at 1815 AST on 6.224 MHz.

USING THE CHARTS

Legend

☐ water depth less than 1 fathom

☐ water depth between 1 fathom and 10 fathoms

– – – large vessel route-6' draft

– · – · shallow vessel route

  +   rock or coral head

++++ reef

═════ road

m   mooring

dm   dinghy mooring

☐ water depth over 10 fathoms

⚲ light

⚓ anchorage

⊕ GPS waypoint

◉ tower

⊥ wreck--above hw

⟨⊕⟩ wreck-submerged

▣ building

The soundings were obtained using a computer-based hydrographic system in my Data Acquisition Vessel, a 12' Carib RIB (*Afterglow*, the tender to *IV Play*) graciously supplied by *Inflatable Xperts* in Ft. Lauderdale, FL. The system consists of an off-the-shelf GPS and sonar combination that gives a GPS waypoint and depth every two seconds including the time of each observation. The software used records and stores this information in an onboard computer. When I begin to chart an area, I first put *Afterglow's* bow on a well-marked, prominent point of land and take GPS lat/lons for a period of at least twenty minutes. I use the average of all these positions to check against the lat/lon shown on the topos, which are very accurate by the way. I also use cross bearings to help set up control points for my own reference. At this point I then begin to take soundings.

My next objective is to chart the inshore reefs. Then I'll plot all visible hazards to navigation. These positions are recorded by hand on my field notes as well as being recorded electronically. I rely primarily on my on-site notes for the actual construction of the charts. The soundings taken by the system are later entered by hand but it is the field notes that help me create the basis for the chart graphics. The computer will not tell me where a certain reef ends or begins as accurately as I can record it and show it on my field notes. Next I will run the one-fathom line as well as the ten-fathom line (if applicable) and chart these. Here is where the system does most of the work though I still stop to take field notes. Finally, I will crisscross the entire area in a grid pattern and hopefully catch hazards that are at first glance unseen. It is not unusual to spend days sounding an area of only a couple of square miles. This takes a lot of fuel as well as a lot of time when transferring the data to the chart!

Due to the speed of *Afterglow*, each identical lat/long may have as many as ten or twenty separate soundings. Then, with the help of NOAA tide tables, the computer gives me accurate depths to one decimal place for each separate lat/long pair acquired on the data run. A macro purges all but the lowest depths for each lat/long position (to two decimal places). At this point the actual plotting is begun including one fathom and ten fathom lines. The charts themselves are still constructed from outline tracings of topographic maps purchased at the Nassau Land And Surveys Dept. The lat/long lines are placed in accordance with these maps which are known for their accuracy. These topos are drawn from aerial photos and are geographically located using ground plane markers at known positions on each of the islands.

These charts are as accurate as I can make them and I believe them to be superior to any others. They are indeed more detailed than all others showing many areas that are not covered, or are incorrectly represented by other publications. However, it is not possible to plot every individual rock or coral head so pilotage by eye is still essential. On many of the routes in my guides you must be able to pick out the blue, deeper water as it snakes between sandbanks, rocky bars, and coral heads. Learn to trust your eyes. Remember that on the banks, sandbars and channels can shift over time so that once what was a channel may now be a sandbar. Never approach a cut or sandbar with the sun in your eyes, it should be above and behind you. Sunglasses with a polarized lens can be a big help in combating the glare of the sun on the water. With good visibility the sandbars and heads stand out and are clearly defined. As you gain experience you may even learn to read the subtle differences in the water surface as it flows over underwater obstructions.

All courses shown are magnetic. All GPS latitude and longitude positions for entrances to cuts and for detouring around shoal areas are only to be used in a general sense. They are meant to get you into the general area, you must pilot your way through the cut or around the shoal yourself. You will have to keep a good lookout, GPS will not do that for you. The best aids to navigation when near these shoals and cuts are sharp eyesight and good light. The charts will show both deep draft vessel routes as well as some shallow draft vessel routes. Deep draft vessel routes will accommodate a draft of 6' minimum and often more with the assistance of the tide. Shallow draft vessel routes are for dinghies and small outboard powered boats with drafts of less than 3'. Shallow draft monohulls and multihulls very often use these same routes.

Not being a perfect world, I expect errors to occur. I would deeply appreciate any input and corrections that you may notice as you travel these waters. Please send your suggestions to Stephen J. Pavlidis, C/O Seaworthy Publications, Inc. 215 S. Park St. Suite #1, Port Washington, WI 53074-5553. If you see me anchored nearby, don't hesitate to stop and say hello and offer your input. Your suggestion may help improve the next edition of this guide.

LIST OF CHARTS

CAUTION:

The Approach and Index charts are designed strictly for orientation and should not be used for navigation.

All charts are to be used in conjunction with the text.

All soundings are in feet at Mean Low Water.

All courses are magnetic.

Projection is transverse Mercator.

The Datum used is WGS72.

Differences in latitude and longitude may exist between these charts and other charts of the area; therefore the transfer of positions from one chart to another should be done by bearings and distances from common features.

The author and publisher take no responsibility for errors, omissions, or the misuse of these charts. No warranties are either expressed or implied as to the usability of the information contained herein.

Note: Some official NOAA and DMA charts do not show some of the reefs and heads charted in this guide. Always keep a good lookout when piloting in these waters.

The prudent navigator will not rely solely on any single aid to navigation, particularly on floating aids.

CHART #	CHART DESCRIPTION	PAGE
THE CAICOS ISLANDS		36
TCI-C1	THE CAICOS ISLANDS	38
TCI-C2	PROVIDENCIALES	40
TCI-C3	NORTH WEST POINT, MALCOLM ROADSTEAD	42
TCI-C4	WEST HARBOUR TO WILEY POINT	43
TCI-C5	SANDBORE CHANNEL, WESTERN ENTRANCE	44
TCI-C6	SANDBORE CHANNEL, SAPODILLA BAY	46
TCI-C7	FIVE CAYS TO LONG BAY	52
TCI-C8	COOPER JACK BIGHT, DISCOVERY BAY	53
TCI-C9	JUBA POINT CREEK, CAICOS MARINA & SHIPYARD	54
TCI-C10	SELLARS CUT, TURTLE COVE MARINA	56
TCI-C11	STUBBS CUT TO PINE CAY	58
TCI-C12	LEEWARD GOING THROUGH	61
TCI-C13	PINE CAY TO PARROT CAY, FT. GEORGE CUT	65
TCI-C14	WEST CAICOS	67
TCI-C15	FRENCH CAY	69
TCI-C16	NORTH CAICOS	71
TCI-C17	MIDDLE CAICOS	73
TCI-C18	EAST CAICOS, SOUTH CAICOS	75
TCI-C19	SOUTH CAICOS, COCKBURN HARBOUR	79
TCI-C20	SIX HILLS CAYS TO LONG CAY	83
TCI-C21	AMBERGRIS CAYS, FISH CAYS	84
THE TURKS ISLANDS		87
TCI-T1	THE TURKS ISLANDS	88
TCI-T2	GRAND TURK	91
TCI-T2A	GRAND TURK, NORTH CREEK ENTRANCE	92
TCI-T3	GRAND TURK TO DUNBAR SHOALS	99
TCI-T4	DUNBAR SHOALS TO SALT CAY	100
TCI-T5	SALT CAY	102
TCI-T6	GREAT SAND CAY	105
THE DOMINICAN REPUBLIC		
DR-1	BAHIA BLANCA, LUPERÓN	113
DR-2	PUERTO PLATA	118

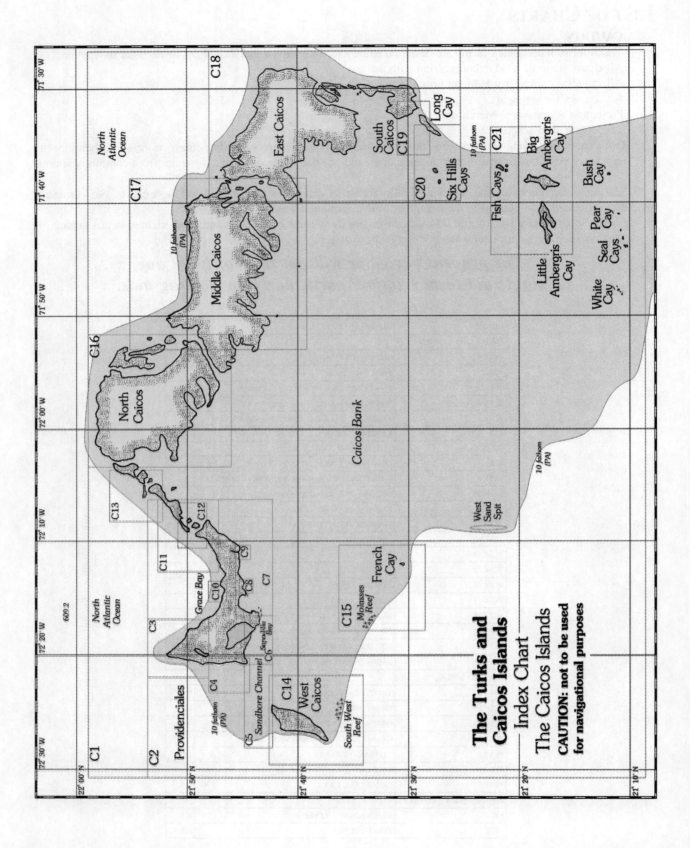

The Turks and Caicos Islands
— Index Chart —
The Caicos Islands
CAUTION: not to be used for navigational purposes

Part I

THE CAICOS ISLANDS

The Caicos Islands lie on the edge of the northern half of the huge Caicos Bank. They lie to the west of the Turks Islands and are separated from their sister cays by the ocean deep Turks Island Passage. The group lies approximately 575 miles southeast of Miami and about 450 miles northeast of Jamaica. The majority of the land area, population, tourist industry, and yachting scene in the Turks and Caicos Islands is located in the Caicos Islands themselves. Some say the Caicos Islands probably derived their name from "Caya Hica", the Lucayan words for "String of Islands" while others say the term is said to be derived from the Spanish "cayos" meaning rocky islands.

Many limestone caves abound on the Turks & Caicos Islands, where spelunking is becoming a popular activity. Some of the best caverns are on East and Middle Caicos, the latter of which is also home to some dazzling surface formations of limestone. Several valuable archeological sites containing pre-Columbian artifacts have recently been found in some of the caves on Middle Caicos.

A very unusual and interesting phenomena occurs on a monthly basis after a full moon throughout the Caicos Islands. Look for an ebb tide about 3-6 nights after a full moon. About 1 hour after sunset, for around 15 minutes, the marine worm *Odontosyllis enopia* performs a sparkling mating ritual. Simply called *Glowworms*, the female of the species releases an egg mass that spirals to the surface emitting a pulsating pale green luminescence. The male, also glowing, does a zig-zag sort of maneuver until he encounters these egg masses, causing an even brighter green flow. The number of mating displays may change from month to month but the spawning cycle is dictated by the lunar and solar patterns happening only a few nights of the month. This is a fascinating ritual to watch and most charter boat operators offer sunset glowworm cruises complete with dinner and drinks.

APPROACHES TO THE CAICOS ISLANDS

Vessels approaching the Caicos Islands from The Bahamas usually make Mayaguana their last stop in this island chain as they work their way south to Provo. From the waypoint at the eastern entrance to Abraham's Bay, 22° 21.70'N, 72° 58.45'W, the entrance to Sandbore Channel lies 46.6 miles away on a course of 150° while Leeward Cut bears 134° at 54.1 nautical miles distant. Bruce Van Sant, in his excellent guide book, *The Gentleman's Guide to Passages South*, suggests using Southeast Point as a staging area and leaving from there instead of the slightly longer run from Abraham's Bay. This is an excellent idea except in southeast winds as Mr. Van Sant also reminds us. In southeast winds the reef gives you no protection whatsoever. The best protection you have at Southeast Point is from winds from the northeast to east. From the GPS waypoint at Southeast Point, Mayaguana at 22° 16.70'N, 72° 48.40'W, Sandbore Channel bears 157° at a distance of 37.6 nautical miles while Leeward Cut bears 135° at 44 miles. The primary hazard on the route from Mayaguana to Sellar's Pond, Stubbs Cut, or Leeward Cut are the reefs of North West Point on Providenciales. A GPS waypoint at 21° 53.10'N, 72° 19.90'W, will place you approximately ½ mile north of the reefs in deep water. If your route takes you to Sellar's Pond, Stubbs Cut, or Leeward Cut, especially at night, do not venture south of this waypoint until east of 72° 17' W. Also, bear in mind that when you head towards Sandbore Channel, sometimes called the Columbus Passage. From the Front Street anchorage at Grand Turk, the waypoint at the entrance to Cockburn Harbour on South Caicos bears 281° at a distance of 21.1 nautical miles. From Salt Cay, Cockburn Harbour bears 306° at 19.3 miles, while from Great Sand Cay it bears 328° at 22.7 miles distant.

Long Cay Cut at the south end of Long Cay bears 275° at 23.4 miles from the Front Street anchorage at Grand Turk, 298° at 20.6 miles from Salt Cay, and 320° at 22.9 miles from Great Sand Cay. Vessels heading to Provo across the Caicos Bank see the section entitled *Routes Across The Caicos Bank.*

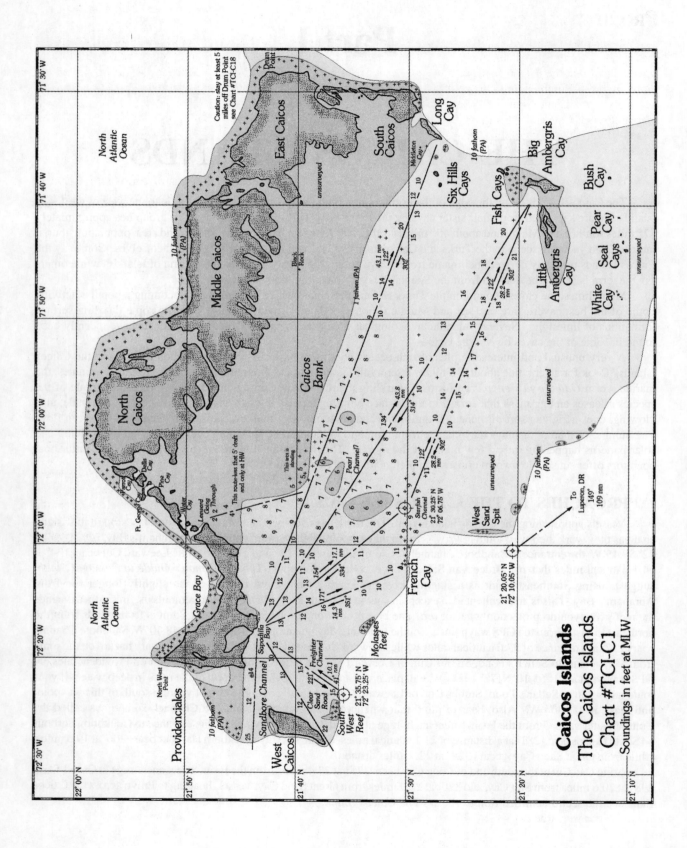

Caicos Islands
The Caicos Islands
Chart #TCI-C1
Soundings in feet at MLW

PROVIDENCIALES

Once known as *Blue Caicos* and *Provident Caicos*, Providenciales, or as everybody calls it, Provo ("Just say Provo mon, don' hurt your tongue."), is the tourist and yachting center of the Turks and Caicos Islands. One local legend has it that the island was named by the survivors of a French boat, *La Providentielle*, that washed up on the shore. In pre-Columbian times there were several Lucayan settlements on Provo; caves dating to that era await your discovery in the Long Point and West Harbour Bluff areas. In later years, Provo, like many of its neighboring cays, such as French Cay, and Parrot Cay, were said to be a stopping place for pirates waiting to ambush treasure laden vessels plying the waters of the Caicos Passage. As in The Bahamas, the Loyalists came and went next. They found less success in the Turks and Caicos Islands than they did in The Bahamas, primarily due to its more arid climate. The ruins of the Loyalist era *Cheshire Hall Plantation* lie near the *Market Place* on Leeward Highway.

The northern and most of the western shore is protected by an almost continuous fringing reef with few breaks. This reef, with its almost vertical thousand foot drop-offs, is the focus for the multitude of dive operations on Provo. The 38 square mile island has over 30 square miles of protected land and sea areas designated by the National Parks system. The protected areas include the Chalk Sound National Park, North West Point Marine National Park, the North West Point Nature Reserve, the Princess Alexandra Land and Sea Park, the Princess Alexandra Nature Reserve, the Pigeon Pond and Frenchman's Creek Nature Reserve, the Cheshire Hall Loyalist Ruins, and Sapodilla Hill, with its stones engraved by shipwrecked sailors.

The three oldest settlements on the island are The Bight and Blue Hills on the northern shore and Five Cays on the southern shore. The Bight and Blue Hills were built around fresh water supplies and these locations give one a real feeling of a Caribbean settlement. Blue Hills had a notorious reputation as the wrecking capital of the island until just after the American Civil War. Nearby North West Reef contributed much to this profession and to the reputation of the community. Five Cays is primarily a fishing settlement with a large Haitian population. As recently as 1960, these three villages were all there was to Providenciales. It was on Provo that the economy of the Turks and Caicos first experienced its rebirth in the late 1960's, as tourism began to take over from the steadily declining salt industry.

In 1966, a Swedish surveyor named Bengt Soderqvist met with Fritz Luddington, who had been flying over the island for many years. These two shared their interests with other developers of vision. The government allowed the group to lease/purchase some 4,000 acres on Providenciales. In October of 1966, the seven investors, or the 'Seven Dwarfs' as they were called, arrived on Providenciales on a boat of the same name. Tommy Coleman was the advance man for Fritz Luddington and his Provident Ltd. group. The other five investors were Julia Barber, Rogers Morton, Peter Thompson, Theodore Roosevelt III, and Richard DuPont. Provident Ltd. had certain obligations to meet to satisfy the government in order to receive the acreage, and these were met by 1971, scarcely five years from the inception of the project. This included the dredging of Sellar's Pond and the creation of a channel to the sea, the building of roads to connect the three settlements of Blue Hills, The Bight, and Five Cays, the construction of a hotel and a jetty at Five Cays, and the employment of a certain number of the local population. The jetty was actually constructed at South Dock as Five Cays was too shallow.

Provident Ltd. laid the early groundwork for the boom that was to come, and Provo is still right in the midst of that tourism boom. Resorts, marinas, restaurants, condos, residential projects, dive operations, a casino, and several shopping centers have all sprung up in recent years, and the end is nowhere in sight. Provo serves more than 100,000 visitors annually and it is a truly cosmopolitan island where you will find native Turks and Caicos islanders (Belongers), American, European and Canadian expatriates, Haitians, Dominicans and a variety of other nationalities and cultures. There are several major resorts, a casino and one posh golf course.

Many cruisers have a love/hate relationship with Provo. Just as you cannot judge The Bahamas by Nassau, if you don't like Provo don't judge all the islands of the Turks and Caicos group by her standards. You'll find that many residents on the other islands in the Turks and Caicos archipelago often say that Provo is too cosmopolitan, that it tries to be too American. Indeed, Provo has a livelier nightlife, and more hustle and bustle than Grand Turk and South Caicos, and may give one the impression of being more of a suburb of Florida than a Caribbean hideaway. You will find that the rest of the islands of the Turks and Caicos have a much more laid-back out-island feel to them. A final note; if you are having any packages or mail sent to you in the Turks and Caicos and especially Provo, have them sent by *UPS* or *Fed-Ex*, never by regular mail delivery - even first class or airmail. It might take weeks. Even going by *UPS* or *Fed-Ex* often poses a danger. I once ordered a part from a major marine supplier and told them to *Fed-Ex* it to me in Provo, Turks and Caicos Islands. Somehow, I still don't know how, it got to me even though it was addressed to the Cocos Keeling Islands. I've had other friends who found their mail had been forwarded to St. Kitts instead of the Turks and Caicos Islands. You'd think in this modern age. . .

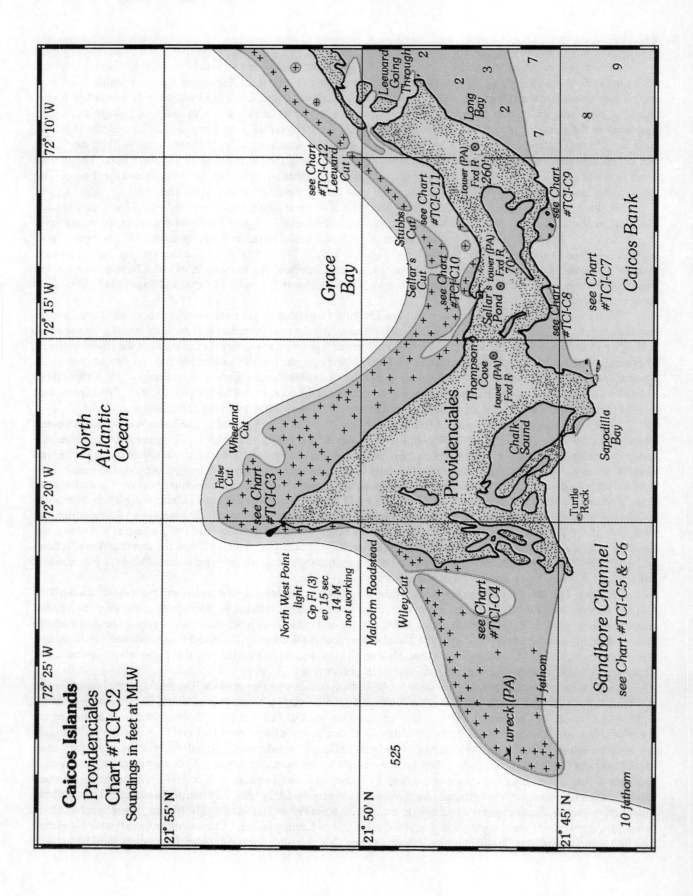

Caicos Islands
Providenciales
Chart #TCI-C2
Soundings in feet at MLW

72° 25' W   72° 20' W   72° 15' W   72° 10' W

21° 55' N

North
Atlantic
Ocean

False
Cut

Wheeland
Cut

see Chart
#TCI-C3

Grace
Bay

see Chart
#TCI-C12
Leeward
Cut

Leeward
Going
Through

2

Long
Bay

2

2

7

3

7

8

9

Stubbs
Cut

see Chart
#TCI-C11

tower (PA)
Fxd R
260

Sellar's
Cut

see Chart
#TCI-C10

Sellar's tower (PA)
Fxd R
70

see Chart
#TCI-C9

Pond

see Chart
#TCI-C8

see Chart
#TCI-C7

Caicos Bank

North West Point
light
Gp Fl (3)
ev 15 sec
14 M
not working

Malcolm Roadstead

Wiley Cut

see Chart
#TCI-C4

wreck (PA)

1 fathom

Providenciales

Thompson
Cove
tower (PA)
Fxd R

Chalk
Sound

Turtle
Rock

Sapodilla
Bay

21° 50' N

525

Sandbore Channel
see Chart #TCI-C5 & C6

21° 45' N

10 fathom

SANDBORE CHANNEL AND SAPODILLA BAY

Vessels approaching Sapodilla Bay and the western shore of Providenciales from Mayaguana or The Plana Cays will have no obstructions. If headed to Leeward Going Through or Turtle Cove Marina at Sellar's Pond on the northern shore of Provo on Grace Bay, you must take care to avoid the reefs off North West Point as shown on Chart #TCI-C2. A good rule of thumb is not to head south of 21° 53'N until east of 72° 17'W.

Tiki huts on Provo.

South of North West Point on the western shore of Providenciales is a great anchorage in prevailing winds with quite an amusing recent history. Malcolm Roadstead offers a deep, reef-clear entrance right up to the beach as shown on Chart #TCI-C3. Columbus is said to have anchored here in October of 1492. You too can anchor right off the beach in 8'-15' of water by the Tiki Huts. A GPS waypoint at 21° 49.85'N, 72° 20.80'W will place you approximately ½ mile west of the Tiki Huts. From this position simply head in towards the Tiki Huts and anchor wherever your draft allows just off the beach. A good landmark to look for is the first large hill south of North West Point: it has a very distinctive white sandy road running vertically down its western face. The Tiki Huts and the anchorage lie about ¼-½ mile south of the hill.

The Tiki Huts, shown on some charts as Atlantic Village, were originally the set of a French game show called Pago. The theme was a South Pacific island where contestants could win various prizes by completing several tasks. Just offshore is a dive site that consists of a large metal cage left over by the show. Contestants were required to dive down into the cage to catch small plastic pearls that were released into the water by a huge artificial "sponge" inside this cage. Nearby were several mermaids with SCUBA tanks to offer air to the divers when they needed a breath, bracelet-like rings that the divers earned were traded underwater for breaths of air. However there was one bad mermaid who would signal a diver over for a breath and then swim away. This was to add a bit of excitement to the show. You can imagine the problems they might have had with this format. The show filmed less than a dozen episodes that are sometimes still shown today on the local cable TV station. You can reach the Tiki Huts by car but it must be a four-wheel drive vehicle as the road leading in from Blue Hills is very rough

Just south of Malcolm Roadstead is narrow Wiley Cut just north of Wiley Point. Vessels with drafts of less than 6', with the tide can work their way along the western shore of Provo from Wiley Cut to West Harbour Bluff on the inside of the reef, but I do not recommend this route for the average cruiser. By using this route you'll save only a little time by not going around the reef to the mouth of the Sandbore Channel and the risk involved is not worth the few minutes saved. I only show this passage because it can be done and several local charter and dive boats use this reef-strewn route. A GPS waypoint at 21° 48.85'N, 72°, 21.35'W, will place you approximately ¼ mile north/northwest of Wiley Cut as shown on Chart #TCI-C4. Never, I repeat NEVER, attempt this route with the sun directly in your eyes, with heavy

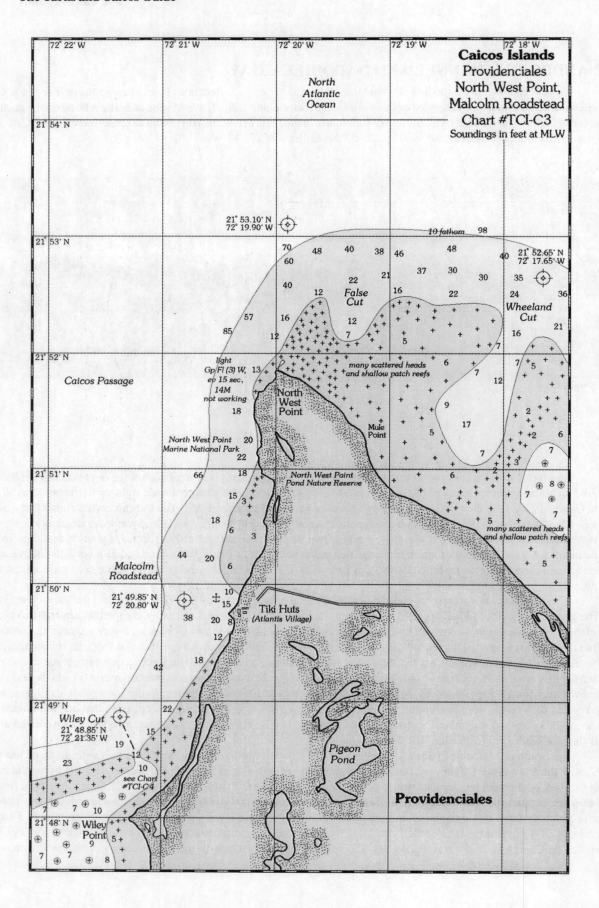

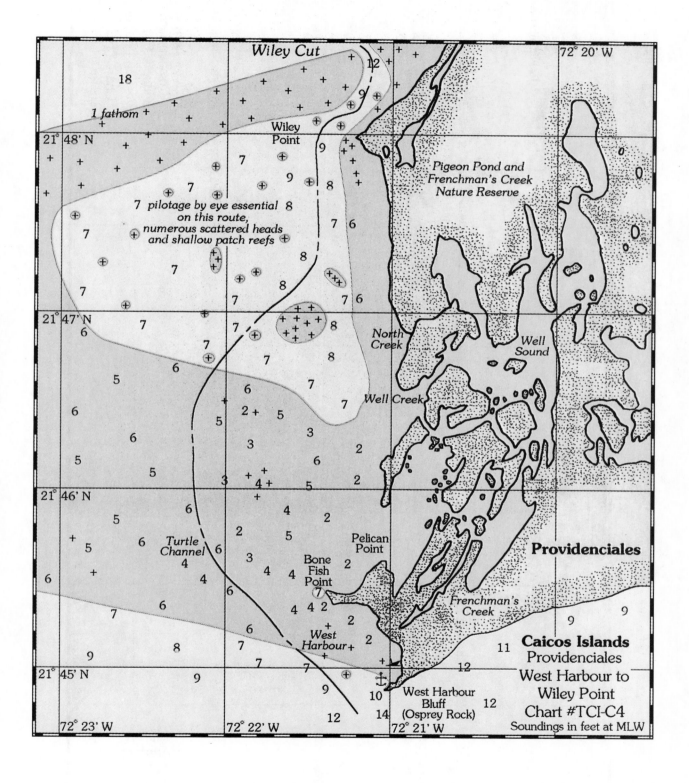

Wiley Cut

72° 20' W

18

1 fathom

21° 48' N

Wiley Point

7 pilotage by eye essential
on this route,
numerous scattered heads
and shallow patch reefs

Pigeon Pond and
Frenchman's Creek
Nature Reserve

21° 47' N

North Creek

Well Sound

Well Creek

21° 46' N

Turtle Channel

Pelican Point

Bone Fish Point

West Harbour

Frenchman's Creek

Providenciales

21° 45' N

West Harbour Bluff (Osprey Rock)

Caicos Islands
Providenciales
West Harbour to
Wiley Point
Chart #TCI-C4
Soundings in feet at MLW

72° 23' W

72° 22' W

72° 21' W

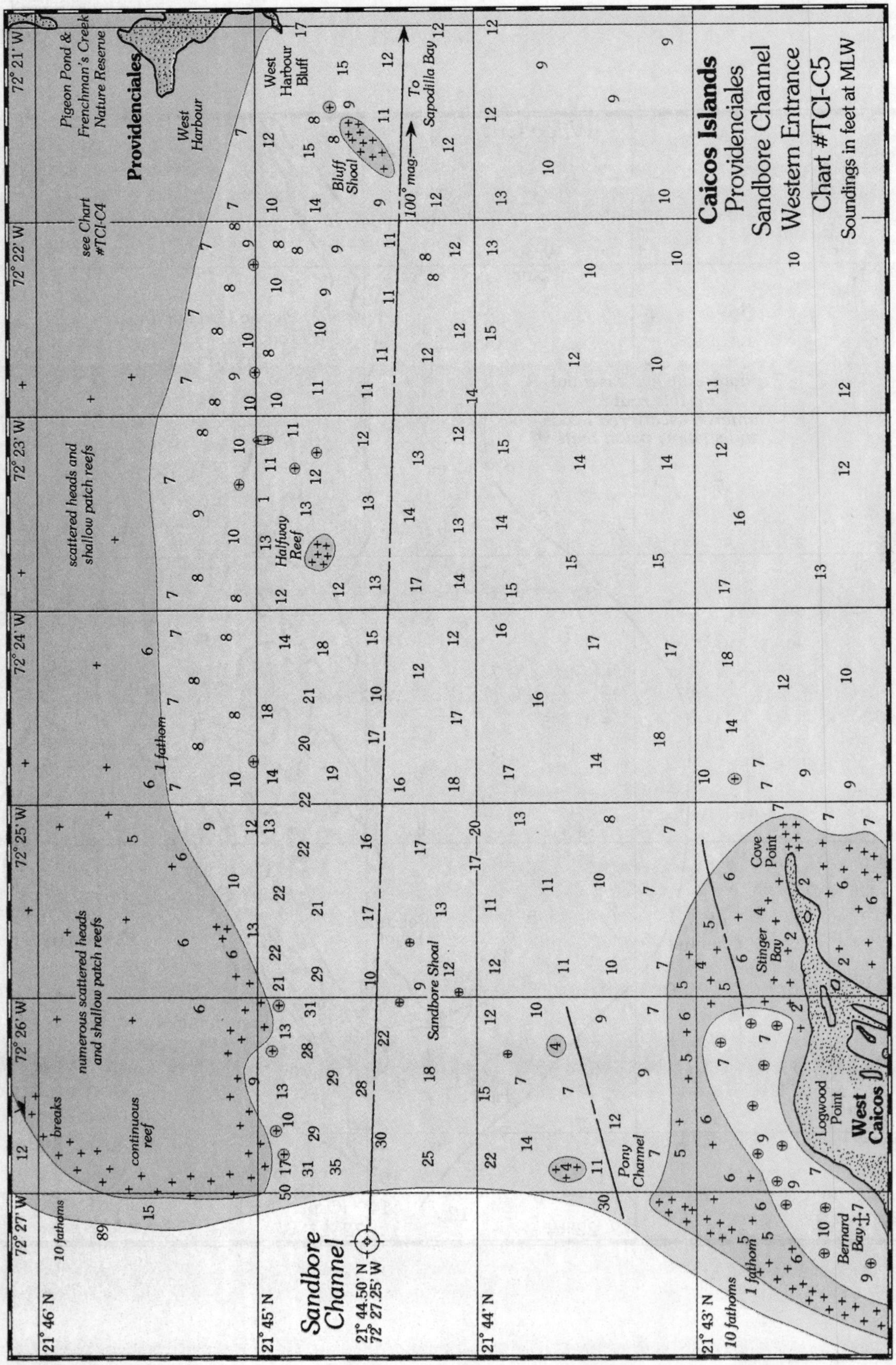

Providenciales

Pigeon Pond & Frenchman's Creek Nature Reserve

West Harbour

West Harbour Bluff

see Chart #TCI-C4

scattered heads and shallow patch reefs

Bluff Shoal

To Sapodilla Bay

100° mag.

Halfway Reef

numerous scattered heads and shallow patch reefs

continuous reef

breaks

10 fathoms

1 fathom

Sandbore Channel

21° 44.50' N
72° 27.25' W

Sandbore Shoal

Pony Channel

Cove Point

Stinger Bay

Logwood Point

West Caicos

Bernard Bay

1 fathom

10 fathoms

Caicos Islands
Providenciales
Sandbore Channel
Western Entrance
Chart #TCI-C5
Soundings in feet at MLW

21° 46' N
21° 45' N
21° 44' N
21° 43' N

72° 27' W 72° 26' W 72° 25' W 72° 24' W 72° 23' W 72° 22' W 72° 21' W

following seas, or during periods of poor visibility and cloudy, murky water. Head in through the cut on a heading of SSE-SE keeping between the two very visible reefs. Work your way around Wiley Point as shown on Chart #TCI-C4 steering between the numerous shallow head and patch reefs that are strewn across the northern section of this route and, believe me, they are thick through here. Keep working your way southward, zigzagging between the heads, reefs, and shallow bars that begin to thin out along with the water around North Creek. Do not attempt to follow the courseline exactly as drawn on Chart #TCI-C4: it is only for reference. Your actual route will be quite a bit more circuitous with little resemblance to the courseline on the chart. Use your eyes through here, nothing else will get you through. Just north of North Creek, boats drawing less than 4' have the option of continuing southward paralleling the shore closer in to work your way through the shallows west of the area between Well Creek and Bone Fish Point. Vessels drawing over 5' are advised to head further west (as shown on the chart) around the shallows and through Turtle Channel. Vessels can anchor on the western side of West Harbour Bluff in prevailing winds but you cannot tuck in close to the beach unless you draw less than 3'. Once past West Harbour Bluff you can turn eastward to proceed to Sapodilla Bay as shown on Chart #TCI-C6.

Vessels wishing to arrive at Sapodilla Bay via wide Sandbore Channel should head to a GPS waypoint at 21° 44.50'N, 72° 27.25'W, which will place you approximately ¾ mile west of the mouth of the Sandbore Channel as shown on Chart #TCI-C5. From this position you can take up your course of 100° for the 9.17 miles to the waypoint just south of the anchorage at Sapodilla Bay. The only obstructions on this route are the couple of shallow rocks at Sandbore Shoal as shown on Chart #TCI-C5, but if you stay on your course you will pass well north of these. Once past this area your only worries are Halfway Reef and Bluff Shoal, both also shown on Chart #TCI-C5. Once past Sandbore Shoal, if you must stray from your course, stray south as that is where the deeper obstruction-free water will be. As you approach the Turtle Rock-Sapodilla Bay area watch out for the scattered heads that will lie well north of your course line as shown on Chart #TCI-C6.

Just south of the entrance to Sandbore Channel is another smaller break in the reef called the Pony Channel. About the only boats that use this channel are the Provo dive boats on their way back from diving the western shore of West Caicos. It is usable and that is why I show it on Chart #TCI-C5, though I suggest that the average cruising boat use Sandbore Channel instead; it is wider, deeper and safer. Pony Channel saves you little in the way of time and distance and once inside the reef you must avoid another smaller rocky bar on the inside.

On the northern side of the Sandbore Channel (as shown on Chart #TCI-C6) the shoreline of Providenciales is generally rocky and steep to. One can anchor along here, but this should only be done in northerly winds or calm weather. In moderate or above prevailing winds, primarily east to southeast, a considerable chop builds up from Sapodilla Bay to the west and makes this shore very uncomfortable. A small canal and swing bridge (vertical clearance only about 5' when closed) has been constructed to connect the Silly Creek area to Proggin Bay. Silly Creek is a private planned community and plans are afoot to build a marina inside. Currently access is limited to boaters who own property at Silly Creek, which is a shame because Silly Creek is a fantastic hurricane hole if you could get in there.

Heading east down Sandbore Channel, a GPS waypoint at 21° 44.25'N, 72° 17.40'W, will place you approximately ¼ mile south of the anchorage at Sapodilla Bay. It is not necessary to keep on the course line all the way from the entrance to Sandbore Channel to this waypoint. Once past Turtle Rock you can begin to adjust your course more north of east to arrive right in Sapodilla Bay but you must keep an eye out for a few scattered, shallow heads.

The anchorage at Sapodilla Bay, as shown on Chart #TCI-C6, although shallow, has very good holding in soft sand, but I see so many skippers anchoring too far south and west, virtually out of the small protection that the point offers, most likely this is due to their deeper drafts. Sapodilla Bay is good in north through east winds, but when the wind goes into the southeast, the waves work their way right around the point and can make it a bit uncomfortable. If you anchor as far as your draft will allow to the north; you will have less wave action in southeast winds. A draft of 5' can tuck in fairly close. If a frontal passage threatens, cruisers in Sapodilla Bay will find good protection in Bermudian Harbour, sometimes shown as Mudjian or Mudjon Harbour, just north of the Five Cays as shown on Chart #TCI-C7. From Sapodilla Bay head east past South Dock, William Dean Cay, Pussey Cay and Sim Cay. Head northward between Sim Cay and Bay Cay and anchor wherever you draft allows and you'll find adequate protection from south through west to north winds. You can also anchor on the northern side of Bay Cay, but you get a little more wave action there in strong west winds. If you anchor in Bermudian Harbour, don't anchor too close in towards the Providenciales shore as the water thins quickly and the bottom is poor holding. Another option is to anchor in the lee of Middle Cay, also shown on Chart #TCI-C7. Again, when the wind moves into the north it will be time to move back to Sapodilla Bay.

On the hill overlooking Sapodilla Bay is the old *Provo Aquatic Center* at the southeastern end of the bay. The center has not been open in a few years and many cruisers are under the mistaken idea that they can clear in there or use the dock. The building is private now and the dock is reserved for the occasional dive boat to load and unload passengers, but several cruisers have been using the dock to tie up while in town. If unsure as to whether or not to use this dock, ask around; those skippers

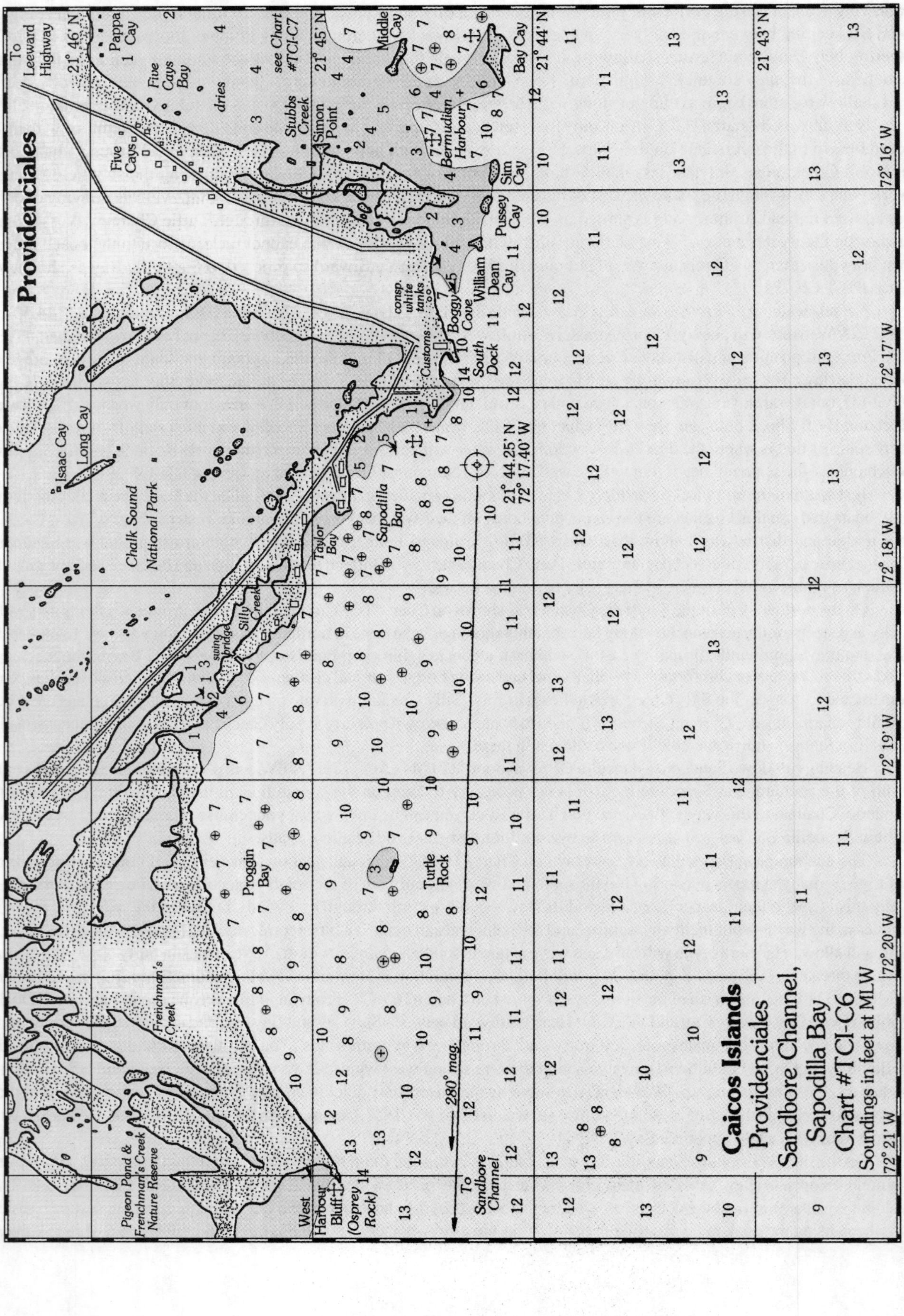

Providenciales

To Leeward Highway

Pappa 1 Cay

Five Cays Bay

dries

see Chart #TCI-C7

Middle Cay

Stubbs Creek

Simon Point

Bermudian Harbour

Sim Cay

Bay Cay

Five Cays

Pussey Cay

William Dean Cay

Boggy Cove

consp. white tanks

Customs

South Dock

Isaac Cay

Long Cay

Chalk Sound National Park

Sapodilla Bay

Taylor Bay

Silly Creek

swing bridge

Proggin Bay

Turtle Rock

Frenchman's Creek

Pigeon Pond & Frenchman's Creek Nature Reserve

West Harbour Bluff (Osprey Rock)

To Sandbore Channel

← 280° mag.

21° 44.25' N
72° 17.40' W

21° 46' N   21° 45' N   21° 44' N   21° 43' N

72° 16' W   72° 17' W   72° 18' W   72° 19' W   72° 20' W   72° 21' W

Caicos Islands
Providenciales
Sandbore Channel,
Sapodilla Bay
Chart #TCI-C6
Soundings in feet at MLW

there before you will probably have the latest information on the status of the dock. Rumor has it that the old *Aquatic Center* is to be torn down and a condo built in its place. On the eastern side of the hill, Sapodilla Hill, is the *Mariner Hotel and Bakery*. While not very busy as a hotel they do serve up some excellent baked goods. On the top of Sapodilla Hill are several stones that were engraved by shipwrecked sailors and can be accessed from the hotel side of the hill or from the gravel road by the old *Aquatic Center* using a steep, rocky trail.

Vessels arriving at Sapodilla Bay and wishing to clear *Customs* are now advised to dinghy in to shore and walk to the *Customs* office, a walk of about a mile. You can still take your dinghy around Gussie Point, less than ½ mile to the east and tie up to the dock if it's empty and no freighters are due and walk the hundred or so yards to the green, multi-story office. It would be a good idea to secure the contents of your dinghy here as I have had cruisers tell me that they had their dinghies searched for valuables when left here; so leave nothing aboard that can wander off easily. I always leave my dink here and have never been troubled by theft or any appearance of attempted theft. Of course, I'm usually carrying all sorts of weapons to leave at *Customs* and that could be why my dink isn't bothered by whoever is messing around in our boats. Clearance itself is usually painless and quick; the fee is $5.00. For more detailed information on clearing in see the section "*Customs and Immigration*" in the chapter "*The Basics*." You can also contact *Customs* by calling *Harbourmaster* on VHF ch. 16, but this is not required unless you arrive after hours in the early evening. If you arrive at night they'll usually suggest that you wait until the morning to come in and clear anyway.

If you plan to stay longer than seven days, you must next visit the *Immigration* office located downtown. *Immigration* is now located in the large gray building that says "*Sam's*" and that sits just east of *Island Pride Supermarket*. From *Customs*, you should dinghy back around to Sapodilla Bay and leave your dink at the north end of the beach and lock it if you can, at least lock your motor to the dinghy. Since the first edition of this guide there have been a couple of dinghy thefts here. From here you can walk about 50 yards to the road and hitchhike into town (they drive on the left here, so hitchhike accordingly). If you would rather have a ride waiting for you, call *Morris Bus* on VHF ch. 16. Mr. Morris will pick you up at Sapodilla Bay and take you downtown for $4.00 per person, round trip. You can place your garbage in the dumpster on the dirt road just in from beach at the southeast end of Sapodilla Bay. Other buses can be called on VHF ch. 70 and taxis monitor VHF ch. 06. The taxis are very, very expensive. You will find out that it is cheaper for four persons to rent a car than to pay for a taxi from one of the resorts to Leeward or Sapodilla Bay. The taxis are supposed to charge $2.00 per person per mile. Some of the buses and jitneys, with the exception of *Morris Bus*, will try to get as much as they can for their service from the unwary tourist. By all means, agree on a price before boarding the bus or taxi or you will find that you may have made a grievous and expensive error. I would just as soon call *Morris Bus* as anyone; Mr. Morris can be trusted. Unfortunately, unless you arrange things in advance, Mr. Morris doesn't work at night, I don't blame him.

If you need a diesel mechanic try *Caribbean Marine Diesel*; they are based at the *Caicos Marina and Boatyard*, you can phone owner Mike Spears at 941-5903. As an alternative, you can phone George Nixon, at 946-5763.

The facilities that abound on Provo itself could fill an entire book, and you will find pamphlets and small magazines and papers all over town advertising this and that. I will endeavor to give you a brief description of what is to be found on Provo, but only if you promise not to swear at me in the event that I missed some special or favorite place of yours. I haven't been to each and every store and building on the island, most perhaps, and I have certainly not eaten at every restaurant; that would take a long time and a lot of money and my publisher would not go for that! So with that in mind, let's head up the South Dock Road from Sapodilla Bay towards the main road on the island, Leeward Highway, and I'll try to give you a mini-tour of what's available.

From Sapodilla Bay and the docking facilities at *South Dock*, the South Dock Road winds up and over the gentle hills northward toward Leeward Highway. Just north of *South Dock* is the large *Shell* complex where you can get your propane filled. As you pass over the hills you'll get an absolutely gorgeous view of beautiful Chalk Sound and its vivid green waters. About a mile or so north of the Shell complex is a Texaco station on your left. Just before the South Dock Road joins the Leeward Highway you'll see Kishco on the right. This is a small dry-goods store with all sorts of home-related goodies for sale. Before long you'll come to the intersection at the Leeward Highway. The Leeward Highway is the main road that stretches from the airport on the western end of the cay all the way to *Leeward Marina* at the eastern end of Provo and this is where you'll find the bulk of the business on Provo located. To your right at the intersection is *Lamont's Barbecue and Grill* for take out food, or if you choose, eat outside at one of their tables.

If you take a left at Leeward Highway you will be on the old Airport Road where immediately on your right you will see *Discount Liquors, Micro 2000 Computer Sales and Service*, a barber shop, and a beauty parlor as well. Past *Micro 2000*, just before the police station and the post office is *Gil's Island Craft*, the only place in the Turks and Caicos to have your sails repaired at this time. Owner Gil Selver repairs sails as well as upholstery, dive suits and Bimini tops.

If you take a right on Leeward Highway from South Dock Road you will have several miles of stores and restaurants before you. On the left, just past *Discount Liquors* is Airport Road which leads (where else?) to the *Fritz Luddington International Airport*. A hundred yards down the road is the large *Walkin Marine* facility. *Walkin Marine* is the only boating supply store on the island and it is a good one. *Walkin Marine*, an *OMC* dealer, carries a good supply of outboard parts as well as most anything you need such as wire, *5200*, SS nuts and bolts, line, anchors, fishing supplies and frozen bait. They also perform service work on all outboard motors at their facility on Blue Hills Road. For more info ask at the store or call *Walkin Marine* on VHF ch. 16 and ask for Sherlock. At the airport you can rent a car, visit any of several small shops, or dine at *Gilley's Restaurant*. *Gilley's* has fine food and is owned by the same folks as the *Gilley's* at *Leeward Marina*. Also on Airport Road is *Tibor's Machine Shop*, the only one on the island. If you're hungry you might want to stop at *Fast Eddies* for seafood and native dishes.

Proceeding eastward on Leeward Highway from the Airport Road, you will now enter the downtown area. "Downtown" is little more than a few stores and small mall-like centers along the Leeward Highway at what is known as *Butterfield Square*. On the north side of Leeward Highway you will see the yellow *Barclay's Bank* building which also houses some government offices, and several other shops. Next door is the *American Airlines* office and the *Public Treasury*. A must stop is *Tasty Temptations*, open at 6:30 every morning until mid-afternoon serving fresh buns, rolls, bread, croissants and sandwiches.

Across the street, on the southern side of Leeward Highway, is the *Town Center Mall* where you'll find a *Donny's Express*, a branch of the *Bank of Nova Scotia*, a computer service shop, and the *Island Pride Supermarket*. *Island Pride* is a great provisioning stop with a good deli and everything from frozen foods to fresh meats and veggies as well as fresh milk, orange juice and ice cream. Just east of *Island Pride* is the new *Immigration* office in a large gray building that simply says "Sam's" on the front.

Just past *Butterfield Square* on the northern side of the road there is a *Shell* station just before the intersection with Blue Hills Road. Blue Hills Road takes you northward along the gorgeous Grace Bay shoreline through Blue Hills and northwards to North West Point and the *Tiki Hut*s via the new Millenium Highway. Blue Hills is a lovely little community, the oldest one on the island, located on the edge of Grace Bay and bordering Blue Hills Road from Leeward Highway all the way to the road turns into a sandy track past Reef Harbour. Here you'll find the *Government Clinic*, the *Provo Food Fair*, *Rigby's Variety Store* and *Where It's At* where you can find fine Jamaican and native dishes. Where Blue Hills Road does a 90° at Grace Bay you'll find *Bugaloo's Blue Water Park* where you can have the freshest conch and conch salad found almost anywhere, right out of the bay to your plate. About a half a mile west sits *Pub on the Bay* offering excellent native cooking and "just catched" seafood served to you right on the beach under palm thatched Tiki Huts. You've gotta try *Pub on the Bay*. Another fine eatery is *Henry's Road Runner Restaurant and Bar* specializing in local dishes. There is a strong Haitian influence in Blue Hills; one gentleman I talked to estimated it to be about 50% Haitian. Further west on Blue Hills road, just past the *Three Queens Bar*, look to seaward and you will see several sailboats in various stages of construction. The Dean family, primarily James Pringle Dean and James Dean, has been building sloops here on the beach for over 30 years and racing them regularly in the local regattas.

Back on the Leeward Highway, as you continue east you'll come to a *CIBC Bank* on the right and across the street is the *Market Place* where the *Bamboo Art Gallery*, *Unicorn Bookstore* and *Mackie's* is located. *Mackie's* is probably one of the best spots on the island for true Turks and Caicos Island cooking and it's a very, very popular spot. Seating is outdoors and the food is piled high on your plate, very tasty and extremely economical. *The Unicorn Bookstore* is the place to go for reading materials (lot's of kid's stuff too!), recent periodicals, used as well as new books, and lot's of guides for the Caribbean. They also carry *The Turks and Caicos Guide*.

Continuing down Leeward Highway the shops begin to spread out more and more. You'll pass places like *Provo Building Supply*, the *Rigby Medical Center* and the local *Fed-Ex* office. Just past the *FedEx* office a road heads off to the south of Leeward Highway, where on the hills above Five Cays, you'll find *Contractors Building Supplies* and *ICS (International Car Services)*: 946-4425 which also has new as well as used auto parts. Next to *ICS*, sometimes called the *Car Doctor,* is *TC Gas* where you can get your propane filled here while you wait

Heading east from Market Square you'll come to a huge *DO-IT Center*, much like a *Home-Depot* in the United States. Next on your right is a large two-story green building with several gift shops, a barber shop, a Realtor, a pharmacy and the *Go-Fish Restaurant*.

Moving eastward once again on Leeward Highway, those provisioning will want to visit the newly opened *Laster's Price Club* with it's huge stock of groceries and dry goods. *Laster's* moved here from South Dock Road and their new large building houses even more goodies than their old place. If provisioning in Provo, you'll find the prices generally equivalent to Nassau prices, with some items priced close to stateside prices.

A little more eastward and you will come to *Quality Supermarket, Menzies Medical Center* and *Hey Jose's Mexican Restaurant*, definitely worth a stop for good Mexican food and great pizzas. Check out the jukebox that was donated by Dick Clark of *American Bandstand* fame. There are several small gift shops next to *Hey Jose's* and at the end of the small strip mall and a photography studio. Directly behind *Hey Jose's* you'll find *Payless Foods*. Here you'll find all sorts of packaged food that you can buy in lots at good prices. Things like cookies, soft drinks, sodas and even some paper products. If you need a coin laundry there is one in this area. Heading westward, from *Hey Jose's* to Sapodilla Bay, take your first left, just past *Quality Supermarket* and *Menzies Medical Center* and then take your first right. Go about ¼ mile and on your left will be a small apartment complex. This complex houses a small coin laundry, and the manager, a young Jamaican man, will gladly sell you tokens for the machines. Another laundry, *Pablo's*, lies a bit eastward on the Leeward Highway.

A little east of *Hey Jose's* you will come to *Suzie Turn* at *Suzie Turn Plaza*. The area around the turn-off from Leeward Highway to *Turtle Cove Marina, Draco Restaurant,* and the *Erebus Inn* is called *Suzie Turn*, because Suzie, a secretary who used to work in *Turtle Cove*, could never remember where the turn was. Her friends felt for her and put up a sign that read "Suzie, turn!" Both the sign and Suzie are long gone but the area still bears her name, as does *Suzie Turn Plaza*. More on *Turtle Cove Marina* a little later. On the southern side of Leeward Highway, next door to *Bayview Motors*, you'll find a *NAPA* auto parts store if you need any items that may be useful on a boat (I can think of plenty). One word of warning however: no refunds, all sales are final, even if they gave you the wrong part. Across the street from *NAPA* is *TC Trading Ltd.*, a restaurant supply house that also sells wholesale to the public. Here you can pick up almost any type of kitchen utensil as well as serving dishes and glasses, bulk quantities of spices and staples and fresh or frozen meats and veggies. Just past *Suzie Turn Plaza*, on the left side of Leeward Highway, is the *Cable and Wireless* office. Here you can purchase telephone calling cards in $10.00 increments or use their Internet kiosk to access your email.

If you take a right at the *Texaco* station you can follow the road to the *South Side Basin Marina*. Just as you turn off onto this road you will notice a sign that points to a local artist's house. This is where Phillip Outten lives. Phillip painted the back cover artwork for this guide and he welcomes folks to his house to sample his paintings and carvings. I urge you to stop by and check it out if you're looking for something to adorn a wall or table or whatever.

On the right hand side of Leeward Highway is the huge *IGA* supermarket, another good place for provisioning in Provo. The store is large, even by U.S. standards, and has just about anything you could want including a deli with fresh baked goods. About ¾ mile past *IGA*, on the left, is *Pablo's Laundromat*.

Still eastward on Leeward Highway is *Kathleen's Seven Eleven Convenience Store*, though it is much more than its name implies. *Kathleen's* is more like a regular grocery store than a convenience store as you might be used to in the U.S. or Canada. Here you can find lots of veggies, packaged foods, drinks, ice cream, and frozen meats, but the prices are slightly higher than *IGA* and *Island Pride*. Nearby, on the northern side of Leeward Highway, by the electrical power station, is *Dora's Restaurant and Bar*. *Dora's* serves up delicious native seafood and chicken dishes for breakfast, lunch, and dinner and the seafood buffet on Mondays and Thursdays is not to be missed: only $22.50 per person.

Very soon the pavement will run out on Leeward Highway; actually Leeward Highway makes a 90° turn to the north and a separate gravel road continues eastward. If you follow the rough gravel road you will soon come to the Long Bay Hills area. Taking a right on Long Bay Hills Road will take you to the *Caicos Marina and Boatyard*. At the crest of a hill on the right is Sea Sage Hill Drive where you'll want to visit *The Hole*, a naturally formed massive limestone hole 40' across and over 80' deep. There's a swimming hole at the bottom for those who dare to climb down the ropes to reach it. If you continue down the gravel road past the Long Bay Hills area you will eventually dead end at the *Conch Farm*. You will learn more about the *Conch Farm* in the section *The Caicos Cay: Leeward Going Through to North Caicos*.

If you turn left and follow the pavement of Leeward Highway you'll pass the *New China Restaurant* on your left, some very nice gift shops on your right, and then a miniature golf course where you'll find the new *Mama's Restaurant* and several more gift shops just before the new *Comfort Suites Hotel*. *Neptune Plaza* lies on the left hand side of the road with the *Dolphin Restaurant and Sports Bar*, the *Grace Bay Medical Center*, a photo studio, and a gift shop.

Straight across from you at the "T" intersection is the *Allegro Resort*, formerly the *Turqoise Reef Hotel and Casino*. If you turn left here you will be on what is called the Bight Road, a major road project completed in 1993 to facilitate access to the resorts on Grace Bay. Immediately on your left is the *Bella Luna* restaurant, a multi-storied, Italian restaurant with a huge area for outside dining and glass walls permitting a wonderful view of Grace Bay even in inclement weather. *Bella Luna* is the place to go for true Italian food and good service in an elegant atmosphere. Heading westward on the Bight Road you will pass the area known as Kingston (where *Bonnie's* or *Annie's* are the places to go for local cooking) and the *Beaches Resort* and *Le Deck* resorts. *Beaches* has a good deal for divers. For $85.00 per person, you get to go on a two-tank dive as well as have the complete use of the *Beaches* complex for one day. Swimming pool, beach, tennis court, and the opportunity to sample some outstanding dining are all yours for this one low price. Nearby is *Smokey's On Da Beach*, serving excellent native cuisine right on the waterfront. Keep heading west and the Bight Road will bring you through the settlement of The Bight and onward to the *Turtle Cove Marina* complex, which we will discuss momentarily.

If you were to turn to the right, eastward, at the *Allegro Resort*, immediately on your right is the *Ports of Call* shopping and dining area. This is one of the most popular stops on Provo and the highlight for most is the *Latitudes,* formerly the *Lone Star Café*. Not to be outdone, *Angela's Delicatessen* (you've gotta try an eggle-bagel), the *Caribbean Kitchen*, and the *Marco Polo Restaurant* give *Lone Star* all the competition that they can handle. Shoppers will delight at the offerings of the *Night and Day Boutique*, *Provo Fun Cycles*, and *the Tattooed Parrot* where sailors can even pick up a replacement *Tilley* hat for the one they lost while beating to windward from The Bahamas. Check out *Provocom Ltd.* or *TCI online* for Internet access. If you wish to work off the fancy meals you've been dining on, there is a gym upstairs at *Ports of Call*.

Heading east from *Ports of Call* you will pass the elegant *Grace Bay Club* with its extremely formal *Anacaona Restaurant*. Formal attire only, no children under 12, needless to say this cruiser did not dine here and I apologize if I have let you down. Tell you what, you go and try it and let me know how it was. Opposite the *Grace Bay Club*, behind the beautiful grounds of the *Sunshine Nursery*, is the *Coco Bistro* where you can dine under the palms. All the brochures about this place never mention the mosquitoes and no-see-ums. If you plan to dine here, and you should perhaps, choose a very windy night. Even better, maybe they ought to put a can of insect repellant on every table. A little further east is the huge *Club Med* complex. *Club Med* is very private, it is not open to the general public, but for a fee you can become a member for a day and have access to their complex. Just east of *Club Med* is the *Provo Golf Club*, an 18-hole championship course with an attractive clubhouse that is open to members and non-members alike. The golf course uses over 300,000 gallons of RO water a day to maintain its lush fairways and greens. The Arab backers that financed the golf course had to do something for the island to be allowed to construct the golf course so he built the *Provo Water Company* which benefits the course as well as the islanders. In 1996 the course was rated one of the top ten golf courses in the Caribbean.

Across the street is the *Ocean Club*, a luxury condominium project. Now you will enter the Leeward area where a huge planned community development project is ongoing. The Leeward Highway ends at *Leeward Marina* and Leeward Going Through which we will discuss in greater detail in the section *The Caicos Cays-Leeward Going Through to North Caicos*.

THE SOUTHERN SHORE

There are two good marine facilities on the southern shore of Providenciales including the only haul-out yard in the Turks and Caicos at this time. These services are easily accessible from Sapodilla Bay with only a few small reefs and shoals, easily seen in good light, to avoid. Don't try to head eastward to the marinas at Discovery Bay or Juba Point with the sun right in your eyes first thing in the morning. Bear in mind that strong northeast winds for a day or two can keep the tides low on the southern shore of Providenciales while strong southerly winds will give the area higher tides than normal.

The closest facility to Sapodilla Bay is the *South Side Basin Marina* in Cooper Jack Bight and usually just called Discovery Bay (a draft of 7' can enter the marina at high tide). To reach *South Side Basin Marina* head east from Sapodilla Bay past the Five Cays, William Dean Cay, Pussey Cay, Sim Cay, Middle Cay and Bay Cay, passing south of them as shown on Chart #TCI-C6 and #TCI-C7. Once past Bay Cay you can take up an approximate northeast heading to a GPS waypoint at 21° 45.05' N, 72° 14.00' W, placing you approximately ¼ nautical mile southwest of the entrance channel into the canals of Discovery Bay and the marina as shown on Chart #TCI-C8. From the waypoint in Cooper Jack Bight you will be able to look northeastward and see the marina complex hiding just inland. At this point, you can head generally NE past Cooper Jack Rock until you pick up the markers leading in to the marina. Watch out for scattered heads and shallow bars on this route, the whole southern shore of Providenciales has numerous scattered heads and bars strewn about that are easily seen in good light and avoided. Be sure to take the point and its shallow sandbar well to starboard. Round into the deeper water of the entrance channel and proceed to the marina that lies straight ahead. To your left, as the canals of Discovery Bay bear away, you will see the new *Provo Marine Biology Education Center*. Turtle Lake at the end of the canals is a good bonefishing spot. The *South Side Basin Marina* lies just ahead and to starboard. Here you can find diesel, gasoline, and dockage alongside though you might wish to call ahead. Facilities are slim at this time as the marina is still under construction with a restaurant, showers and a laundry planned. For transportation call *Morris Bus*.

Well east of Cooper Jack Bight is Juba Point and the well-marked entrance to the *Caicos Marina and Boatyard* where a draft of 6' can enter just past low tide. Canadian investor Ted Trump built this marina in 1986 with the goal of making it the largest marina complex in the Caribbean and today, new owners are in the process of upgrading and expanding the services with plans for more slips and a even a playground for the kiddies. *Caicos Marina and Boatyard*, the only place to haul a boat (a 75-ton travelift and a 20-ton forklift) between Stella Maris and George Town in the Bahamas, and Puerto Rico, sells diesel, gas, ice, sodas, and RO water. The marina also has a small laundry, public telephone, and will handle your mail and fax needs. The yard can handle all sorts of hull related work such as fiberglass repairs, strut work, welding, painting, interior repairs, and even motor work in their newly refurbished eco-friendly yard. Dockage is side-to along their 500' dock and with the installation of their new floating docks, *Caicos Marina and Boatyard* are able to accommodate approximately 24 vessels with full electric and RO water. Their large shed has now been converted into stacked dry-storage for smaller boats and the marina now offers long-term wet and dry storage of cruising boats including a care-taking service to run your engine, pump the bilge, and charge the batteries. The *Caicos Marina and Boatyard* can be reached by VHF on Ch. 16, or by phone at 649-946-5600, by fax at 649-946-5390, and by email at caicosmarinashp@tciway.tc. Marine parts and any type of groceries require a healthy cab ride into town so again it's best to call *Morris Bus*.

Housed on the marina property is Mike Spear's *Caribbean Marine Diesel* where you can have your engine serviced or replaced, welding done, and have your prop straightened. You telephone *Caribbean Marine Diesel* for service if your boat can't make it to the marina at 941-5903. There is another gentleman on the island that handles diesel repairs, his name is George Nixon and you can phone him at 946-5763.

Photo Courtesy of Lenny Williams

Entrance to Discovery Bay.

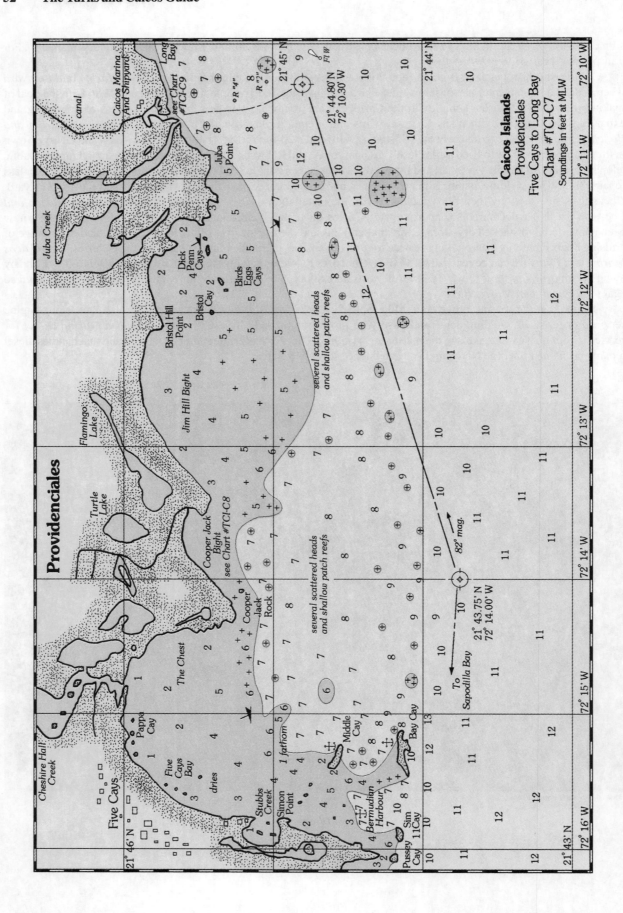

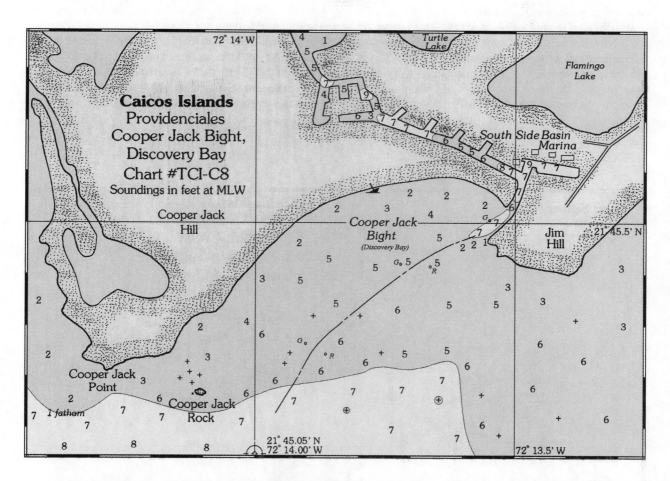

To find Juba Point and the *Boatyard* from the Sapodilla waypoint steer 108° for 3.2 miles, past the Five Cays, William Dean Cay, Pussey Cay, Sim Cay, Middle Cay, and Bay Cay, to a GPS waypoint at 21° 43.75'N, 72° 14.00'W, as shown on Chart #TCI-C7. The best way to describe the route to the *Boatyard* is to use the natural land formations themselves instead of GPS waypoints. From the waypoint southeast of Bay Cay, look to the north and east. That last point of land that you see to the east is Juba Point. Heading just north of east on a course of approximately 82°, a line of dark spots, shallow patch reefs and rocky bars, will lie parallel to this route. Keep south of all the dark spots that you see (the line of shallow reefs) keeping them well off your port side as the deeper, obstruction free water lies to their south. The actual course line has you passing north of one of the dark reefs, but it is fine to pass it to the south as well. The course here is not as important as staying in the clear blue/green water and avoiding any dark patches that you see. As you approach Juba Point you will notice what looks like a huge white "I" seemingly carved into the hillside. Actually it is a sandy road with a vertical trail leading down to a sandy beach. As you take the huge white "I" on your port beam, the *Boatyard* entrance channel lies approximately ¾ mile to the east. At this point you should be able to make out the cranes and perhaps even the entrance channel markers of *Caicos Marina and Boatyard*. From here you can work your way to a GPS waypoint at 21° 44.80' N, 72° 10.30' W, which will place you a little over 1 nautical mile south of the entrance channel leading into the *Caicos Marina and Boatyard* as shown in the blow-up on Chart #TCI-C7 and #TCI-C9. From this waypoint you should see the outer sea buoy (white light atop) and the two red markers between it and the shore. From this position, the entrance channel is approximately 1 nautical mile distant on an approximate course of 345° magnetic (but as you will notice, the course actually bends more northward after R "4"). The channel mouth is marked by tall red and green striped pilings (red-right-returning) and as you approach the entrance keep a lookout for any stray heads in the surrounding waters. There is a shallow spot between the channel markers that carries 6' at low water. The channel curves to the east as you approach the marina complex with its huge building and tall cranes that are usually the first sight of the marina from seaward. The two small coves southeast of the marina dock and lift are private and are not part of the marina complex; they would make a fair hurricane hole if needed. A canal heads northward from the marina past a small bridge towards a number of private homes in the Long Bay Hills area, but draft is limited to about 3'-4' at MLW. This too would be a nice spot to ride out a hurricane.

Now if you insist on waypoints for this route then here you are: from the Sapodilla Bay waypoint head 108° for 3.2 nautical miles to a waypoint southeast of Bay Cay at 21° 43.75'N, 72° 14.00'W, as shown on Chart #TCI-C7. From this waypoint steer 82° for 3.6 nautical miles to a waypoint at 21° 44.80' N, 72° 10.30' W. This is the outer waypoint for your route to the *Boatyard*. From this waypoint keep the red markers to starboard as you approach the entrance channel as shown on Chart #TCI-C9. If you plan to run waypoint to waypoint through here keep a sharp lookout for the scattered heads and small patch reefs that abound on the north side of this courseline.

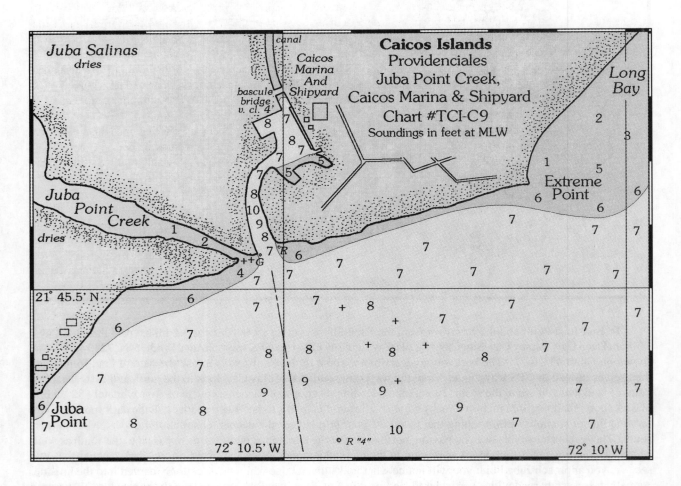

THE NORTHERN SHORE

As mentioned earlier, vessels approaching Sapodilla Bay and the western shore of Providenciales from Mayaguana or The Plana Cays will have no obstructions. If headed to Leeward Going Through or *Turtle Cove Marina* at Sellar's Pond on the northern shore of Provo on Grace Bay, you must take care to avoid the reefs off North West Point as shown on Chart #TCI-C2. A good rule of thumb is not to head south of 21° 53'N until east of 72° 17'W. A GPS waypoint at 21° 53.10'N, 72° 19.90'W, will place you approximately ½ mile north of the reefs in deep water. If your route takes you to Sellar's Pond, Stubbs Cut, or Leeward Cut, especially at night, do not venture south of this waypoint until east of 72° 17' W.

Just east of North West Point as shown on Chart #TCI-C3, is Wheeland Cut. Vessels drawing less than 4' can enter this cut and pass eastward between the outer reef and the northern shore of Providenciales, that is if they can pick their way through the shallow reef that winds itself from Provo out to the barrier reef just southeast of Wheeland Cut. I do not recommend this route as there is nothing to gain by taking it, but everything to lose. There are numerous shallow patch reefs, coral heads, and rocky bars between the reef and the shore that you must avoid along this route. The best water is just inside the reef, staying north of the shoreline until in the vicinity of the high hills just west of Sellar's Pond. The only boats that actually use this route are the local fishermen and a few of the dive boat operators. And by all means stay out of False Cut - it is exactly that. It can lead even small outboard powered boats (yes, I mean dinghies) to destruction. From False Cut to North West Point the area is literally STREWN with dangerous shallow reefs, many of which dry out at low water or lie just inches below the surface. This area is a great snorkel spot in settled weather, but use extreme caution; these waters are thick with heads just waiting for the unwary dinghy. The heads are especially thick in the close in to the point. The North West Point Light, Gp Fl (3) W ev 15 sec 14M, is not working as of this writing, hasn't worked in years, and probably cannot be counted upon to work in the near future.

Grace Bay, the large body of water on the northern shore of Providenciales, is the location for most of the tourism infrastructure as well as being a fantastic sailing ground in its own right. Here you can get the full effect of the prevailing east/southeast winds, but with very little sea. Grace Bay is named after Gracie Jane Hinson, usually just called Grace, who was born in Grand Turk in 1873. In 1892, Grace married Hugh Houston Hutchings, also a native of Grand Turk. The couple spent their honeymoon at a small cottage on the beach on the north shore of Providenciales near the settlement called The Bight, then called Blue Hills. Grace was a very beautiful woman and the couple's visit was quite an occasion for the few inhabitants of the area. After the couple returned to Grand Turk, the people of Blue Hills referred to the beach as Grace Beach and the waters as Grace Bay, as they are known today.

The center of the yachting scene in Grace Bay is located at Turtle Cove Marina in Sellar's Pond. There are two routes to Turtle Cove Marina from outside the reef. The main route is through Sellar's Cut as shown on Chart #TCI-C10. A secondary route - and this one is usually only used by those skippers with good weather and visibility who wish to sail along the beach - is to enter via Stubbs Cut and head westward towards Sellar's Cut on the inside of the reef. We will discuss entering Stubbs Cut in a moment, but for now, let me just say that once inside Stubbs Cut, the skipper can parallel the beach close in, keeping all the white dive site buoys to starboard as you approach Sellar's Cut. Off the Beaches Resort you will have to keep further offshore and steer between several small patch reefs and heads to gain English Cut as shown on Chart #TCI-C10.

For those skippers wishing to enter through Sellar's Cut, a GPS waypoint at 21° 48.40'N, 72° 12.40'W, will place you approximately ¼ mile north of the red and green daymarks that define the entrance channel through Sellar's Cut as shown on Chart #TCI-C10. Always remember that any floating aid to navigation mentioned in this book is subject to disappearing or moving between the time we go to print and the time you arrive at your destination. Storms, high winds and seas, all combine to play havoc on floating aids along the northern shore of Provo from Sellar's Cut to Leeward Cut.

From the waypoint at Sellars Cut head generally southward until you can pass between the outer red and green daymarks (red right returning), in 13'-22' of water and follow the rest of the markers in as shown on the chart. Once inside the reef there are actually two routes to take. Once inside you have the option of turning northward around the "hairpin" back out towards the reef, or heading westward in the narrower but deeper English Cut. I much prefer and certainly recommend English Cut. If you follow the markers back out towards the reef you will quickly come across a narrow, shallow area with 5'-7' over a rocky bottom just east of the first green marker. This is the shallowest part of the hairpin route. English Cut on the other hand, though narrow (a 52' long by 30' wide trimaran comes through here all the time folks) has a minimum depth of 7' and is far shorter. Almost all boats heading to Sellar's Pond use English Cut. Once through English Cut keep the green markers to port as you head towards the marina entrance. Watch out for the shallow heads lying just north of the shoreline about 100 yards northeast of the entrance to the pond. The winding entrance channel itself is narrow and has a shallow sandbar at its eastern entrance, on your port side when entering, and a rocky bar across the channel on your starboard side. Once inside, give the final inner turn on your port side a wide berth before rounding to port into the pond itself.

Never attempt Sellar's Cut with a strong northerly swell; in these conditions the cut will break all the way across and any mishap at this point could be disastrous. If unsure about how to enter Sellar's Cut and the entrance to *Turtle Cove Marina*, call the marina on VHF ch. 16 and Dockmaster Winston Rigby will be happy to have someone come out to lead you in. At this time there is no charge for this service but a tip is expected, and very well deserved as you will see.

There is a nice anchorage in Sirus Cove just west of the entrance to Sellar's Pond and *Turtle Cove Marina*. This is a calm spot in moderate prevailing conditions, though the bottom is a bit grassy. It offers an excellent opportunity for cruisers to avail themselves of all that *Turtle Cove* has to offer by dinghy. Another good anchorage is in The Bight just south of the *Beaches Resort*. This spot has good holding and adequate protection from the prevailing wind and swell. Snorkelers will love to investigate *Smith's Reef*, the large area lying between English Cut and the shoreline.

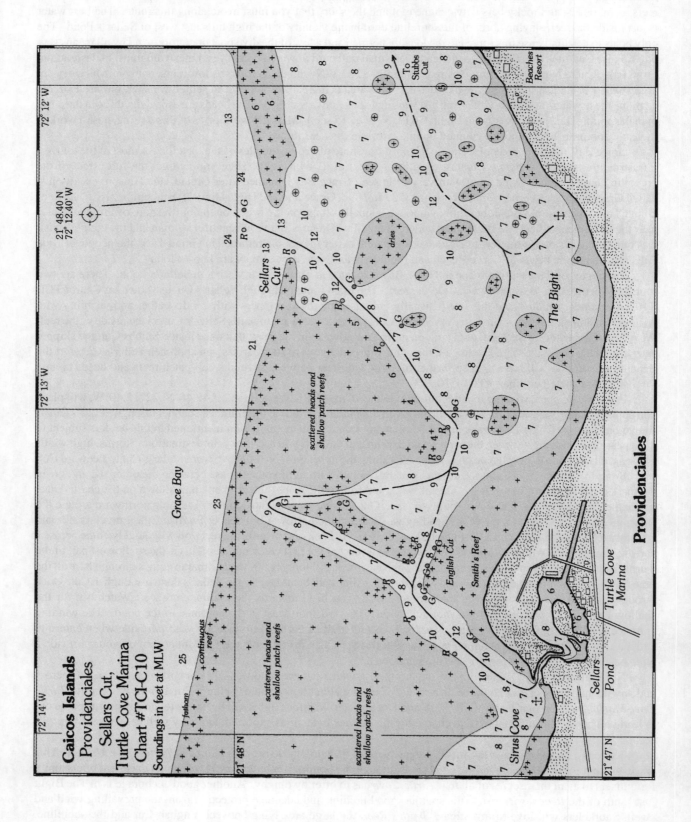

Caicos Islands
Providenciales
Sellars Cut,
Turtle Cove Marina
Chart #TCI-C10
Soundings in feet at MLW

Smith's Reef is a favorite local dive spot where you can explore several shallow water patch reefs and numerous scattered heads that are frequented by snorkelers from both the resorts and the local dive operations. In fact, between the barrier reef and the shoreline are many shallow reefs marked by white buoys. These are all active dive sites and the buoys are for the dive boats to tie to. You can take your dinghy out to these reefs and see for free what the charterers and other tourists pay a lot of money to view.

Turtle Cove Marina has 40 slips, sells diesel and gas, and can handle a 110' vessel with a 6' draft at MLW. The marina is a port of entry so if you need to clear in the dockmaster can assist you in reaching *Customs*. The marina hosts the annual *Provo International Billfish Tournament* in mid-summer and sells fishing licenses year-round. In years past cruisers could anchor in Sellar's Pond, but the sandbar that once filled the center is now part of the marina, and docks are being constructed around it's circumference effectively ending the anchoring in the pond. *Turtle Cove Marina* can be reached by phone at 941-3781 or by email at TCMarina@provo.net.

The complex surrounding the marina has just about anything a cruiser could want; what isn't there is only a short taxi ride away, or perhaps you would rather rent a scooter or car from *Scooter Bob's* on the marina grounds. *Scooter Bob's* has the most economical rental prices on the island and also has a good line of fishing tackle and baits.

Also on site is the *Turtle Cove Inn* with its swimming pool and tennis court, *The Tiki Hut* and *The Banana Boat,* both very nice outdoor bar and grill combos, and *The Terrace Restaurant* serving economical lunches and eloquent dinners with great homemade ice cream. *The Banana Boat* also has an Internet kiosk for email access. *Art Pickering's Turtle Divers* operates out of *Turtle Cove* for those wanting to explore the fine reef diving in Grace Bay or West Caicos. There are numerous other small gift shops, boutiques and salons in the surrounding complex.

Across the street from the marina you'll find the steep natural stone stairs that lead up to the *Erebus Inn*. The *Erebus Inn,* named after a giant butterfly which when touched brings you good luck, is a truly elegant establishment and the bar and restaurant is first class with an absolutely stunning view of Grace Bay. I suggest going there just for the view, but I personally avoid the staircase from *Turtle Cove Marina*. Perhaps if I made better use of *Bodywise*, the complete gym that is located at the *Erebus Inn*, the steep staircase known as *Cardiac Hill* might not be so exhausting. Of course, the time I spend at *Turtle Cove* in *Sharkbites* probably doesn't help. Situated on the eastern end of the marina property, the Friday evening happy hour with two for one drinks and complimentary munchies is a regular stop for *IV Play*. I sincerely believe, and I may have tried them all, that *Sharkbites* has THE BEST chicken wings on the island of Providenciales, though the fellows at the *Lone Star Café* will likely disagree with me. Check out the money shark and the card shark hanging from the ceiling in *Sharkbites*. If you need any welding, fabrication, minor rigging repairs, woodworking, and minor hull repairs you can seek out Mike Robertson on the trimaran *Minx* at the *Turtle Cove Marina*. Mike is one of the best welders and fabricators on the island.

About a mile to the west of Sellar's Pond, around the next point (Cove Point), lies the almost hidden entrance to the dredged creeks of Thompson Cove as shown on Chart #TCI-C2, a very, very private residential community. The sign that welcomes you at the entrance says it all: "Private. Unauthorized boats will be removed." Thompson Cove would make a great hurricane hole with excellent protection in its narrow creeks (5'-7' at MLW) that are protected on all sides by high hills. If you had permission you could probably tie up to someone's unused dock or simply head up one of the channels to secure yourself. Drafts of less than 5' can wiggle their way into Turtle Cove on a high tide by heading west from Sellar's Pond in 7' of water dodging the occasional head or small reef that you will come across. As you approach the next point there will be a rocky bar that works its way west/northwest from the point. A small white buoy marks a narrow cut through the reef to port. Enter the cut at high tide and work your way in towards the narrow entrance to Thompson Cove. Five feet can make it in with a good visibility and a high tide of at least 2 ½'; needless to say the ability to read the water is essential here.

To the east of Sellar's Cut is the wide and deep Stubbs Cut, sometimes called Club Med Cut. When Leeward Cut and Sellar's Cut are breaking, Stubb's Cut may still be passable. A GPS waypoint at 21° 48.93'N, 72° 11.30'W, will place you approximately ¼ mile northwest of the cut as shown on Chart #TCI-C11. From this waypoint look ashore and you will see a large red and white tower, the Cable and Wireless tower that sits in the Long Bay Hills area (260' with a fixed red light at night). Put the tower on your bow and steer 140° magnetic to enter the cut. An alternative method of entry is to line up the tower and the red roofed building that lies just below it on the beach. The eastern end of this building is elevated and pointed. Line up the tower directly behind this raised portion of this roof or slightly to the east of it, between the roof and the trees, and come in on that heading. Once inside, watch out for the shallow bars to starboard. Once inside Stubb's Cut you can head northeastward to Leeward Going Through as shown on Chart #TCI-C12 or southwest towards English Cut as shown on Chart #TCI-C10. If heading to English Cut you can cruise close in to shore keeping the line of white dive buoys to starboard. Once in the vicinity of the *Sandal's Beaches Resort* you will have to keep offshore a little more as shown on the chart. If headed to Leeward Going Through there are fewer obstructions as shown on the charts.

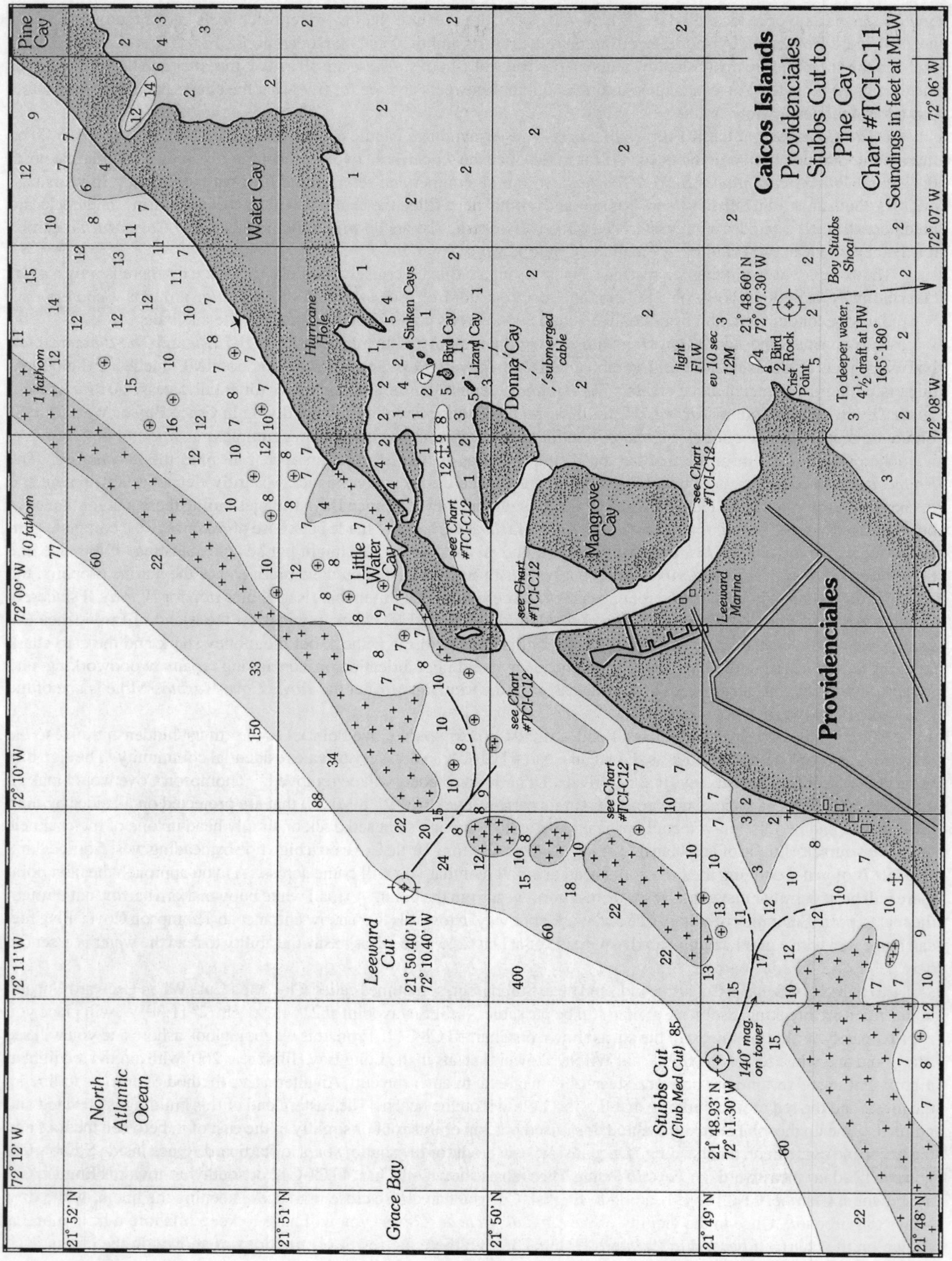

Caicos Islands
Providenciales
Stubbs Cut to
Pine Cay
Chart #TCI-C11
Soundings in feet at MLW

Pine Cay

Water Cay

Hurricane Hole

Sinken Cays

Bird Cay

Lizard Cay

Donna Cay

submerged cable

Mangrove Cay

Leeward Marina

Providenciales

Boy Stubbs Shoal

21° 48.60' N
72° 07.30' W

Bird Crist Rock Point

To deeper water, 4½' draft at HW 165°-180°

light Fl W ev. 10 sec 12M

see Chart #TCI-C12

Little Water Cay

North Atlantic Ocean

Grace Bay

Leeward Cut
21° 50.40' N
72° 10.40' W

Stubbs Cut
(Club Med Cut)

21° 48.93' N
72° 11.30' W

140° mag. on tower

1 fathom

10 fathom

72° 12' W
72° 11' W
72° 10' W
72° 09' W
72° 08' W
72° 07' W
72° 06' W

21° 52' N
21° 51' N
21° 50' N
21° 49' N
21° 48' N

THE CAICOS CAYS: LEEWARD GOING THROUGH TO NORTH CAICOS

Stretching from the northwest of Provo to the tip of North Caicos are a small group of barrier islands. These unassuming little gems surrounded by settings of finely powdered beaches and warm, blue waters, are some of the prettiest sites in the entire archipelago. From the air, they take on the appearance of a delicate necklace suspended between the two points of land. Little Water Cay, Water Cay, Pine Cay, Fort George Cay, Dellis Cay and Parrot Cay: these names include both uninhabited wild life preserves (the domain of the *Turks and Caicos National Parks*) as well as award-winning and internationally recognized luxury resorts. Each island is blessed with gorgeous beaches, swirling sand flats, and plenty of shallow coral reefs. The most beautiful and protected anchorages in the Caicos Islands can be found in between these cays and all are within a short dinghy ride of each other. A word of warning: the ability to read water is essential here as you will travel over some shallow sandbars before you will be able to enjoy the deeper protected water of the anchorages. Never try these entrances with the light in your eyes; you'll have little chance of discerning the shallow water from the deeper water.

The area that is sometimes called the Caicos Cays, stretches from the northeast end of Providenciales to North Caicos. The best anchorage for those wishing to spend time on Provo is at Leeward Going Through as shown on Chart #'s TCI-C11 and #TCI-C12. A 7½' draft, sometimes 8' (if you've got a really high tide), can enter this harbor at high tide and the protection is excellent in all conditions short of a hurricane (even though I know of several skippers who have ridden out one here). Here you'll find Leeward Marina, a primary building block of the planned Leeward Community. Leeward Marina currently has a fuel dock with over 8' at MLW, diesel, gas, oil, RO water, ice, a washing machine but no dryer, and the marina offices carries limited marine and fishing supplies as well as charts, oil, and The Turks And Caicos Guide. Gilley's Restaurant has fine local fare as well as burgers and steaks. Try Gilley's in the morning (or any time for that matter) and sample their excellent boiled fish n' grits. Leeward Marina has no transient slips at this time but has installed a floating dock for smaller vessels; all of their current dock space is taken up by small charter boat operations but big plans are in the works. The marina is far behind its deadline to construct the planned 140 slips to accommodate boats of up to 150' in length and drafts of up to 10' with all amenities: showers, laundry, 110v and 220v electricity, water, phone, cable TV, and a dredged (10' at MLW) entrance channel that is to be buoyed and lighted. A seven-day-a-week fresh fish market supplied by local fishermen and a fresh produce market featuring local grown North Caicos crops is also planned, but as of 2002 remains but a plan. Ashore are planned 520 condos, a 450-room hotel, 35,000 square feet of retail space taken up by bars, Cafés, a grocery store, a liquor store, and a marine supply store. The marina complex will take approximately 2-3 years to complete, the hotel and condos, 5-10 years. Included in the marina area, but not slated for construction until the marina is completed, is dry storage, and a boatyard with haul-out facility. An annual billfish tournament is also planned. If you intend to clear in at Leeward Marina, a port of entry, give Dockmasters Dwayne Pratt or his brother Denver a call on VHF ch. 16 as you approach Leeward Going Through so that they can inform Customs and have an officer on the way as you arrive. Boaters should be aware that Leeward Marina does charge a fee for dinghy landing. You can pay by the day, week, or month and privileges include the use of the dock and garbage disposal; unfortunately there are no showers for boaters at this time.

The entrance to Leeward Going Through is tricky and it changes frequently. What is shown today may be different tomorrow or next week. As *Leeward Marina* completes its expansion a well-marked dredged channel is planned here to permit ease of entry for even the largest mega-yacht. If you are unsure about entering the entrance to Leeward Going Through, call the marina on VHF ch. 16 and someone will come out to guide you in. At present there is no charge for this service, but a tip is expected and certainly well deserved. As a general rule, the tides around Providenciales are approximately ½-1 hour after tides at Nassau, but this is not always the case at Leeward. The tides here are erratic at best. For the most part, the flood tide does not flow as long as the ebb tide. I have seen the flood last only three hours in strong southeast winds. Use caution if attempting to figure the tides.

If bound for the anchorage at Leeward Going Through there are several entrances through the reef. Leeward Cut is the closest but in a strong northerly swell it breaks all the way across, effectively closing the cut. Stubbs Cut or Fort George Cut would be better in those conditions, though not much better. A GPS waypoint at 21° 50.40'N, 72° 10.40'W, will place you approximately ½ mile northwest of Leeward Cut as shown on Chart #TCI-C11. This is where it begins to get tricky. The last time I checked, in the summer of 2001, there were no markers and there may not be any by the time you arrive. The markers have a reputation for disappearing shortly after they are set in place, often moved or destroyed by huge northerly swells. Use your eyesight and depthsounder to get you through here. If in doubt call *Leeward Marina* for assistance. From time to time there will be a combination of red and green markers through here. They were here in 1998, but they were missing in 2002. Bear in mind that buoys may or may not be there as you approach. If in doubt, call *Leeward Marina* on VHF for the latest information.

From the waypoint, enter Leeward Cut on an approximate heading of 135°-140° magnetic. The heading here is not as important as staying south of the very shallow reef on the north side of the cut. This reef is easily seen in good visibility and is usually breaking. Once inside the reef you will see a small patch reef as shown on Chart #TCI-C12. Keep this reef to port and turn to starboard to steer towards the huge red and whited striped *Cable and Wireless* tower (260', Fxd R) to the south on a heading of approximately 180°-190°. As you are heading south look ashore and you will see a string of houses leading south from the northeast tip of Providenciales. There is one residence that is almost hidden by trees with several palms lining the shoreward side of the home. Just in front of this house is a shallow sandbar that works southward from Little Water Cay. Round this shoal well to the south and head northeastward between the sandbar and the shore. If you can't discern the shoal, head in on the house that I just mentioned on an approximate heading of 90°-115° keeping an eye out for the shallow bar to port. Pass between the shallow bar to port and then, swinging wide back towards Leeward Cut, avoid the shallows off the beach as shown on the chart and work your way towards the cut between Little Water Cay and Providenciales. Pass between the two and then you can turn to starboard to head into Leeward Going Through and the anchorage.

The best anchorage is just to the north of *Leeward Marina*. If you wish to anchor south of the marina, be advised that about 150 yards south of the marina the bottom gets rocky with scattered coral heads littering the bottom. There are small, scattered heads throughout the anchorage at Leeward Going Through, even north of the marina, but they are a little thicker south of the marina. Diving to check on your anchor here is advised. There is a fair bit of current in Leeward Going Through and two anchors set in a Bahamian moor are absolutely necessary, unless you like to untangle your lines when they get wrapped around the stray head.

Now let's take a brief look at the down side of Leeward Going Through. At the time of this writing *Leeward Marina* is still far from being complete, it is primarily a working marina. There is a considerable amount of small boat traffic, several outboard powered charter boats and a few boats picking up supplies to deliver to North, Middle and South Caicos. The skippers of these vessels are for the most part very knowledgeable, cautious and courteous, but the occasional boat passes through that will wake you. Wake is a fact of life near a working marina. I suggest that if you do not like where you're anchored, simply move. Probably 99% of these boat operators are great guys, friendly, good to meet and know, but a few of them do not understand that our vessels are our homes and that their wake is very disturbing to life aboard. It's that 1% that simply doesn't give a flip. You'll be gone soon, they'll still be here. They've been running these waters since long before we arrived and they'll continue to run them long after we're gone. Unfortunately, this is not an excuse for a lack of courtesy, whether it be in Provo or Nassau or Ft. Lauderdale. I have sat down and talked to some of these operators who are adamant that they will do exactly whatever they want; it is their country and we are visitors and they don't want to hear another bleeping word about it. If you hang out on Providenciales long enough you will come to learn that there is often a bit of on-island versus off-island intolerance that is very disheartening. I've seen a lot of this prejudice on Provo, but only on Provo, and this bias does not just come from Belongers. There is a large ex-pat population of Americans, Canadians, and Brits that are equally cliquish. The other islands of the Turks and Caicos group do not suffer from this narrow-minded disorder.

A new development came about in the Spring of 1998; a PWC rental facility opened on the *Leeward Marina* property. This is considered bad news by many cruisers who like to use this anchorage. I have been advised that the ride area runs from Little Water Cay southward through Leeward Going Through to the *Conch Farm* and that the PWC operators are instructed to stay a minimum of 100' away from any anchored vessel and that they must also obey the no-wake zone that has just been implemented in front of the marina. Of course, some cruisers (I include myself) feel that a 100' minimum is about a mile too close.

When anchored at Leeward Going Through and bad weather threatens, you will need to keep an eye out for incoming vessels, as the skippers of many of the local dive boats bring their craft in here to anchor when inclement weather threatens. While many of these skippers have a captain's license and are in fact veteran seamen, a captain's license is not required in the Turks and Caicos Islands and a few of these "captains" have little concern about where and how they anchor their unattended boats. Some of these guys simply drop an anchor and head to shore. The *Dive Provo* and *Beaches* boats are the best; the worst are the *Club Med* boats. I once questioned one of these "skippers" when, with a major front approaching, he showed absolutely no concern that he was anchoring his huge metal boat two boat lengths away from me on one anchor when I had been there riding on two for weeks. I suggested that his swing radius would bring his vessel into contact with mine at the next turn of the tide and that I would be extremely unhappy at best about the situation. The French "captain" looked down his nose at me and proclaimed he knew what he was doing, had a 50-ton license, lived on the island and even once owned a 60' boat, implying that I was simply a transient,

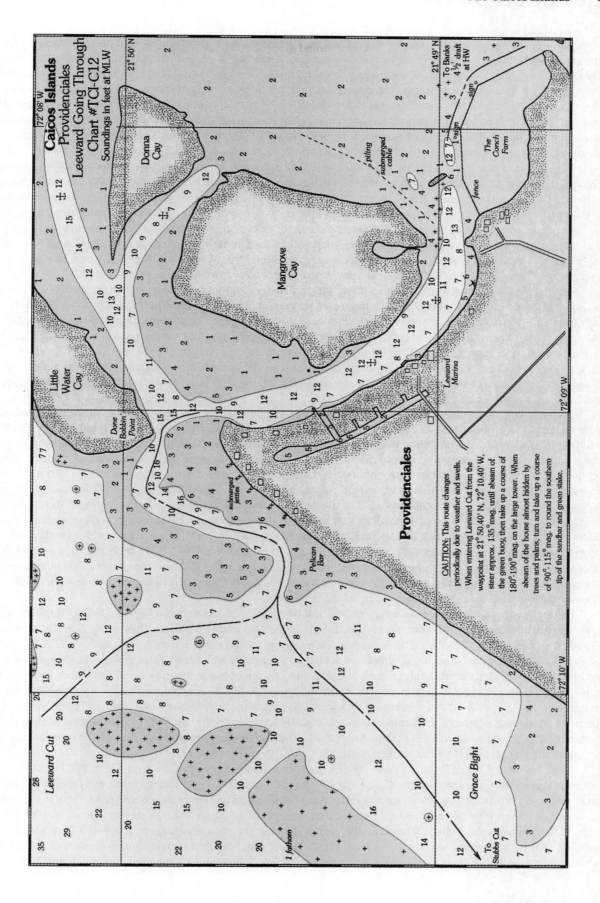

inexperienced, and therefore not important. I replied, in a pleasant tone, that although what he said would make an excellent résumé, it did not mean diddly-squat (not the actual words I used) and that it did not indicate that he was either knowledgeable or courteous when it came to anchoring his vessel. He exhibited neither of those qualities. I brought up the point that his anchoring "technique" showed that he either did not know what he was doing or that he did not care. I finally asked if he actually had to demonstrate how to safely anchor a vessel to acquire his license. His employer finally arrived to pick him up from the boat and after many angry looks toward my boat, they grudgingly set out a second anchor. I often wondered why he no longer owned that 60 footer (perhaps his anchoring technique?). Be sure to keep an eye on these unattended boats when the wind pipes up (as if you didn't have enough to watch out for).

By now dear reader you probably have assumed that I am a major grump and want the anchorage to myself. WRONG! Leeward Going Through is a wonderful, well-protected anchorage with good facilities that are only going to get better. I love the anchorage at Leeward and I urge more people to take advantage of it, but I am obligated to warn the potential visitor of what they can expect, whether it be good or bad. *Leeward Marina* has established a no-wake zone just off the marina which should help alleviate matters for all concerned. My intent here is not to discourage you from visiting Leeward Going Through; far from it. But if you get tired of the PWC's and the occasional small boat traffic you can always head over to the less trafficked anchorages between Little Water Cay, Donna Cay, and Mangrove Cay, as shown on Chart #TCI-C12. From here you can dinghy over to *Leeward Marina* at your leisure.

South of Heaving Down Rock, the ramp where the small barges load and unload about ½ mile south of the marina, you will notice a large area with pilings in the water and nets stretched between them. This is the *Conch Farm*, established in 1984 to commercially grow the queen conch, *strombas gigas*. The life cycle from egg to adult takes about four years. The *Conch Farm* has successfully developed hatchery and juvenile rearing techniques and the Farm has a current inventory of approximately 1.5 million conch in all stages of their growth cycle. Theirs is the only such facility in the world. The *Conch Farm* has guided tours for $6.00 a person and a *Conch Boutique* and restaurant. South of Mangrove Cay and east of the Conch Farm is a submerged cable in 1'-3' of water at low tide. This cable is easily seen and definitely something to avoid.

From *Leeward Marina* you can get on any one of several charter boats for a wonderful day trip to North Caicos or if you desire, any other island in the chain from Middle Caicos, to South Caicos and even Grand Turk. Allen Ray Smith's *Sanddollar Cruisin* runs trips to North Caicos whenever weather permits. For $99.00 per person you get transportation to North Caicos, a scooter to ride, and lunch. If you wish to rent a car instead, you can opt for a Suzuki jeep for $50.00 or a van for $70.00. Transportation is then $40.00 per person, but no lunch is included; not to worry, there are several places on North Caicos to stop for a great lunch (for more information on North Caicos, see the section "North Caicos"). For more info, call 946-5238 or stop in at the *Sanddollar Cruisin* office at *Leeward Marina*. *Silver Deep* has a similar deal. But *Silver Deep* will also take you just about anywhere you want to go in these islands: Middle Caicos, East Caicos, South Caicos, Grand Turk, and even to Salt Cay. Owner Arthur Dean and his brothers will be happy to take you to any of these spots from Leeward. For more information call 941-5595 or check in at the *Silver Deep* office at *Leeward Marina*. Not to be outdone, *J & B Tours*, also at *Leeward Marina*, has several Island exploration charters that will take you in and around Provo and all the way to South Caicos if you like. For more info, check their office or call 946-5047. *J & B Tours* also sells fishing licenses.

Vessels drawing 4½' or less and wishing to head out onto the Caicos Banks from Leeward Going Through can do so at high tide, and only at high tide. Since it is easy to get Nassau tides by SSB and ham radio (see the section on "Weather" in the chapter "The Basics"). A vessel drawing 4½' will need a tide of over 2'-2½', that is a 2.6'-3.1' above datum Nassau tide or equivalent. Remember that tides here are generally 6' less than tides in Nassau and approximately one hour later. A 5' draft needs a tide of the equivalent of a Nassau above datum tide of 3.6' and more, not rare, but definitely not common. I have traveled this route with a Nassau tide of 3.8' above datum and saw nothing less than 5' the entire route. Bear in mind that wind direction sometimes affects the tides on the banks south of Provo. A few days of northwest through northeast wind may cause an unusually low tide on the southern shore of Provo while a strong southeast to southwest wind will have the reverse effect. The prudent mariner will likely check the route at high tide by dinghy the day prior to his planned departure.

From Leeward Going Through, head south toward the *Conch Farm* as shown on Chart #TCI-C12, passing between the small unnamed cay and the *Conch Farm* (You really shouldn't try this route in the early morning with the sun in your eyes; you won't be able to see a thing). Keep the first sign and the conspicuous brown shoal that parallels the *Conch Farm* fence to starboard. Once past the first sign, head for the second sign staying about 75'-100' off the fence. There are a couple of shallow heads on this part of the route, but they should lie well to port if keep your course close in to a line between the two signs that parallels the fence. Once past the second sign, keep parallel to the fence as you head towards Bird Rock keeping about 50-100 yards east of the rock. As you come abeam of Bird Rock steer approximately southeast until about two hundred yards or so south of the rock, to avoid a shallow sand patch lying just south and southeast of Bird Rock. From this position you can take up a course of anywhere between 165°-200° to cross shallow Boy Stubbs Shoal; the deeper water seems to be on a course of about 180°-200°. The shallowest part of this route lies between ½ mile and 2 miles south of Bird Rock across shallow Boy Stubbs Shoal. The bottom is not quite flat through here, there are several "humps" in the bottom and if you are too early or if the tide is too low, you will likely keep bumping over them as you power your way through, but don't worry as they're all soft sand. Keep on your course for several miles, dodging any black or brown patches you see, until you reach deeper water, anywhere from 7' and above, generally in the area of 21° 45.50' N-21° 46.00' N. This route is a terrific shortcut if you're headed to Sapodilla Bay. I believe that if enough sailboats come through here we'll eventually have a pretty nice channel dredged (but don't try it with a winged keel, they tend to act as an anchor).

If you are in Sapodilla Bay or *Caicos Marina and Boatyard* and wish to avail yourself of this shortcut to Leeward, head ENE past the Boatyard to a GPS waypoint at 21° 45.50'N, 72° 07.00'W. Watch out for scattered heads and shallow patch reefs along this route. Once in the general vicinity of the waypoint, head for a GPS waypoint at 21° 48.60'N, 72° 07.30'W, approximately ¼ mile east/southeast of Bird Rock. From this position simply follow the above mentioned directions in reverse.

Just North of Leeward Going Through lies Little Water Cay, a very popular picnic spot for locals and cruisers with 1995/1996 showing visitation by over 17,000 tourists. The island lies within the boundaries of the Princess Alexandra National Park and has been set aside as a nature reserve for about 1,500-2,000 of the rare and endangered Turks Island rock iguanas (*Cyclura carinata*) as well as a variety of bird life. When Loyalists and Salt Rakers first inhabited the Turks and Caicos Islands, their pet dogs decimated the indigenous iguana population on these cays, until the only place you can find them today is on the uninhabited cays such as Little Water Cay. As the *Meridian Club* was being built on Pine Cay in 1973, an iguana survey showed a population of 15,000 on the cay. By 1976 nearly all the iguanas were gone due to predation by cats and dogs introduced during construction. A 1995 survey showed only one iguana, a few burrows, and several tracks along the northeast coast. A new problem has occurred by the creation of the sand bridges between Little Water Cay, Water Cay, and Pine Cay over the last several decades. Speculation concerning the feral cats on Pine Cay suggests that it is only a matter of time before they work their way down to Little Water Cay.

From the small beach on the southern shore of the cay there is a nice boardwalk that takes you through the interior of the cay to view the local vegetation and the island's population of iguanas. The nature trail on the northern shore of the island, best reached from the Grace Bay side of the cay and within easy dinghy distance from Leeward, is the most scenic in terms of animal life. If you visit the cay, please stay on the boardwalk; do not feed, touch, or harass the iguana in any way, and please do not bring a cat or dog ashore. A bit of Turks and Caicos Island folklore that has to be seen to be believed has it that the iguanas in these islands will dance to music. Try it and see, grab a few cans or bottles and tap out a rhythm, or perhaps bring along a boom box with your favorite CD and play DJ for these creatures. The waters between Little Water Cay, Donna Cay, and Mangrove Cay as shown on Chart #TCI-C12 are deep and make for a very good though current-ridden anchorage. Two anchors are a must here. The only problem with this anchorage area occurs on the weekends when the locals tend to water ski through here. Donna Cay was once part of Mangrove Cay until Hurricane Donna changed the landscape along these islands, hence the name of the cay.

North of Little Water Cay, and connected to Little Water Cay since Hurricane Donna, is the uninhabited Water Cay. Just off its western shore, as shown on Chart #TCI-C11, is the wreck of an old barge in 4' of water. The barge was being towed along the shore when it broke loose and came to rest in its current location. On the northern shore of Water Cay are some very nice beaches and sheer rock ledges that are wonderful for snorkeling or just swimming. In prevailing winds these beaches are very calm, though sometimes a swell can work its way over the reef to push your anchored dinghy ashore. These very beaches were the background for the 1987 *Sports Illustrated Swimsuit Edition*.

Pine Cay lies just to the north of Water Cay and is named after the Cuban Pine which thrives on the edges of the island's freshwater ponds. Once a separate cay, Pine Cay was joined to Water Cay by Hurricane Donna, as was Little Water Cay. Pine Cay is best known for being the home of the *Meridian Club*, an extremely exclusive total-getaway resort constructed in 1973. No phone, no TV, just peace and quiet and pristine beach. No loud vehicles are allowed, only golf carts and bicycles. The island itself has several distinctive zones of vegetation, shared mainly by palmettos and pines. On the islands northern end there are a few brackish lakes inhabited by several species of (once) saltwater fish, also a legacy of Hurricane Donna. Pine Cay was also the site of an ancient Lucayan settlement, and in the 18th and 19th centuries is said to have been used as a hideout for pirates. Pine Cay is private and visits ashore must be by invitation only, although access to the beach up to the dune line is allowed. You can anchor off the beach, a somewhat surgy anchorage at times, on the western shore of Pine Cay wherever your draft allows, but only in prevailing winds.

If you're interested in name-dropping, it is said that Bill Cosby and Denzel Washington frequent Pine Cay, and that Jimmy Buffet has a passion for bonefishing in the nearby waters.

Further north, the Pine Cay, Fort George Cay, Dellis Cay, and Parrot Cay anchorages can be easily accessed by sea via Fort George Cut as shown on Chart #TCI-C13. Vessels wishing to visit the area from Leeward Going Through can do so by venturing northeast inside the reef. As shown on Chart #'s TCI-C11, C12 and C13, the route lies between the reef and Water Cay and Pine Cay. There are only a few shallow reefs and a couple of sandbars to watch out for. Stay away from any dark spots you see; these will likely be heads or small patch reefs. For skippers entering through Fort George Cut, a GPS waypoint at 21° 53.70'N, 72° 07.90'W, will place you approximately ½ mile northwest of Fort George Cut. Enter the cut on an approximate heading of 130°-140° magnetic. The heading here is not so important as simply staying between the reefs, but not to worry, Fort George Cut is wide and deep. Once inside you can head southward to Leeward or Water Cay, or northward to Dellis Cay and Parrot Cay. About a mile southwest of Fort George Cay is another smaller break in the reef known as Andy's Alley. This very visible bright blue cut is about 100 yards wide and has a minimum depth of 11'. To find Andy's Alley look for the southern end of the beach on Pine Cay, and when approaching the usually breaking reef, look for the bright blue cut.

Fort George Cay is a National Historic Site that dates back to 1798-1812. To protect the cotton production on North and Middle Caicos, settlers built Fort George and set up cannons to defend their main port of export in anticipation of attack by pirates and Americans. Today, thanks to Hurricane Donna, the same cannons that were poised to protect the islands now lie in about 3'-4' of water, making for an excellent snorkel. Look for them about 50 yards south of the small beach on the northwestern tip of Fort George Cay about 50' offshore. There are three of these two hundred-year-old cannons, all pointing to seaward; you can't miss them. You can anchor west of Fort George Cay wherever your draft allows, but only in settled weather, and watch out for a surge coming in over the reef. There is a wonderful, deep, uncrowded anchorage between Fort George Cay and Pine Cay that only sees some small boat traffic from the resort on Pine Cay. This is an extremely difficult anchorage to enter: it has shallowed to the point that only drafts of less than 5' can enter, and that's on a high tide. As little as three or four years ago, drafts of 5'-6' could enter, but as with all the cuts along this section of the Caicos Cays, what is deep today may be quite shallow tomorrow. After entering Fort George Cut head northeastward until you can take up an approximate southeast heading towards the point on Pine Cay as shown on Chart #TCI-13. There is really no way to describe the entrance here other than to say that it curves around generally back towards the northeast until you reach the darker, deeper water between the cays. A high tide, excellent visibility and the ability to read water are what will get you through here. There are several sandbars that you must zig-zag between and some shallow grassy patches that give a false impression of being deeper than they look. Once inside you will find a deep anchorage that goes well eastward between Pine Cay and Stubbs Cay and even out onto the Caicos Bank a bit. As usual, put down two anchors for the current.

Dellis Cay, named after a Greek sponger from Hydra named John Dellis, was the center of a small but thriving sponging industry on the cay in the late 1800's. The cay is subject to a unique pattern of tide and current, giving this island the nod when it comes to some of the best beachcombing in the Turks and Caicos Islands. Beautiful white sandy beaches surround Dellis Cay; ashore you may find the ruins of an old fish processing plant. There is a good, deep anchorage between Dellis Cay and Fort George Cay that can be accessed by vessels with drafts of less than 5'. Excellent, and I do mean excellent, visibility as well as a healthy dollop of patience is required to find the channel, as the sandbars change often and you will have to do quite a bit of zigzagging. Only try this just before high tide and remember that there may be no one around to help you should you run aground. The cay is currently owned by the wife of a former president of Italy who proposes to develop the small island in four phases over the next decade.

As shown on Chart #TCI-C13, head northeastward from Fort George Cut between the reef and Fort George Cay, avoiding the large shallow bar that sits northwest of Fort George Cay and the small shallow reefs between the bar and the outer barrier reef. Line up the southwestern tip of Dellis Cay and head in on it on a heading of 140° magnetic. You will probably have to dodge some shallow spots as all these sandbars change frequently in this stretch of cays. As you approach the southwestern tip of Dellis Cay you will find that you also have to pass between two shallow yellow colored sandy bars, 1'-2' at MLW. One works out westward from Dellis Cay, the other also lies east/west just a little northwest of the first bar. You will have to turn to starboard to pass between the two to make it into the deeper water at the entrance to the anchorage. The anchorage itself has two arms, one on the Dellis Cay side, one on the Stubbs Cay side. Both offer good protection, though I prefer the anchorage on the Dellis Cay side.

North of Dellis Cay and southwest of North Caicos lies Parrot Cay. Some say that Parrot Cay is a corruption of "Pirates Cay", where legendary pirates such as Calico Jack Rackham, Annie Bonney, Mary Read, and Blackbeard are said to have visited. An 18th century house still stands on this 300-acre private island. There was an attempt at growing cotton on Parrot Cay in 1918, but it lasted only a few years until the operators gave it up in 1922. Along Parrot Cay's

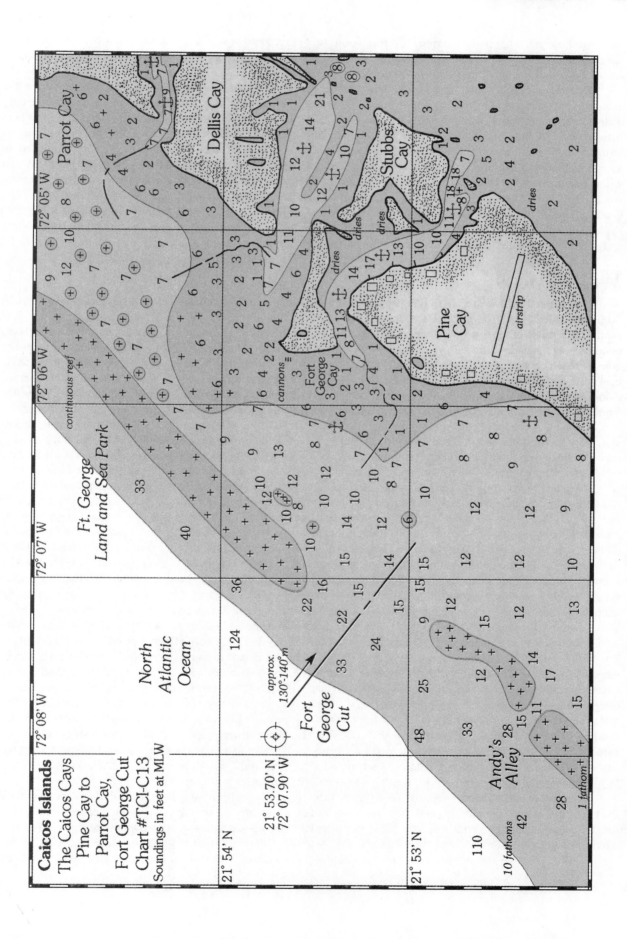

northern shore you will see the red roofs of a prestigious modern resort that was deserted but is now being reopened. It has been said that the multi-million dollar *Parrot Cay Resort* project, set to begin construction in 1998, is going to create an "island paradise with all the most modern facilities."

There is an excellent anchorage lying between Parrot Cay and Dellis Cay that is much easier to access than the anchorage between Fort George Cay and Pine Cay. A vessel with a draft of 5'-6' can enter here with the tide; the only dangers are the numerous (though easily seen in good light) shallow heads and small patch reefs that dot the waters between the reef and Dellis Cay and Parrot Cay. Good visibility is essential but a cool head and nerves of steel are just as important. As shown on Chart #TCI-C13, work you way north inside the reef from Fort George Cut, taking care to avoid the many shallow heads and patch reefs. When you are north of the cut between Parrot Cay and Dellis Cay you will notice the darker water inside the cut and a small arm of it heading out north/northwest towards the reef. You will want to line up the northern point of Dellis Cay and take up an <u>approximate</u> heading of south/southeast on it. The heading here is not so important as trying to picture how the deeper water flows out over the sandbar. This channel, 4' in places at MLW, is your only way in if you draw 5'-6'. Once inside, the deeper water goes well eastward to the eastern end of Dellis Cay, with only a slight zig-zag. Use two anchors, there is a lot of current here.

WEST CAICOS

Uninhabited wild West Caicos, lying approximately 10 miles southwest of Providenciales and Sapodilla Bay, was originally called *Macubizza* by the Lucayans and *Petite Caique* by the French. The waters off the western shore of the island offer miles of superb wall diving and imposing limestone cliffs, a favorite spot for the numerous dive boats operating out of nearby Provo. In years past, West Caicos was allegedly a haven for pirates that would attack homeward bound French boats returning from Haiti. A French Captain in 1753 wrote that West Caicos was "abounding in the white beaked Bahamian parrot." It is said that Nelson captured a French sailing vessel off West Caicos in 1777 when he commanded the sloop *Little Lucy*. The tourist brochures say that Delvin's Cove at the northern end of West Caicos was a hideout for the infamous pirate Delvin or Dulien but I was unable to find any reference to a pirate by that name.

On the western shore you will find the ruins of Yankee Town where in the mid-1800's a flourishing community of sisal workers lived. In 1849, 18 acres were planted at Spencerville on the northern coast of West Caicos and proved so successful that over 1,000 acres of sisal were eventually being grown on the island. If you look around you will find the ruins of a sisal press, railway, steam engines, and several limestone buildings dating to the late 1800's and early 1900's when 70 salt and sisal workers lived and worked here. At a cost of over $30,000, the government constructed the railway and a saltwater canal to the salinas but the sisal project was halted at the beginning of the American Civil War. The old railway stretches across West Caicos in an east/west direction and if you hike the causeway you may see some of the pink flamingos, osprey, and herons that live along the shores of Lake Catherine, a nature reserve. The Dominican dictator Trujillo tried to buy West Caicos a few years prior to his assassination. It is believed that he wanted the island for a hideaway, but the deal fell through when clear title could not be found. In 1973 *Esso* planned to build a huge oil refinery on the cay, but plans were abandoned when the owner suddenly died. You can anchor off Yankee Town in settled weather or in light to moderate prevailing east/southeast winds. Stronger winds create a bit more surge in the anchorage. Any northerly swell tends to make this area uncomfortable and sometimes downright dangerous.

There is a nice lee anchorage off the northwestern tip of West Caicos that is often used by locals as well as the dive boat operators working out of Provo. The anchorage in Bernard Bay that is shown on Chart # TCI-C5 and #TCI-C14 lies just off a beautiful beach and is a great spot in settled weather and in east to southeast winds. The anchorage can be gained through a small winding break in the reef off Company Point as shown on Chart #TCI-C14 and from the Sandbore Channel area directly from Sapodilla Bay as shown on Chart #TCI-C5. Both routes require good light and you'll have to dodge several coral heads and small patch reefs in water that is less than 6' deep (at MLW) in places, but you may find that the end result is worth your effort. If you don't wish to try the cut at Company Point, you might consider anchoring south of Company Point along the western shore of West Caicos as shown on the chart and taking a short dinghy ride in to the beach. There are great plans afoot for the construction of a new marina somewhere between Company Point and Logwood Point in Bernard Bay. Dredging is scheduled to begin in 2002. For more information check my website at http://www.islandhopping.com and I'll pass along any information as soon as I receive it.

The eastern and northern shores of West Caicos offer miles of beautiful sandy beaches with a few rocky cliffs at the northeastern and southern tips and the rusty ruins of an old freighter about midway down the eastern shore. It is said that when this freighter was wrecked, the crew opened the safe aboard and removed a quantity of silver bars. Atop a bluff on the southeastern shore of West Caicos stands Star Town, the ruins of an old DEA base during the 1970's and early 1980's. The site got its name from the two quonset-hut-style buildings that are laid out in a star pattern. At the

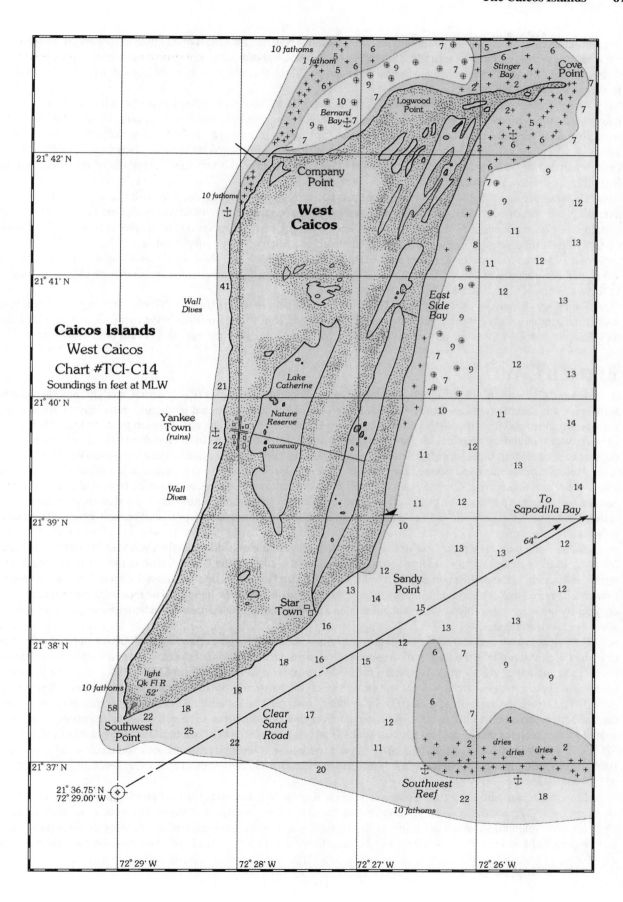

10 fathoms
1 fathom

Stinger
Bay
Cove
Point

Bernard
Bay

Logwood
Point

Company
Point

**West
Caicos**

21° 42' N

10 fathoms

Caicos Islands
West Caicos
Chart #TCI-C14
Soundings in feet at MLW

21° 41' N

Wall
Dives

East
Side
Bay

Lake
Catherine

21° 40' N

Yankee
Town
(ruins)

Nature
Reserve

causeway

Wall
Dives

To
Sapodilla Bay

21° 39' N

64°

Sandy
Point

Star
Town

21° 38' N

light
Qk Fl R
52'

10 fathoms

Clear
Sand
Road

Southwest
Point

Southwest
Reef

21° 37' N

21° 36.75' N
72° 29.00' W

10 fathoms

72° 29' W   72° 28' W   72° 27' W   72° 26' W

northeastern end of West Caicos, just south of Cove Point, it is possible for a draft of less than 6' to work its way within a few hundred yards of shore to gain some lee from west through north/northwest winds. You'll have to pick your way through some heads and reefs here to anchor in close and you'll never find your way out at night if the wind should shift to the northeast or east.

Along the eastern shore of West Caicos is the popular Clear Sand Road, the channel from the ocean across the banks that is often used by the freighter traffic that uses South Dock on Providenciales. This is also an excellent route for skippers heading to Provo from Inagua, Cuba, or the Windward Passage. A GPS waypoint at 21° 36.75'N, 72° 29.00'W, will place you approximately ¾ mile south of Southwest Point on West Caicos as shown on Chart #TCI-C14. From this position you can take up a course of 64° for 13.1 miles to the waypoint just south of the anchorage at Sapodilla Bay with no obstructions.

The area between Molasses Reef and Southwest Reef along the edge of the Caicos Bank is generally clear of shallow patch reefs though there is a rocky bar stretching between the two. In most places this bar has 15'-20' over it and does not pose a navigational hazard to the average cruising boat. There is a channel through here as shown on Chart #TCI-C1 that is simply called the Freighter Channel. It is often used by commercial vessels headed to South Dock on Provo and leads in from the sea between Southwest Reef and Molasses Reef with a least depth of 12' near South Dock. A GPS waypoint at 21° 35.75' N, 72° 23.25' W. From this position you can take up a course of 41° for 10.1 miles to the waypoint at Sapodilla Bay with no obstructions.

Capt. Dave Matthews of the trimaran *Tao* has been sailing these waters for over 20 years and suggests that if you are off the southern end of West Caicos and cannot find refuge from strong northeast winds you can tuck up under the lee of Southwest Reef for some protection from the seas (parts of the reef and bars to its north dry at low water).

FRENCH CAY

French Cay was originally called Cay Blondell at the beginning of the 1600's. Blondell was a French surveyor in Haiti who was commissioned to study the feasibility of building a navigational landmark on the cay to assist those vessels enroute to and from the Windward Passage. The French lost several ships in the vicinity of the small rocky islet over the years, including one three-decked merchantman laden with treasure from Hispaniola. Blondell stressed the importance of building some sort of structure on French Cay to keep mariners from confusing it with West Caicos and West Sandspit, but nothing ever came of his efforts. Over the intervening years, French Cay's greatest claim to fame is that the pirate Francoise L'Olonnois is said to have occasionally used the island as a base from which to raid ships enroute to and from the same nearby Windward Passage. There is no proof of this and the gentleman who started that rumor has since withdrawn his original statement though all the tourist literature touts French Cay as L'Olonnois' hideout.

Today French Cay is a protected bird sanctuary and you will understand why when you visit. Hundreds of gulls, boobies, and terns call this tiny sliver of rock and sand on the edge of the Caicos Bank home, swarming over and around it throughout the day. A permit from the DECR is required to set foot upon the island. In the waters surrounding French Cay nurse sharks mate each summer so give them a wide berth if you happen to be there at the same time; they are usually not aggressive unless molested. The island itself is rather low-lying and sandy, with excellent snorkeling along its southwest side.

As you approach French Cay, you will probably not sight this low-lying island until about five miles away. Your first sight of it will probably be the top of the wrecked tug on the eastern shore of the cay. From the GPS waypoint just south of the anchorage at Sapodilla Bay, steer 171° for 14.3 miles to a GPS waypoint at 21° 30.60'N, 72° 12.70'W, which places you approximately ½ mile west of the anchorage on the western shore of French Cay as shown on Chart #TCI-C15. On this route the water depths range from about 16' just south of Sapodilla Bay to about 10' just north of French Cay, and there are no obstructions. As you approach French Cay from these 10' depths, the water gets progressively deeper as you head for the edge of the Caicos Bank. If arriving from offshore head to a GPS waypoint at 21° 29.75'N, 72° 12.65'W, which places you approximately ¾ mile southwest of the anchorage area and on the edge of the Caicos Bank. From the entrance waypoint to *Caicos Marina and Boatyard* at Juba Point, French Cay bears 197° at a distance of 14.8 nautical miles.

If headed to Sapodilla Bay from French Cay you will begin to make out the hills of Providenciales from more than 10 miles away. The conspicuous twin white fuel tanks at the *Texaco* yard east of the green customs building at South Dock are your landmarks if you are making for Sapodilla Bay, but don't confuse them with the several white houses that lie to the easy of Sapodilla Bay. Another good landmark as you get closer is the huge crane at South Dock just west of the white tanks. As I said, there are no obstructions on this route; I have run this route at night from French Cay to Sapodilla Bay, but I cannot recommend that others do so.

The northern section of the anchorage area tends to be rocky and grassy, but if you set your anchor well in the surrounding sand you will stay put. The best holding is in the sandy holes in the grassy areas in the center of the anchorage area.

A bit of a lee anchorage is available from southwest through west winds off the northeastern shore of French Cay. Entrance is gained by heading north around the shoal of the northern tip, and then heading in as close as your draft allows on the northeastern side. The holding here is fair to good depending on how well you are able to set your hook in the rocky/grassy bottom. A better idea is to head northward towards Sapodilla Bay and anchor in Bermudian Harbour.

Excellent snorkeling can be found on the reef that lies south and southeast of French Cay. Another reef lies well southeast of French Cay and is also worth exploration.

Just a few miles to the north/northwest of French Cay is the *Molasses Reef Wreck,* the oldest shipwreck in the Americas and the first shipwreck site in the Caribbean to be scientifically excavated and exhibited. Measuring just 19 meters long, the caravel, having safely crossed the treacherous Atlantic, ran aground on the reef and became stranded in sand in about 15'-20' of water, laying undiscovered for some 400 years until it was found by treasure divers in 1976. Some unscrupulous salvager tried to gain financially from the excavation by claiming the ship was the Pinta, one of Columbus' original three ships. The claim was soon proven to be false and the government of the Turks and Caicos Islands took over the salvage and identification process. A government permit was issued to the Institute of Nautical Archaeology at Texas A &M's National Museum under the direction of Dr. Donald H. Keith. Irate treasure hunters then tried to dynamite the site with, fortunately, minimal damage. Dating of Lucayan pottery pieces found on the site placed the ship on the reef prior to 1513 (remember, all the Lucayans were forcibly removed from the Turks and Caicos Islands by 1513) and researchers speculated that the ship was a slaver enroute to Hispaniola. The ship was armed with state-of-the-art weapons of the period and the national museum on Grand Turk now displays the largest selection of 16th century wrought iron breech loading cannons in the world.

From French Cay, with the right wind, you can sail right off the bank for Inagua, Little Inagua, Haiti, Manzanillo or Luperón in the DR, or to the Windward Passage and Cuba. If you are bound for Manzanillo, a course of 179° for 101.5 nautical miles will bring you to the entrance to Manzanillo. If bound for Luperón from French Cay, head out into the deeper water off the Caicos Banks and head for a GPS waypoint at 21° 20.50'N, 72° 10.05'W. This will place you approximately two miles southwest of West Sand Spit, a shallow

Caicos Islands
French Cay
Chart #TCI-C15
Soundings in feet at MLW

area on the western edge of the Caicos Bank as shown on Chart #TCI-C1. From this waypoint take up a heading of 149° for the 109 miles to Luperón. If you intend to sail the entire way you'll need a northeast wind. For the first half of this route you will be sailing in the lee of the Caicos Banks so expect the seas to build once you pass out of its lee.

If headed west across the banks from French Cay you must first clear the shoal north of French Cay and then head for a GPS waypoint at Star Channel at 21° 30.25'N, 72° 06.60'W. You will steer approximately 102° for almost six miles to this position. For more information on Star Channel see the section "Routes Across the Caicos Bank." From this waypoint you can take up a course of 123° for 28 miles to the waypoint one mile northwest of the anchorage at Big Ambergris Cay or 104° for 29.7 miles to the anchorage at the southwestern tip of Long Cay. From here you can pass out into the Turks Island Passage to head northward to South Caicos or eastward to the Turks. Also from the Star Channel waypoint you can steer 113° for 28.1 miles to the waypoint just north of the Fish Cays. From here you can head out across the Turks Passage to Great Sand Cay if you choose.

NORTH CAICOS

North Caicos, located only 12 miles from Provo, is about 44 square miles in area. Its 1,500 inhabitants primarily live in the four settlements that are connected by the King's Highway, which runs the length of the island. The southern shore of the island is primarily mangroves and tidal flats, home to flocks of flamingos, bonefish, and tarpon. Thanks to its abundant rainfall, North Caicos is known as the garden center of the Turks and Caicos Islands. At one time, extensive farms fed all of the islanders with crops transported by inter-island trading sloops.

There are no deep draft anchorages at North Caicos; the closest for a 5'-6' draft is between Parrot Cay and Dellis Cay as shown on Chart #TCI-C13. There are several day charters that run out of *Leeward Marina* that can provide lunch and transportation, either scooters or jeeps, for those interested in taking a tour of this beautiful cay. The entire northern shore of North Caicos is protected by an offshore barrier reef, but a vessel with a draft of less than 6' can work its way through the reef at Ropier Cut (see Chart #TCI-C16) in an emergency. That route, as are almost all the inshore routes between Parrot Cay eastward to East Caicos, is literally strewn with shallow coral heads and shoals. If you choose to dinghy to the island you can rent a car from Pat Hamilton at 946-7141 or from *Old Nick Rental Cars* at 946-7284.

Along the northwestern shore of North Caicos, Three Mary's Cays is a great snorkeling spot near Sandy Point where you'll also find ospreys and their nesting sites. The cays are a protected sanctuary and visits ashore are by *DECR* permit only. Sandy Point is a small fishing/farming community of only about 40-50 residents, where, in the early 1900's, guano miners discovered a cave containing ancient Lucayan artifacts, including a stone idol. The community is tucked in behind the lush vegetation of the cay and the casual visitor might not even see the buildings. At the dock by the small harbor sits an old rusting crane, while to the right sits a huge old wooden hull. There used to be a blue hole tucked into the mangroves right off this harbor, but it was filled in during the last hurricane. You'll want to check out nearby Cottage Pond, a large pool surrounded by tropical vegetation and protected Nature Reserve.

Most visitors make their first stop at Whitby where you'll find *Whitby Plaza*, a resort area located along the northern shore. Three hotels here offer fine lodging and meals to those who wish to get away from the hustle and bustle of Provo. Here you'll find a tourist information center; a great spot to begin your exploration of North Caicos. You'll probably want to check out the *North Caicos Art Center*, where you can find great buys on very nice native arts and crafts as well as silk paintings and pareos by local islanders. You might want to call ahead to make sure they'll be open as they really don't stick to a schedule. Call Alveira at 946-7120 or Regina at 946-7360. Don't miss dining at *Papa Grunt's Seafood Restaurant* for great food. You might also want to sample the choices at *Marina View* and the *Ocean Club*. Directly across from *Whitby Plaza* is Flamingo Pond where you can view and photograph hundreds of West Indian flamingos. To find the pond, take the Whitby Highway heading east to the beach roads and you will come to Flamingo Lookout with its sign and small covered viewing platforms. Aircraft flying out of the nearby airstrip have been restricted from flying across the pond to the delight of the flamingos and flamingo enthusiasts. The *Prospect of Whitby Hotel* serves Italian Cuisine with dinner reservations requested at what is really *Club Vacanza*, a mini-*Club Med* for Italians just west of Whitby. The *Prospect of Whitby Hotel* is named after the famous *Prospect of Whitby Pub* that overlooks the Thames River in London. The nearby *Pelican Beach Resort* has a great view overlooking the pine-fringed shore. The family-run resort has 12 rooms and serves excellent native meals in a modern restaurant. The bar attracts locals as well as tourists and guests on the cay. If you need fresh bread look up Wealthy Forbes in Whitby; just ask anyone in the village where to find her. For those who prefer a bed and breakfast inn, try *Joanne's Bed and Breakfast*. Horsestable Beach on the northern shore east of Whitby offers miles of beautiful private beaches. For groceries try *KJ Variety Store*.

The settlement at Kew, the agricultural center of North Caicos, is named after the botanical gardens at Kew, England. There is a clinic, a post office, and a public phone on Forbes Street in the heart of Kew. Between Bellefield Landing and Kew you will find the *Cosmic Farm* where North Caicos farmers grow fresh fruits, vegetables, and herbs and welcome all visitors. Another mile up the Cosmic Farm Road are the ruins of Wade's Green. As the road ends you will find a sign with a map and instructions on how to proceed by foot. Bring a good pair of shoes for the walk from the road to the ruins can be rough. A team of archaeologists from UCLA excavated the ruins in 1989 and now visitors can see some of the finest Loyalist ruins in the Turks

and Caicos Islands including a court-yard and jail. A small general store is on the left as you approach the Wade's Green ruins. Stop in for a cold drink and meet Cecelia, who sells her own wonderful basketwork. If you feel adventurous, spend the night in Kew as their only tourist and don't miss eating at *Ma Sue's* where Susan Butterfield will serve you up some truly authentic North Caicos fare, as well as sell you groceries, fruit, veggies, and frozen goods. At the other end of Kew, on the road from Whitby, you'll find *Forbes' Variety Store* where owner Elizabeth Forbes sells a wide range of household and auto supplies. If you wish to purchase fish and veggies in season, try Farmer John at 946-7381.

Further east along the main road, Bottle Creek offers up its own Loyalist ruins at the Belvedere Plantation. Bottle Creek is a small fishing community that borders Bottle Creek on the King's Highway. The creek is protected from the North Atlantic Ocean swells by the Bay Islands and their fringing elkhorn reefs. In case of emergency there is a small medical facility by the high school in the heart of Bottle Creek at High Rock, just up from the government dock, or you can call *Government Nurse* on VHF ch. 16. At the airport north of Bottle Creek you will find some pretty good food at the *Super D Café*. Along Creek Road, the lower road in Bottle Creek, are several old, historic houses, many of them in-

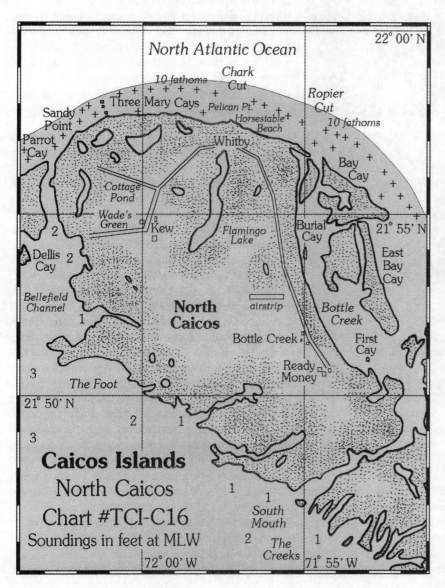

habited. If you need fresh fish and veggies in season contact Peter the Haitian at 946-7303. If you want a loaf of fresh bread try Iona Gardiner (who also offers some very nice basketry) at the *Aquatics Restaurant* at 946-7187. You can also get some fine native cuisine at *Titter's Restaurant* ran by "Titters" whose pea soup and steamed conch is to die for. *Titter's* is right next to the airport. If you're into dominos you'll want to visit the *Two Son's Restaurant*. Another good eating establishment is *Wendy's Restaurant*, no relation to the chain though. If you plan to stay overnight try *Gordon Black's Guest House*. For groceries try *Speed's Grocery* or *My Dee's Variety Store*. For those in search of cool libation, try *Ellie Smith's*, *Albert Grey's*, *Dar Williams'*, and *Nash's Bar and Pool Hall*. South of Bottle Creek, near Ready Money, stand the tallest pine forests in the Turks and Caicos Islands. Off the eastern shore of North Caicos, the Bay Islands are a national park boasting miles of pristine beaches. Iguanas on the nearby East Bays Cays are an outstanding example

Regatta boat, Bottle Creek, North Caicos.

of the natural diversity of this green island. Towards the mouth of Bottle Creek sits the small village of Major's Hill, where everyone is named Gardiner.

Divers will want to note that diving along the north shore of North Caicos, as in the other islands, takes the form of spur and groove formations that drop in a mini-wall from 30 - 70 feet. This is the same barrier reef that stretches across the entire northern boundary of the Caicos Islands, and the diving is similar to that found on the north shore of Providenciales. This area sees far fewer divers than the sites at Provo or West Caicos, with a subsequent increase in marine life. Expect an excellent fish population with the occasional larger visitor.

MIDDLE CAICOS

Middle Caicos, often called Grande Caicos, is the largest cay in the Turks and Caicos Island group and the least exposed to tourists of all the inhabited cays. Middle Caicos can boast the most dramatic shoreline of any of the Caicos group with towering limestone cliffs along its windward shore, only broken by a few small beaches with gentle rolling hills in the background. A vessel with a draft of 6' or less can work its way through the offshore barrier reef at Ferguson Cut (see Chart #TCI-C17) to anchor off the northern shore in an emergency. The area is littered with shallow coral heads and shoals, so good light is necessary. The anchorage would be a lee at best and only in south to southwest winds. There are also cuts northwest of Gambol Point (Gamble Cut) and just off the northeastern tip of the island (Big Cut). For the most part these cuts are usable and should only be attempted in an emergency and preferably if you can get some local assistance by VHF. Vessels heading east or west in the vicinity of Middle Caicos must give the northeastern tip of Middle Caicos just east of Gambol Point a wide berth of three miles or more. The water is shallow, about 20'-35', northeastward from Middle Caicos in this vicinity (see Chart #TCI-C17).

There are only three villages on the island, home to about 270 people and recently linked with a new paved road. In a recent nationwide cooperative effort, pastel colored paints have been provided to the island's homeowners to paint all the inhabited homes on Middle Caicos. Daily air service and weekend ferry service to North Caicos are the only links to the other populated islands in the Turks and Caicos Islands. Between North Caicos and Middle Caicos is an area that is known as the *"Crossing over place."* Here you'll find a trail where, at low tide, one can walk from North Caicos to Middle Caicos just as the residents have been doing for centuries. The trail begins just west of the *Blue Horizon Resort* and meanders along the bluffs along the northwestern shore of Middle Caicos. If you don't feel like walking across, a ferry at Pine Barrel Landing provides service between Middle and North Caicos on Fridays, Saturdays, and Sundays.

Middle Caicos is a spelunker's delight where the 120,000 year old *Village Cave* or *Conch Bar Caves* (a national park) offer over 15 miles of above sea level caves. For a local guide, try Herbert Niat; his intimate knowledge of these caves is worth the trouble of seeking him out. Ask him to take you to *Indian Cave* at King Hill where you will see an impressive 60' high cathedral ceiling. Here you'll find roots spiraling down from the ceiling to the rich soil of the floor between massive limestone arches. Artifacts found in these caves by a team from the University of Indiana headed by Sean Sullivan prove that Middle Caicos had an estimated 4,000 Lucayan Indians that thrived in pre-Columbian times.

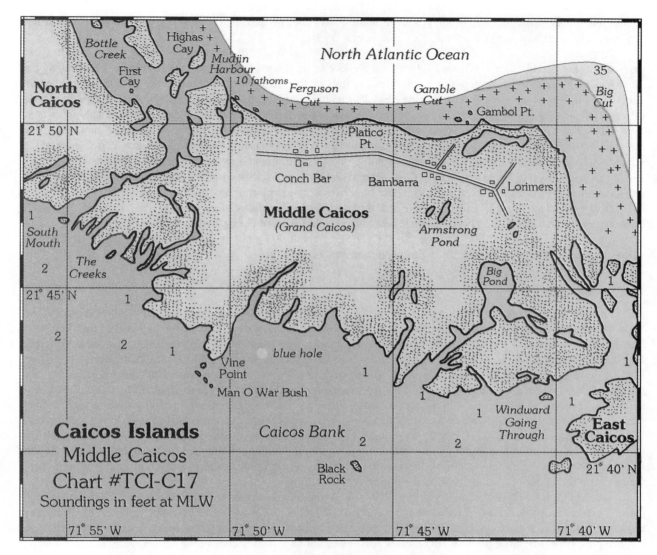

There is also evidence of a Lucayan ceremonial and trading center. Researchers have discovered over 38 Lucayan sites on Middle Caicos alone. And in 1977-1978, archaeologists unearthed a rare Lucayan ball court near Armstrong Pond. Ball courts have been found in Puerto Rico and points farther south, but never this far north. For great description of the ball game and how it was played by the ancient Lucayans, read the first chapter of James Michener's *Caribbean*.

The island's Northwest Point is a combination of beautiful inlets, marshes, mangroves and inland ponds that serves as a haven for birdlife. Conch Bar is the largest of the three settlements on Middle Caicos and is home to the island's only airstrip. Both *Taylor's Guest House* and *Arthur's Guest House* offer fine accommodations for the weary visitor. Nearby Mudjian Harbour, a corruption of the name Bermudian Harbour, offers a beautiful half-moon beach set against a backdrop of breathtaking limestone cliffs and is one of the most photographed sites in the Turks and Caicos Islands. On the front cover of this guide is painting of waves breaking in Mudjin Harbour. The nearby *Blue Horizon Resort* offers five fully equipped villas overlooking this scenic panorama. Future plans call for condo building sites and an enlarged resort. For good local food try *Carey's Restaurant* or *T&J Boutique*, which doubles as a gift shop.

East of Conch Bar, just a scant distance from the northern reef-fringed shore, sits Bambarra, a small community with a very unique history. In 1841, the Spanish slaver *Esperanza* wrecked on the reef at Breezy Point. The surviving freed slaves settled in the Caicos Islands, while some of the survivors traveled to Grand Turk for employment. The following year another Spanish slaver, the *Gambia,* with a hold full of slaves from Bambarra in Africa, wrecked in The Bahamas. The survivors were sent to Middle Caicos, where they founded the settlement of Bambarra situated about five miles east of Conch Bar. The name refers to the Bombarra people who lived on the shores of the Niger River in West

Africa. From offshore, Bambarra is barely visible, some of its buildings dotting the high ridge behind some casaurinas. The only store is Emmanuel Hall's well stocked little grocery store.

Bambarra is home to the *Middle Caicos Expo*, an annual event held in mid to late August that some say is the best party in the Turks and Caicos. The *M.C. Expo* is a homecoming of sorts for Bambarrans who have moved away for employment. The activity centers along the thatched huts in the shade of the casaurina trees on the beach where vendors set up shacks to serve food and drink. Events include a sailing regatta, dominos, a beauty pageant and a tug of war. Pelican Cay, about ½ mile offshore, can be reached at low tide by a sand "road" that disappears at high water.

Further east is the third and most remote of the Middle Caicos settlements, Lorimers, a very traditional settlement named after Dr. John Lorimers, a Loyalist plantation owner whose grave is nearby. Lorimers has a school, a church, a clinic with twice-weekly visits by a doctor from South Caicos, a government built water tank and two wells - "Big Well" and "Dark Night Well." There are no stores, but several residents will sell you items that you may be in need of. The creeks to the east of Lorimers offer some excellent bonefishing and exploring possibilities.

Divers will want to explore the blue hole near the south shore of middle Caicos just northeast of Man O War Bush as shown on Chart #TCI-C16. This dive site is best visited from Leeward Going Through by small boat or from one of the anchorages in the area of Fort George Cay. The hole is about 400 yards in diameter and over 200' deep and is surrounded by shallow banks rich in sea life, including sharks and rays.

EAST CAICOS

East Caicos holds the distinction of being the largest uninhabited island in the Turks and Caicos Islands. Like West Caicos, East Caicos is now an uninhabited paradise, though there was once a considerable bit of industry here. The ancient Lucayans once settled here and there are several caves on the island adorned with Lucayan artwork. Near Jacksonville there are several caves where skeletons have been found. In a cave known as "New No. 1," there are prehistoric petroglyphs on the walls. Loyalists settled here in 1791, but as elsewhere, didn't last more than a few decades. The sisal industry flourished following the Loyalists, finally collapsing in the late 1820's. In the 1960's, a newspaper Tycoon rebuilt the ruins of the old Jacksonville Plantation on the northern tip of the island where railroad tracks stand in silent testament to a former life. Jacksonville was once the home of the *East Caicos Sisal Company* and the *J. N. Reynolds Cattle Farm*. Today the most noteworthy inhabitants are the feral cows and donkeys that still roam this island's 18-square miles, descendants of the animals used by the early farmers. Nearby Iguana Cay boasts, as you have probably guessed by now, a large colony of iguanas. Due to the shallow waters and even shallower reefs, East Caicos is rarely visited, except by small boat or dinghy.

A vessel with a draft of less than 6' can work its way through Jacksonville Cut to anchor between Iguana Cay and East Caicos in Jackson Cut Bay. A GPS waypoint at 21° 47°.00'N, 71, 34.90'W places you approximately ½ mile north/ northeast of the cut as shown on Chart #TCI-C18. After you work your way through the break in the reef you will then have to pick your way through a field of shallow coral head until you can anchor in the deeper water between Guana Cay and the mainland. This anchorage is great in winds from east through south to west though a bit of swell works through from the open Atlantic in moderate and stronger winds. Guana Cay was the site of Lucayan settlement over 600 years ago.

Though swamps and mangroves inundate much of the island, you can find the highest point of the entire Turks and Caicos Islands here on East Caicos: Flamingo Hill, which rises to a height of 230' and overlooks the deadly Phillip's Reef. Phillip's Reef and nearby Haulover Point were the sites of numerous wrecks over the years. When transiting the area north and east of East Caicos, mariners are advised to pass to the east of Phillip's Reef. It is possible to pass inshore of Phillips Reef in water from 22'-30' deep but it is so much safer to pass east of Phillip's Reef, even though you'll travel a few more miles.

There is a splendid 17 mile beach on the north coast of the island that is usually only used by sea turtles to lay their eggs because of the large mosquito population.

In the late 1990's, feasibility studies were completed, and developers are currently deeply involved in the decision-making process that may eventually lead to the re-settlement of East Caicos. Plans are said to include making a part of East Caicos into "the world's largest cruise port." What an effect that would have on the economy of the Turks and Caicos Islands!

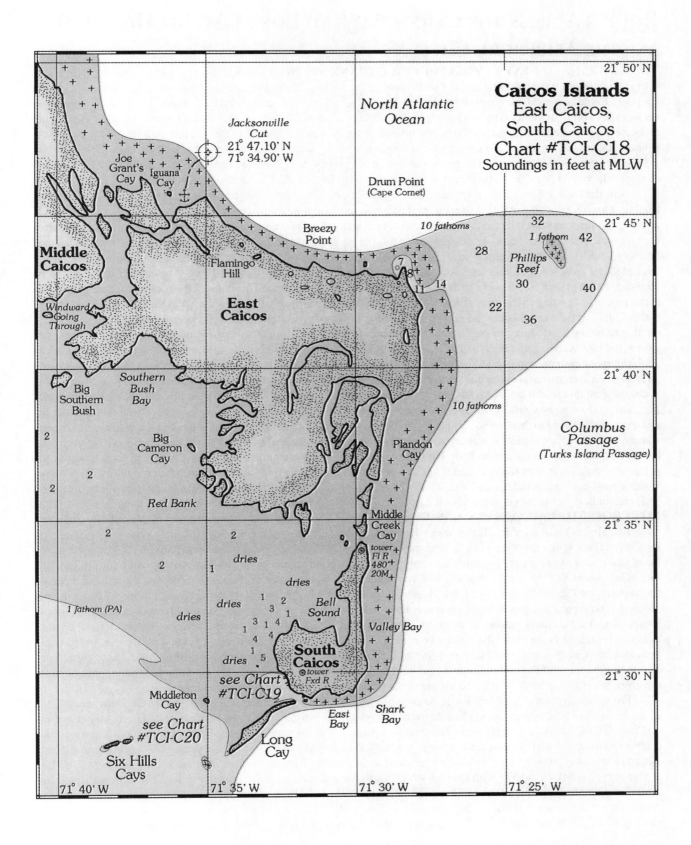

ROUTES ACROSS THE CAICOS BANK TO LONG CAY, SIX HILLS CAYS, AND THE AMBERGRIS CAYS

NEVER, I repeat, **NEVER CROSS THE CAICOS BANK AT NIGHT!** I just thought I would mention that right at the start so maybe you won't forget it and tempt the fates. I am writing this as I sit anchored out off Long Cay in Cockburn Harbour. Looking over at the government dock at South Caicos I see a 42' catamaran that attempted to negotiate the area between Six Hills Cays and Long Cay last night in a nice east wind of 25 knots on the nose, no moon, and only a spotlight to locate the scattered heads and reefs that you often find on the Caicos Bank. Please note that on a moonless night you cannot pick out the reefs with a spotlight unless they are breaking and they probably won't be doing that. The cat, with a delivery crew aboard, promptly ran aground on one of the several reefs in the area and the Captain put out a MAYDAY distress call on VHF. ch. 16. They immediately received word from South Caicos that help was on the way.

Now the folks at South Caicos are seamen; they make their living from the sea and they know what it is like to be in trouble at sea. Soon two small boats set out to render assistance in the rapidly deteriorating weather. Before they could arrive at the stricken vessel the captain was able to get his boat off the reef and the mate suggested that they anchor where they were in 15' of water. The mate also suggested this before they ran aground. He knew there were reefs around but the delivery skipper wanted to keep going. The captain, with that special wisdom that only captains sometimes have, overruled the mate's suggestion and decided that they would keep going on past Long Cay and up into Cockburn Harbour. Meanwhile the fellows from South Caicos arrived, one had damaged his engine on a rock and the other his hull in the process of getting to the once-stricken vessel. The delivery skipper had canceled the MAYDAY but the men from South Caicos in their small boats had no way of knowing it. The captain told them he no longer needed their assistance, but that he would like to hire a pilot. Captain Willis Jennings, the South Caicos Harbour Pilot, boarded the catamaran and guided the hired captain, and his much wiser mate, safely into Cockburn Harbour in the middle of a moonless night with 25-30 knots of easterly wind and 8' seas on the outside. The skipper paid the Harbour Pilot his fee but when presented with a bill for the other assistance that he requested, said hired skipper hit the cabin top making all sorts of snide remarks about the gentlemen who had risked their lives and their boats to come out and help a boat that did not need help in the first place. Do not put yourself in a similar situation. Those men put their lives on the line for a vessel that was not in distress, only uncomfortable. Who can put a price on the service they rendered? In my tenure as a volunteer assistant warden at Exuma Park I went on a dozen rescue calls similar to this one and I can tell you from experience that you do it because you have to, because somebody has to help and you are the only one there to do it. Were the warden and I to put a price on the services we rendered, I am sure it would seem staggering to the average boater, but then again they weren't out there in the wind and the seas. I know a certain salvager in The Bahamas who would not have stirred from his bed without being guaranteed twice what the good men of South Caicos asked for. Do not let this happen to you. **DO NOT CROSS THE CAICOS BANK AT NIGHT!** There, now that I'm finished getting up on my soapbox, let us continue.

I've always considered local knowledge the best knowledge when it comes to navigating any waters anywhere, and the Caicos Bank is no exception. The local knowledge here is that when crossing the Caicos Bank, if you can see land to the north, you are too far north towards the shallower water - good advice when crossing from Provo to South Caicos, Long Cay, Six Hills Cays, or the Ambergris Cays. There are several routes to choose from depending on your draft as shown back on Chart #TCI-C1. As I just mentioned, and probably cannot repeat often enough, none of these routes should be attempted at night as you may come across the stray coral head or small patch reef anywhere on the Caicos Banks. If you see any dark patches of water, by all means steer around them. Even in areas on the Caicos Banks where the heads and patch reefs are particularly thick you can always find deeper water between them and plenty of room to steer around them. One pleasant sight that you'll find on the Caicos Bank is the phenomenon of the Emerald Cloud. On certain days when the sun and the clouds are right the bottoms of the clouds take on a lovely green hue. What happens is that the green water of the bank is reflected off the underside of the cloud giving its emerald appearance.

From the waypoint at Sapodilla Bay, a heading of 122° for 43.1 nautical miles will bring you to a GPS waypoint at 21° 27.40'N, 71° 34.75'W, approximately ½ mile inside Long Cay Cut and just west of the southern end of Long Cay as shown on Chart #TCI-C20. In the first edition of this guide I mentioned that this route across the Caicos Banks could accommodate drafts of less than 7' at MLW and drafts of up to 8½' with the tide and was the easiest and preferred route across the bank. Although still easy, areas of the route have shallowed to the point that the controlling depth as shown on Chart #TCI-C1 is a bit over 5' at MLW and 6½' with the tide, which limits the use of this route to fewer vessels. The shallower areas are on the northern side of this route between 72° 07' W and 72° 00' W, so if you find the water getting progressively thinner, try heading a bit south of the courseline. You will still have to steer through some scattered heads in the vicinity of 72° 05'W through 71° 55'W, but once east of this area you will find the heads more scattered. Depending on the wind direction, you can anchor north or south of the Six Hills Cays. This pair of cays with a small rock between them is easily identified, the six hills, three hills on each cay. Here you'll find good snorkeling on the reefs on the southern side of the cays but getting the hook to set here can sometimes be a pain. There are several areas of rock and grass but if you look around a bit you'll find a good sandy spot in which to drop your hook.

You can anchor in the lee of the southern tip of Long Cay in easterly winds, but keep a good eye out for the scattered heads and patch reefs in the area, as shown on the chart. If you have enough time you can head out Long Cay Cut into the deeper water of the Turks Island Passage and head northeast to enter into protected Cockburn Harbour at South Caicos (see next section *South Caicos*). When heading out through Long Cay Cut, watch out for the rocks south of Long Cay and the large breaking reef lying southwest of the cay as shown on Chart #TCI-C20. Skippers with shallow drafts or those who love a challenge can pass north of Middleton Bar and then parallel it on its north shore to work in along the northwestern tip of Long Cay into Cockburn Harbour. I do not recommend this route unless you: A) you absolutely have to be in South Caicos and conditions do not allow an outside transit of Long Cay; B) you have a draft of less than 5' and you are attempting to round or cross the bar at high tide; and C) you are simply adventurous and like a challenge. If you are attempting to round Middleton Bar, a GPS waypoint at 21° 30.90'N, 71° 36.10'W will place you approximately ¼ mile northwest of the shallow northwestern end of the bar. From this position head generally southeast keeping in the deeper water on the northern side of the bar until you begin to find the deeper water closer in towards Long Cay. If you headed south from Leeward Going Through across Boy Stubbs Shoal and enjoyed that passage, you'll love this one. You would not be able to guess by looking at the island, but Middleton Cay was once home to Lucayan Indians. Recent digs have unearthed a Lucayan site on this tiny cay.

Vessels heading to the Ambergris Cays from Sapodilla Bay (as shown on Chart #TCI-C1) can steer 134° for 43.8 miles from the Sapodilla waypoint to a GPS waypoint at 21° 19.75'N, 71° 39.75'W. This waypoint places you approximately 1 mile northwest of the anchorage between Little Ambergris and Big Ambergris as shown on Chart #TCI-C21. Of course, if you are heading from Big Ambergris to Sapodilla Bay you will steer 314° for 43.8 miles to reach the waypoint south of the Sapodilla Bay anchorage. This route takes you through the Pearl Channel, which lies between two relatively shallow banks with about 6' at MLW.

The more traditional routes across the Caicos Bank make use of the Starfish Channel, which lies south of the major area of shallows on the bank. From Sapodilla Bay take up a course of 154° for 17.1 nautical miles to a GPS waypoint in Starfish Channel at 21° 30.25'N, 72° 06.75'W. If bound for Long Cay from Starfish Channel, take up a course of 104° for 30 nautical miles, which will bring you to the anchorage off the southwestern tip of Long Cay. A note of caution on this route; take care not to run up on the Six Hills Cays, you can pass them on either their north side or their south side, but you cannot go straight through them. Your course north or south of the Six Hills Cays will depend on whether you are heading for the waypoint at the anchorage off the southwestern tip of Long Cay, or if you are heading for the deep water waypoint at Long Cay Cut.

From the waypoint at Starfish Channel a course of 122° for 28. 2 miles will bring you to the anchorage between Big Ambergris Cay and Little Ambergris Cay. If you're at French Cay and wish to head to Ambergris Cay, this is also a good route to take. One can also head east of French Cay, past the shallow reefs to work your way up onto the banks about 4-5 miles east/southeast of French Cay where you can take up a course to the Ambergris anchorage. There will be several areas of heads lying just to the east of French Cay that you will have to dodge.

Vessels heading toward Long Cay and the route across the Caicos Banks towards Sapodilla Bay and Providenciales can head to a GPS waypoint at 21° 26.55'N, 71° 34.15'W placing you ½ mile southeast of Long Cay Cut. Pass between the southern tip of Long Cay (watch out for the rocks off its southern tip) and the reef lying just southwest of Long Cay as shown on Chart #TCI-C20. Work your way up inside of Long Cay, as shown on the chart, to take up your course of 302° to Sapodilla Bay.

SOUTH CAICOS

South Caicos, or Big South as some of its residents describe their island, is relatively small, only 8½ square miles, but it is quite densely populated by Turks and Caicos Islands standards. Most of the island's 1,200 inhabitants live in Cockburn Harbour, which should not be confused with Cockburn that boils out contains a high degree of salinity, making it perfect for salt production. The Boiling Hole fed the salt pans that once made South Caicos the Turks and Caicos' largest producer of salt. Today most of her people rely on the sea for their livelihood and South Caicos exports large numbers of conch and lobster to the United States and France through her two fish processing plants. Some sport-fishermen call South Caicos the big fish capital of the Turks and Caicos, with the larger pelagics often seen here in great numbers. A vertical wall wraps around the southern edge of South Caicos, then extends the length of Long Cay and is often reputed to have the finest diving in the Turks and Caicos. On the northern tip of the island is the 480' tall red and white antenna of the old U. S. Coast Guard Loran Station, NMA-5, that is now a Vessels heading toward Long Cay and the route across the Caicos Banks towards Sapodilla Bay and Providenciales can head to a GPS waypoint at 21° 26.55'N, 71° 34.15'W placing you ½ mile southeast of Long Cay Cut. Pass between the southern tip of Long Cay (watch out for the rocks off its southern tip) and the reef lying just southwest of Long Cay as shown on Chart #TCI-C20. Work your way up inside of Long Cay, as shown on the chart, to take up your course of 302° to Sapodilla Bay.

Town on Grand Turk. Cockburn Harbour, or East Harbour as it is sometimes called, dates to Bermudian Salt Raker days. private station that transmits in Spanish at 50,000 watts - a great landmark that flashes red at night. Don't confuse it with the much shorter (260') red and white *Cable and Wireless* tower at the southern end of the island at Cockburn Harbour that has a fixed red light at its top.

Cockburn Harbour, one of the best natural harbors in the Turks and Caicos Islands, is a working harbor with a regular fleet of fishing boats and trading vessels bound to and from Haiti and the Dominican Republic. It's not unusual to walk down the streets of town and hear Creole on one corner and Spanish on the next. The entrance to the harbor is lighted and easy to enter, even at night. If approaching Cockburn Harbour from the north, stand off South Caicos at least a mile or more to avoid the fringing reefs. The entrance to Cockburn Harbour will lie about a mile or so south of the long unfinished hotel on the southeastern shore of South Caicos. A GPS waypoint at 21° 28.70'N, 71° 31.70'W, will place you approximately ¼ mile southeast of the entrance channel between Long Cay and Dove Cay as shown on Chart #TCI-C19. A good landmark is the huge green house with the pointed roof on the hill and the conspicuous white concrete light tower. The light tower shows a fixed white light at 90' above sea level from 90°-180°. Dove Cay is marked by a flashing green light every 2½ seconds, while Long Cay is marked with a red flashing light every 2½ seconds as per *IALA Region A* regulations. TAKE NOTICE! This is not red, right, returning as boaters from the States and The Bahamas may be used to. Upon entering Cockburn Harbour you will take the red light to port. Head in between Long Cay and Dove Cay in 20'-25' of water and proceed westward into the harbor. New lights have been purchased and are to be installed while this publication goes to press. I have been assured that the new lights, when they are replaced, will change to the American system of entry, *IALA Region B*, in other words, red-right-returning. For more information check the *Newsflash* page on my website at http://www.islandhopping.com and I'll relay whatever information I get on the subject as soon as I receive it.

Cockburn Harbour has received a bad rap as having poor holding but those that reported bad holding have simply been anchoring in the wrong spots. I have ridden out fronts with prolonged winds of over 30 knots here without a problem. The holding, if your anchor is set well, is good throughout with the exception of a few places. At the eastern end of the harbor near Dove Cay, and close in along the southern shore of South Caicos, there are several areas of what the locals call "slate," hard, crusty, scoured sand that is difficult to get an anchor to set in. The best holding is at the western end of the harbor, between the remains of an old buoy and the shore. You will notice that this is where the locals anchor their boats, even during hurricanes. I am told that the old buoy drifted into Cockburn Harbour from Puerto Rico during Hurricane David back in the 1970's and has been in its present position ever since.

Close in to the South Caicos shoreline you must avoid several submerged railways west of *Sea View Marina* between the marina and the wooden dock with the small wooden building on the end. Cockburn Harbour offers excellent protection, even in strong winds, as the banks to the west and northwest dry in places at low water. However, if I knew a strong front was heading my way with westerly winds of 40 knots or more, and if I had the time, I would try to get over to Grand Turk to tuck into North Creek for the best protection and the most comfort. In periods of light or no wind, you might need to set a bridle to keep from rolling as there is a little current in the harbor. If you need a pilot or crew for your voyage you can contact Captain Willis Jennings on VHF ch. 16 by calling *Pilot House* or by telephone at 946-3308. Willis knows the waters well, having over 20 years experience as the South Caicos Harbour Pilot. For a good diving and bonefishing guide try Willis' nephew Gilbert Jennings at *Lightbourne Taxi*.

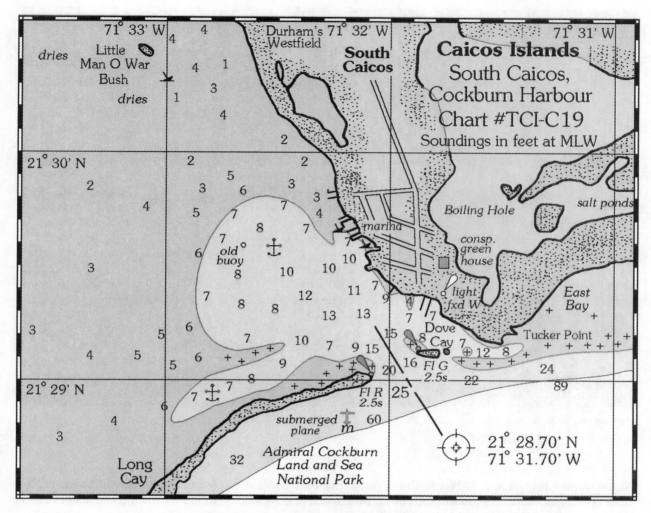

Caution: Lights may be red-right-returning by late 2002. Use caution when entering at night.

Strong east through southeast winds bring swells directly into the harbor; in these conditions it is best to anchor in the lee of the north end of Long Cay instead of in Cockburn Harbour proper. This is my favorite anchorage whenever I visit South Caicos. As shown on Chart #TCI-C19, head along the shore of Long Cay between the shallows west of the cay and the dark patch that is a rock and grass shoal a little to its west. If you are having trouble finding your way in here, simply put the white concrete tower (that houses the white light) on the hill on South Caicos on your stern and steer approximately 250°-255° as a guideline (you must still use your eyes here) and anchor wherever you feel comfortable. About ½ mile or so south of the northern tip of Long Cay are two wedge-shaped rock formations about 50 yards apart along the western shore. I usually anchor off the southernmost of these, about halfway between the grassy shoal and Long Cay.This spot offers great protection from just north of east through south to southwest, and the holding is excellent in soft sand. I have ridden out several fronts here with sustained southwest through northwest winds of 30-40 knots and my one CQR did not budge; yes, the holding here is excellent. Long Bar and Middleton Bay break the larger seas and all you wind up with off Long Cay is a 2'-3' chop. When the wind goes into the northwest the best spot is at the far western end of Cockburn Harbour, where you can find good protection in the lee of Man O War Bush and the large bank area surrounding it that dries at low water. You'll get some chop in a strong westerly here, but nothing dangerous. The School for Field Studies at South Caicos wishes to remind boaters to please not anchor in the large turtle grass beds in the area west of Long Cay; these are study sites for their students. There is plenty of good clean sand to drop the hook in, so please avoid the large turtle grass beds.

Vessels drawing less than 4' can find a nice alternative anchorage west of Cockburn Harbour, but for safety's sake you should check out the approach by dinghy beforehand. Just before high tide head towards Little Man O War Bush, keeping it just off your port bow. Most of the water around this cay dries at low water, but there are two small channels of deeper water that wind around the southwest side of South Caicos between South Caicos and this cay.

Photo Courtesy of Nicolas Popov

South Caicos Light.

As you approach Little Man O War Bush and the conspicuous wreck just southeast of it, you will notice a deeper channel of slightly bluer water snaking around the eastern side of Little Man O War Bush. You will also notice a second blue water channel branching out to the right of this one and heading more northerly, closer in between Little Man O War Bush and South Caicos. Follow this channel, keeping an eye out for shallow spots, as it winds around the southwestern tip of South Caicos. Here you will find a few pockets of deeper water, enough for a 4' draft to anchor. If you take your dinghy further northward along this channel you will come to two conspicuous plane wrecks just west of the airstrip. The first one you come to is little more than a few pieces of metal jutting above the surface. The second wreck lies another half mile or so northwards and reminds one of the plane at Norman's Cay in the Exumas. This plane is a little larger than the one at Norman's Cay, sits higher rests in shallower water, and is missing sections of its wings and fuselage. Capt. Willis Jennings of South Caicos tells me the plane crashed in the 1970's when it ran out of fuel just short of the runway while bringing in a shipment of generators.

South Caicos is dominated by a Bermudian style of architecture. The eastern end of town is home to the government buildings, the post office, Courthouse, government clinic, and the water and fisheries departments. High on a hill to the east of these buildings is the Residency, an 18th century structure that was the district commissioner's home and is now *Mae's Bed and Breakfast*. You can't miss *Mae's*. It's the huge green house with the pointed roof that was your landfall as you approached Cockburn Harbour. Call first if you wish to dine here. Just to the east is a cemetery with several old gravestones. Throughout town you'll see many wooden jetties, warehouses, and churches that date back over 200 years. Along the eastern shore of South Caicos northeast of *Mae's* are the unfinished remains of a huge hotel complex sitting on the ridge above the beautiful beach at East Bay where you'll find good beachcombing after a northeast through southeast blow. The Norwegian investors backed out of this hotel project around 1988; today it stands unfinished, but it remains a great landmark. There is a trail from *Mae's* leading to the beach.

On the northern shore of Cockburn Harbour you will see a large concrete dock with several conspicuous storage tanks. This is the *Sea View Marina* where owner Captain Lewis Cox and his son Norman are your hosts. You can get fuel right at the dock, or, if you draw too much to come alongside (7' at low water), either Lewis or Norman will be glad to meet

House on South Caicos.

you at the government dock with their 2,500-gallon fuel truck. The marina offers free overnight dockage, yes, that's right, free overnight dockage with or without fuel purchase, but the dock can only handle up to three boats - weather permitting. When was the last time you heard of a marina offering free dockage? Thirty-amp 110v power is available and fresh water can be trucked in with a 55-gallon minimum. If you need just a few gallons, Norman says he can help you right from his tank. *Sea View Marina* can also hold your mail for you, arrange a *Fed-Ex* or *UPS* package delivery through Provo, supply a diesel or outboard mechanic, arrange a propane tank fill, and even rent you a car. There's little that Lewis and Norman can't do for visiting boaters. Their very well-stocked *Sea View Market* is the best on the island with fresh fruits and veggies, frozen meats, ice cream, all sorts of dry goods, some small boating supplies, and a phone just outside the front door. Next door, their *Café Columbus* is currently closed and they don't know when they will re-open it. For more info call *Sea View Marina* on VHF ch. 16. You can also call *Charlie Alpha*, Captain Bruce Lightbourne and his *ESSO* fuel truck on ch. 16, for fuel delivery to the government dock. For a taxi you can use ch. 16 to raise *Glinton's Taxi*; owner Bertram Glinton will be happy to take you all over the island at a very reasonable price. For an interesting history lesson, ask Bertram about his years in salt production. You can also try *Lightbourne Taxi*, *Hillside Taxi*, or *Wee 10 Base*. Garbage can be placed in the dumpsters on the street in front of the *Sea View Marina* or by the fish factory docks. Across the street from the *Sea View Marina* is *Anita's Bakery* at *Anita's on the Bay* where owner Anita Clarke bakes wonderful fresh bread; she can even whip up something for you to eat in a pinch.

You will notice that almost everyone in South Caicos has a smile and a hello for you. This community is as far from Provo in distance as it is in atmosphere. I cannot say enough about the wonderful people that is South Caicos' true treasure. This is my favorite island in the entire Turks and Caicos archipelago. I once found myself in dire straits in my data acquisition vessel when my automatic bilge pump burned out and my sixteen-footer was swamped at dawn after all-night 40-knot squalls. I received more than enough help from the good people of South Caicos and none wanted anything in return. All they wanted was the chance to help somebody. They informed me that, after all, that's what we are all here for, to help each other. South Caicos and her people will always hold a dear spot in my heart, especially my good friends Capt. Willis Jennings and Marvin. By the way Marvin, if you're reading this, I still have those plugs and they're still working fine. Oh, and hello to you too, Willis!

As you walk around town it's not unusual to see donkeys, cows, or dogs competing for the road with you and the occasional car or motorcycle. As for bars, *Miss Trudy's Jetaway Bar* is the place for nightlife in South Caicos. For good native food *Muriel's* is the best and she is just east of the immigration office and government dock. Another stop is *Carver's Restaurant* behind *Bayside Auto Parts* across from the *Wee 10 Market* also just east of the *Sea View Marina*. You can also try the *Eastern Inn* for good takeaway food. *Barclays' Bank* has an office in town, though they are only open on Thursdays from 9 till 1. Next to the bank is *Myrna Lee's Restaurant*. For hardware or lumber try the new *G & H Hardware and Lumber Co*. On the airport road at the salt pans is the *Pond View Restaurant*, a good choice for lunch or dinner.

High on a hill above the harbor is the *Admiral's Arm Inn*, a charming and historical location that was the first hotel built in the Turks and Caicos Islands. Until about 35 years ago, the *Inn* was being used to process cotton. With the disappearance of the owner, Diane, her brother could not keep the inn going, and despite his best efforts, the inn and its garden became a pasture for goats and donkeys. Today the inn serves as housing for students in the School for Field Studies Program and its still worth a visit. The large pink two-story building next door is the *Club Caribe Harbour and Beach Resort*, the only hotel on the island. The *Club Caribe Sunset Bar and Restaurant* has large glass windows with a stunning view of the rocky cliffs and turquoise waters of the harbor below.

Club Caribe has the only dive operation on the island and it is here that you can get all your diving questions about South Caicos answered. The diving off South Caicos includes wall dives as well as some beautiful shallow water reefs and coral gardens teeming with marine life. Just off Long Cay, as shown on Chart #TCI-C19, is a dive site known as the Plane Wreck, a Convair 340 lying in about 60' of water. The wreck is situated approximately 300 yards off the cay, actually just opposite the first rock formation on the shoreline south of the entrance to Cockburn Harbour, and is marked by a buoy. Please don't tie your big boat to this buoy, it is only strong enough for small boats and dinghies. Another interesting site is the Eagle's Nest, named for the community of stingrays that lives amidst its unusual seascape of sand channels and ledges. Ask about the shallow water dive sites such as Lion's Head Rock, Boulder Ground, and the Admiral's Aquarium. As I mentioned earlier, ask for Gilbert Jennings at *Lightbourne Taxi* for a knowledgeable diving guide.

Just west of the *Sea View Marina* are several concrete and rip-rap jetties for small boats to tie to; this is where you'll want to tie up your dinghy, but be sure to use a stern anchor to keep your bow off the concrete wall in the surge. At the head of the docks is one of the two fish factories in town. The second, just to the west, lies at the head of the wooden dock with the small wooden building on the end. Just up the hill from the fish factories is the *Cham B Grocery Store* and around the corner is *Hillside Grocery*.

In late May, South Caicos is host to one heck of a big party, the annual *South Caicos Regatta*. People from all over the Turks and Caicos Islands flock to Cockburn Harbour for this colorful, energetic festival. The excitement builds during the Saturday morning sloop races and climaxes Saturday afternoon and night with music, dancing, donkey races, and maypole dancing. If you are in the area do not miss this event.

THE SOUTHERN CAYS

The Southern Cays is the name given to cover the numerous small islands and rocks that lie on the Caicos Bank to the south of Six Hills Cays and Long Cay, stretching about 20 miles south and southwest of Cockburn Harbour on South Caicos. There are three groups, the Fish Cays, the Ambergris Cays, and the Seal Cays. With the exception of the Ambergris Cays these cays are rarely visited except by local fishermen and divers.

The Fish Cays are small, rocky, and offer little to passing yachtsmen. The largest of the three is worthy of a dinghy trip if you are interested in cactus and lizards, and there is a beautiful elkhorn coral reef off this cay's northwest shore. You can actually anchor on the western side of this cay in settled weather or prevailing winds, but you'll have to thread your way through some coral heads and small reefs. The cay is covered in prickly pear cactus and is a nesting site for sooty terns in the summer months. There are three small beaches on the western shore and several shallow reefs that are excellent for snorkelers and fishermen. If passing through from Sapodilla Bay to the Turks Island Passage, a GPS waypoint at 21° 23.50'N, 71° 37.25'W, will place you approximately ¾ mile north of the Fish Cays in good water as shown on Chart #TCI-C21. From here you can head straight out into the Turks Island Passage and on to the Turks Islands or Luperón in the Dominican Republic.

Between the Fish Cays and the Ambergris Cays are numerous coral reefs and heads, some lying just inches below the water's surface; the water in between them, though 25'-35' deep in places, is affected by strong and sometimes confused tidal currents. If you are headed west onto the Caicos Bank and wish to anchor south of the Fish Cays between the Ambergris Cays, the best idea is to do the shallow reefs that lie between the Fish Cays and Big Ambergris

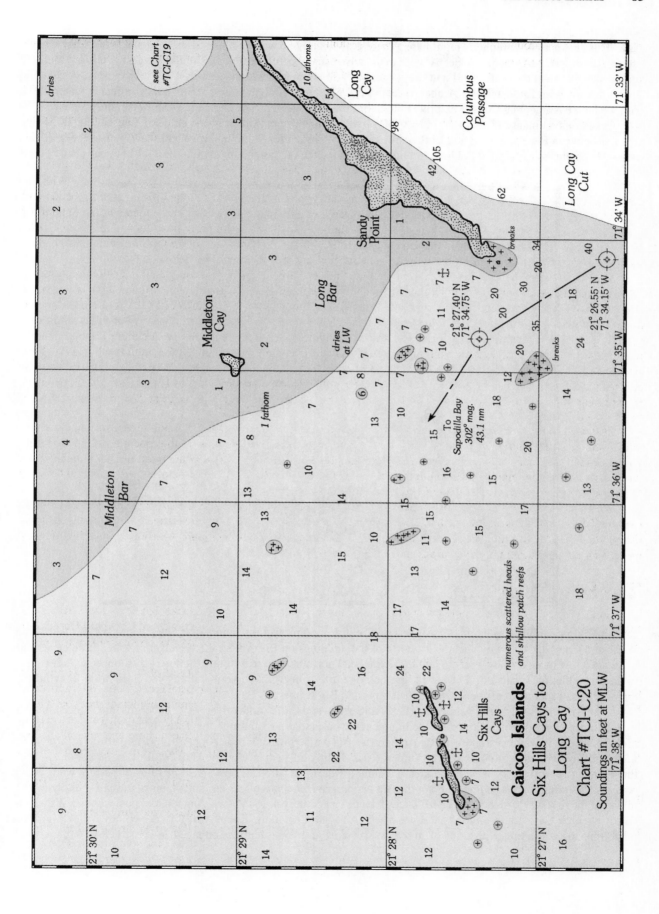

Caicos Islands

Six Hills Cays to
Long Cay

Chart #TCI-C20

Soundings in feet at MLW

Cay. This area is a cartographer's nightmare. There is absolutely no way that I could show each and every reef in this area on Chart #TCI-C21 at that scale. A word to the wise usually being sufficient, I would suggest you avoid this area unless you can read the water well and don't mind a little white knuckle maneuvering. It is possible to leave the anchorage between Little and Big Ambergris and work your way through these reefs to gain the deeper water of the Turks Island Passage, but it might be prudent to avoid them altogether. The choice is yours; I can only advise.

A GPS waypoint at 21° 19.75'N, 71° 39.75'W, will place you approximately one mile northwest of the anchorage that lies between Big Ambergris and Little Ambergris Cay. Watch for scattered heads and shallow patch reefs in this area. The anchorage has great holding, but the shallows stretch out a good bit off the shore of both cays. A 5' draft

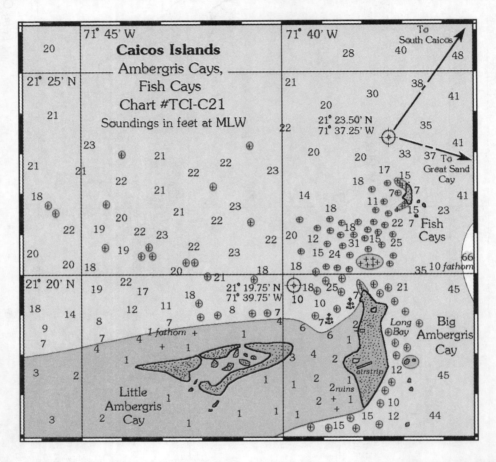

can usually get within ½ mile of Big Ambergris Cay for good protection from east and southeast winds just off the house and small dock. If you anchor just north of the buildings on Big Ambergris, you can tuck in a little closer but there are a few more shallow reefs to avoid. If you head north from here to round the Fish Cays, once again it is best to do it just like the locals do. Put the eastern end of Little Ambergris on your stern as you head north to avoid the majority of the shallow reefs between the Fish Cays and Big Ambergris Cay.

The Ambergris Cays, Big Ambergris (East Ambergris) and Little Ambergris (West Ambergris) are named after the wax-like substance that is excreted by the humpback whales that pass through the Turks Island Passage and that is often found on the windward shore of Big Ambergris. Big Ambergris and Little Ambergris are as distinctly different as night and day. The easternmost cay, Big Ambergris, is slightly hilly (max. elevation 96') while its neighbor one mile to the west, Little Ambergris, is larger in area but quite lower in elevation. There are some ruins of pasture walls and a couple of buildings on the southern end of the Big Ambergris, remnants of earlier inhabitants of the cay. Following the taking of the first whale in the Turks and Caicos Islands on February 4, 1846, a whaling lookout post was established on Big Ambergris Cay. Later on the island was used as a sisal plantation. Today you'll find a colony of rock iguanas inhabiting the cay along with a lot of turk's head cactus and some humans engaged in construction. A group is planning to open a marina here sometime in the future, and if the construction that I witnessed in the Spring of 1998 is any indication, the plan may soon become a reality. On the eastern shore is a beautiful beach in Long Cay that is excellent for beachcombing. Grab a comb and have at it!

Little Ambergris consists mainly of tidal creeks and mangrove flats. The shoreline is very shallow around the entire island and it is best explored by dinghy on a rising tide. Off the northeastern tip of Little Ambergris Cay is an area that is shown on the topographical maps as the Conch Ground. You'll know why it's called that when you investigate pile after pile of conch shells that are probably hundreds of years old. These piles are much taller than I am and there must be at least two dozen of them along the eastern shore of Little Ambergris; it is quite a sight. The surrounding dune and rock structure support a large colony of rock iguanas. Hawksbill and green turtles use the western shore of Little Ambergris Cay for nesting sites during the spring and early summer months; please do not disturb any turtles you may see there and don't dig in the sand for their nests.

Bruce Van Sant in his *Gentleman's Guide to Passages South,* touts these cays as a stopover before heading to Luperón. Good advice Bruce. The reef snorkeling, at its worst, is fantastic.

South of the Ambergris Cays the banks are studded with numerous coral heads that reach up from 20' depths to break the surface. Just south of Big Ambergris Cay lies Bush Cay (as shown on Chart #TCI-C1), a protected Sanctuary. Visits ashore require a permit from the *DECR*. This tiny island is tree covered and has a tiny light tower. The Seal Cays, a protected Sanctuary named after the now extinct West Indian monk seal, are primarily used as fishing ground by Caicos fishermen along with White Cay. These cays lie south and southwest of the Ambergris Cays and stretch for 10 miles between Bush Cay and White Cay. The waters surrounding these cays are strewn with shallow reefs that rise from 40'-60' to dry at low water in numerous places. Travel at night on the Caicos Bank south of this area, as well as on any part of the Caicos Bank, is not advised.

Photo courtesy of Nicolas Popov

Humback Whale tail slapping, Columbus Passage.

Part II

THE TURKS ISLANDS

To the east of the deep Turks Island Passage, sometimes called the Columbus Passage, lies the Turks Bank and the Turks Islands themselves, once called the "Salt Islands." Here you will find the capital of the Turks and Caicos on Grand Turk, the largest of the Turks Islands and one of only two inhabited islands in the group. The Turks Bank is some 36 miles long and varies in width from three to fifteen miles. The sandy bottom is littered with coral heads and patch reefs making for some excellent diving opportunities. The name of the group is said to come from Sir William Phipps, who named them after the native turk's cap or turk's head cactus (*Melocactus intortus*) in 1687. Phipps and his men were in the area recovering 26 tons of gold and silver from a wrecked Spanish galleon when he noticed the cactus that reminded him of a Turkish fez. Sadly so many of these turk's cap cactii have been dug up that except for the few in private gardens and establishments, they are only found growing in the more remote sections of the island group. Another opinion as to the origin of the name suggests that it comes from a time when the islands were used as hideouts for various pirates, some of whom were said to be of Turkish descent. It has been suggested that in the 16th and 17th centuries, under the leadership of the two Barbarosa brothers, a band of Barbary pirates operated out of these waters. Originating in Constantinople, the brothers eventually settled on an uninhabited salt island that the Spanish later referred to as Grand Turk. There is no concrete proof of that occupation but either way, an occasional letter or parcel sometimes is mistakenly sent to Istanbul or Ankara for processing.

APPROACHES TO THE TURKS ISLANDS

The Turks Island Passage, is a 25 mile wide, 7,000' deep trench connecting the Caribbean and the southwest north Atlantic and separating the Turks Islands from the Caicos Islands. The tidal current in the Turks Island passage is often fickle; usually it flows northward through the passage at ½-1 knot, but at other times, depending on the wind strength and direction, it's speed increases and it's direction may vary from north/northwest to northeast. During the months of January through March, an estimated 3,000 humpback whales traverse the Turks Island Passage to their winter breeding grounds that stretch from the Silver Banks to Samaná in the DR. Use caution when around these magnificent creatures and please don't harass them.

From the waypoint at the mouth of Cockburn Harbour on South Caicos, the Front Street anchorage at Grand Turk bears 101° at 21.1 miles, South Dock bears 107° at 21.2 miles, and the western entrance to Big Cut bears 110° at 21.3 nautical miles distant. From South Caicos the waypoint for entry into the protected anchorage at North Creek on Grand Turk bears 93° at a distance of 21.8 miles, but don't simply plug in that waypoint and go. As you approach Grand Turk you must take care to avoid the reef off the northwestern point of Grand Turk that is marked by the steel remains of an old ship. Also from South Caicos, Salt Cay bears 126° at 19.3 miles, while Great Sand Cay bears 148° at 22.7 miles distant.

From Long Cay Cut on the western edge of the Caicos Bank the Front Street anchorage bears 95° at 23.4 miles, South Dock bears 101° at 23.3 miles, and the western entrance to Big Cut bears 104° at 23.3 miles. The entrance waypoint for North Creek bears 88° at a distance of 24.3 miles. Once again, you must avoid the northwest reef off Grand Turk so use caution as you approach Grand Turk. Also from Long Cay Cut, Salt Cay bears 118° at a distance of 20.6 miles while Great Sand Cay bears 140° at 22.9 miles distant.

If approaching from the Luperón in the Dominican Republic, a course of 176° for 77 miles will bring you to a GPS waypoint at 21° 10.80'N, 71° 15.50'W, which lies approximately ¾ mile southwest of the reef at the southern end of Great Sand Cay. From Puerto Plata, a course of 167° for 86 miles will bring you to the same position. Near this waypoint be sure to keep west of the small trio of rocks shown on Chart #TCI-T6 as the Three Marys. From Luperón, the GPS waypoint at 21° 17.60'N, 71° 14.10'W that lies approximately ¾ of a mile southwest of the reef south of Salt Cay, bears approximately 178° at a distance of 83 miles while from Puerto Plata it bears 170° at 92 miles distant.

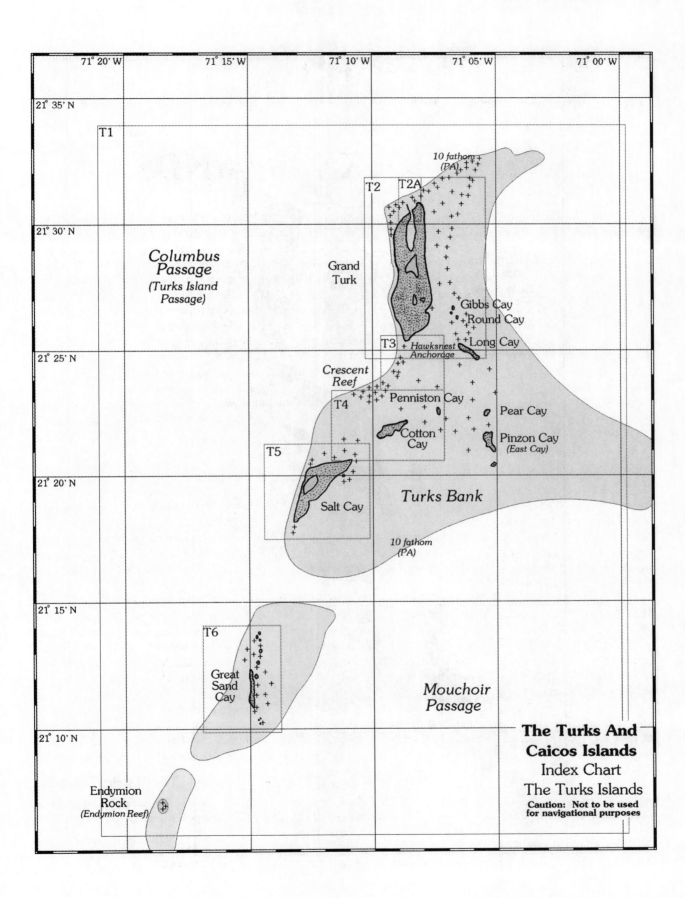

Columbus
Passage
*(Turks Island
Passage)*

T1

T2 T2A

10 fathom
(PA)

Grand
Turk

Gibbs Cay
Round Cay
Long Cay

T3 *Hawksnest
Anchorage*

*Crescent
Reef*

Penniston Cay

T4

Cotton
Cay

Pear Cay

Pinzon Cay
(East Cay)

T5

Salt Cay

Turks Bank

10 fathom
(PA)

T6

Great
Sand
Cay

*Mouchoir
Passage*

**The Turks And
Caicos Islands**
Index Chart
The Turks Islands
**Caution: Not to be used
for navigational purposes**

Endymion
Rock
(Endymion Reef)

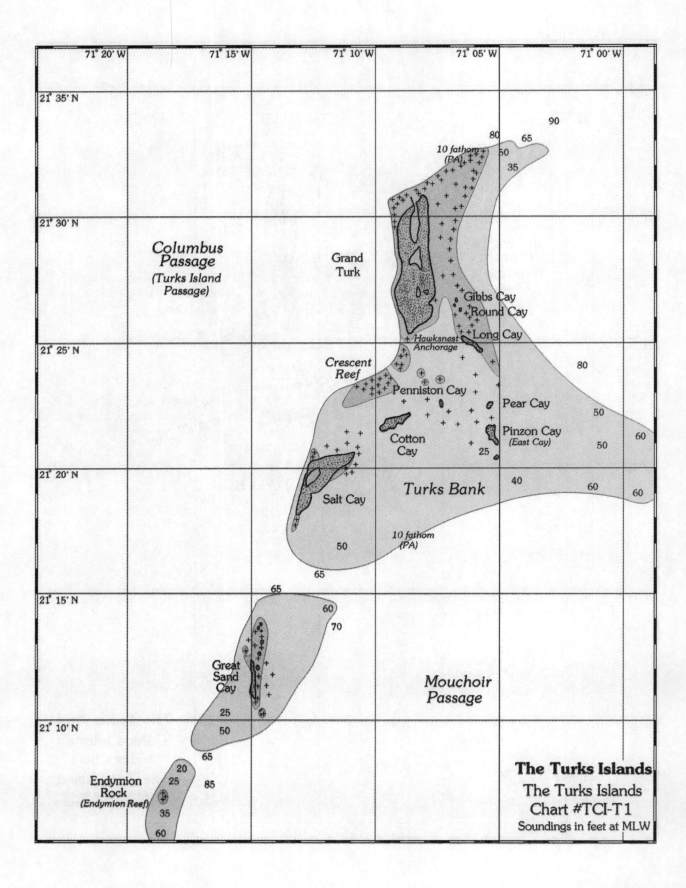

71° 20' W   71° 15' W   71° 10' W   71° 05' W   71° 00' W

21° 35' N

90

80 65

10 fathom   50
(PA)   35

21° 30' N

Columbus
Passage
(Turks Island
Passage)

Grand
Turk

Gibbs Cay
Round Cay

Long Cay

Hawksnest
Anchorage

21° 25' N

Crescent
Reef

80

Penniston Cay

Pear Cay

50

Cotton
Cay

Pinzon Cay
(East Cay)

60

25   50

21° 20' N

Turks Bank   40   60   60

Salt Cay

50

10 fathom
(PA)

65

65

60

70

21° 15' N

Mouchoir
Passage

Great
Sand
Cay

25

21° 10' N

50

65

20

Endymion   25   85
Rock
(Endymion Reef)   35

The Turks Islands

The Turks Islands
Chart #TCI-T1

60   Soundings in feet at MLW

GRAND TURK

Twenty-two miles east of South Caicos, across the 7,000' deep Turks Island Passage, lies the historic, commercial, cultural, and political capital of the Turks and Caicos islands, Grand Turk. Approximately six miles long and three miles wide, Grand Turk is often argued as Columbus' first stop in the New World. Most accounts put Columbus' first landfall at San Salvador, his *Guanahani,* but there is a growing movement, particularly amongst Turks and Caicos Islanders that *Guanahani* was in reality Grand Turk. The theory has been getting some acceptance and in December of 1989 a Grand Turk Landfall Symposium was held in Grand Turk. Several experts in the field, leading Spanish historians, and even a direct descendent of Christopher Columbus were in attendance.

The Grand Turk landfall theory was first put forward by the nineteenth century Spanish historian Fernandez de Navarette and is supported, among others, by the works of Robert Power in 1982 and local Turks and Caicos historians Josiah Marvel of Providenciales, an associate of Power, and the late Herbert E. "Bertie" Sadler of Grand Turk. This theory has gained much in the way of acceptance in the last two decades but, as with all theories concerning Columbus' *Guanahani,* its basis lies in the descriptions of the islands as laid down in Columbus' log, the *Diario* (for more information on this theory you can visit the *Public Library* on Grand Turk and check out Herbert E. Sadler's seven volume *Turks Island Landfall* series on the history of the Turks and Caicos Islands). The descriptions of *Guanahani* in the *Diario* can be interpreted to give a strong argument to a Grant Turk landfall theory but there is absolutely no physical evidence whatsoever pointing to Grand Turk as a possible *Guanahani.* The Lucayan sites that have been found on Grand Turk predate Columbus by almost 500 years though many valuable sites, including the one that may have proven the theory, could have unknowingly been destroyed by the Bermudian Salt Rakers when constructing Cockburn Town in the 17th and 18th centuries. The descriptions in Columbus' log are simply not enough to classify any one particular place as the true *Guanahani* as they can be interpreted to fit several locations. Most experts point to San Salvador in the Bahamas as being Columbus' *Guanahani* and they are supported by some strong physical evidence. Archeologists have dated Lucayan sites on San Salvador to the end of the 15th century and have also found small beads and brass bells that were similar to the types used by the Spanish for trading that date to the same period. This firmly establishes the Lucayans and the Spanish on the island at the same time and presents the most compelling argument for San Salvador being *Guanahani.* But until some researcher somewhere digs up some artifact saying "Columbus arrived here on October 12, 1492," or something to that effect, all these theories will remain exactly that - just theories.

Grand Turk first gained prominence in the 1600's for its salt-making stations. There was a time when Grand Turk's harbor was the main shelter for British vessels out on the business of the empire in this particular part of the world. In more recent times, the United States Air Force had a base on the southern end of the island, while the U.S. Navy had a base (Pan Am Base) at the northern end. In 1950 the United States built a missile tracking station on Grand Turk which remained until 1981. In 1962 John Glenn, after his famous space flight, first set foot back on planet Earth at Grand Turk. LBJ, the Vice President at the time, came to Grand Turk to welcome home the first American to orbit our planet. Glenn was picked up approximately 160 miles east of Grand Turk. Over the next few years five Gemini and one Apollo craft splashed down in the waters north, northeast, and east of Grand Turk.

Sailors might be interested in next bit of Turks Island trivia. The first great American Merchantman to trade with the Orient was the *Grand Turk.* The 300-ton three-masted vessel boasted 22 guns and was originally designed as a privateer. The *Grand Turk* is probably better know as the ship seen on bottles of *Old Spice* after-shave and cologne.

THE NORTH CREEK ANCHORAGE

North Creek is sometimes called Columbus Lake by followers of the Grand Turk landfall theory. If at all possible, I suggest that everyone who visits Grand Turk, if your draft allows, should anchor in this well-protected harbor to explore this marvelous island. Here boats with drafts of 6½' will find excellent holding in 10'-15' of water with protection from every direction and only a relatively few bugs on calm nights. Have I convinced you yet? Sounds too good to be true - right? It almost is.

The hardest part about gaining this anchorage is finding a weather window to permit entry at certain times of the year, primarily the winter months. The entrance channel is easily blocked by northerly swells that tend to break all the way across the narrow mouth, making the channel impassable. Now just because you have light east or southeast winds as you approach Grand Turk, do not assume you can easily enter the channel. Swells from frontal passages that did not make it as far south as the Turks and Caicos Islands or from large storms to the north can easily build and spend themselves along the northern shore of Grand Turk. One day I approached the entrance with a long, lazy 8' northerly

Photo courtesy of Nicolas Popov

Northeast Point Lighthouse, Grand Turk.

swell running in calm wind conditions and could not even get close to the cut. That lazy swell had been transformed into huge crashing breakers along the entire northern shore of Grand Turk. On another occasion I had a light east/southeast breeze of less than 10 knots and a 4'-6' northeasterly swell and had no problem entering. Sometimes you just have to get close enough to take a good long look at the cut before deciding to proceed. Or you can call *Flamingo Cove* or *MPL* on VHF ch. 16 and perhaps if they have seen the cut that day they can tell you whether the cut is passable; they can also arrange a pilot for a fee. Some yachtsmen enter North Creek under the mistaken impression that they can clear *Customs* and *Immigration* once inside. If you need to clear in at Grand Turk you must do so at the new freighter dock on the southwestern side of the island at South Base.

When approaching the northern shore of Grand Turk from the west or the north your landmarks will be the large red and white checkerboard water tower, the old and unused lighthouse on Northeast Point, and the radio antenna that shows a fixed red light at night. As you approach the northern shore from the west, the actual entrance will be hard to discern against the background of the shoreline, but it will appear to lie below the white-roofed building that sits about ¼ mile south of the water tower. A GPS waypoint at 21° 31.10'N, 71° 08.50'W, will place you approximately ½ mile north of the narrow entrance channel and the jetty as shown on Chart #TCI-T2 and on the blow-up, Chart #TCI-T2A. At the time of this writing (Winter 2002) there are two white PVC stakes near the end of the jetty that lies on the western side of the entrance channel. Captain Bob Gascoine set these PVC stakes up as a range to help you line up your entry. This may change at any time, so use caution. In normal conditions the swells will break across the reefs to the east and the west of the channel with lighter action actually in the channel itself. The prudent mariner will likely pass by the entrance once or twice at a close but safe distance to get a good feel for the way the channel lies. The channel is the only entrance to the lake inside and all the water goes in and out of this one channel with the tide, so expect a lot of current. You'll have better steerage if you go against the tidal flow but I have done both and had no difficulties. However, if it is your first time, I recommend going against the flow, or if possible to time you entry for high water slack or just as the tide begins to ebb. Never attempt this entry with the sun directly in your eyes.

When you have decided to enter the channel, line up and approach the entrance keeping the jetty close to your starboard side. The entrance channel is narrow, about 75' wide along the end of the jetty but it widens inside. You should be able to discern the deeper, bluer water alongside the jetty and the yellow and brown of the shallow rocky water to the east of the channel. The reefs to the east and west of the entrance channel stretch farther northward than the end of the jetty so keep your eyes open to avoid them. Enter the channel keeping close to the jetty, but not too close; you'll have 6' just inside the entrance and 8' in places through this first section at MLW. The jetty is made up of large rocks, blocks of concrete, dredged materials, and numerous rusty car and truck frames, engine blocks, axles, and one small front-end loader. Any of these can easily damage the inattentive skipper's vessel if too close. The jetty has a small break in it as it reaches the shore, so don't confuse this with the channel you are in. The break is shallow and has the top of a large rock in the center of it at high water. Both sides of the channel shallow slightly at this break so keep to the center of the visible channel if at all possible and you'll have 6' at MLW. Proceed along the entrance channel paralleling the jetty and as you pass between the jetty and the shoreline to the east the channel will widen a bit. Favor the jetty side as the eastern shore is very shallow and the channel still follows close to the jetty.

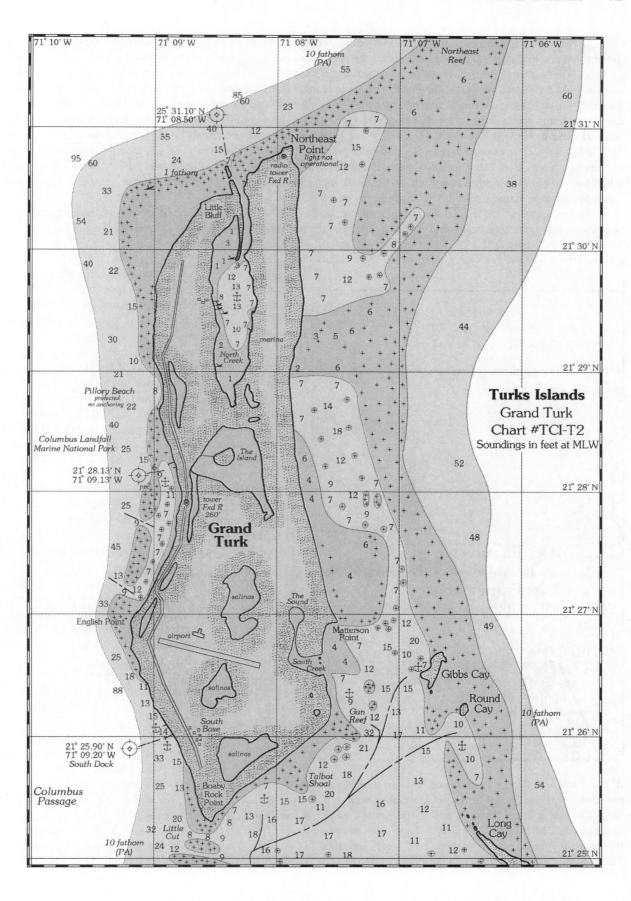

71° 10' W   71° 09' W   71° 08' W   71° 07' W   71° 06' W

Northeast Reef

10 fathom (PA)

25° 31.10' N
71° 08.50' W

Northeast Point
light not operational

radio tower
Fxd R

Little Bluff

North Creek

marina

Turks Islands
Grand Turk
Chart #TCI-T2
Soundings in feet at MLW

Pillory Beach
protected,
no anchoring

Columbus Landfall
Marine National Park

21° 28.13' N
71° 09.13' W

The Island

tower
Fxd R
260'

Grand Turk

salinas

The Sound

English Point

airport

salinas

South Creek

Matterson Point

Gibbs Cay

Round Cay

South Base

Gun Reef

10 fathom (PA)

21° 25.90' N
71° 09.20' W
South Dock

salinas

Boaby Rock Point

Talbot Shoal

Long Cay

Columbus Passage

Little Cut

10 fathom (PA)

21° 31' N
21° 30' N
21° 29' N
21° 28' N
21° 27' N
21° 26' N
21° 25' N

As the anchorage comes into view you will notice that the jetty has a large rusty crane on it as well as a barge at its southern end that also has a crane on it. Between these two cranes you will find the shallowest spots in the entrance channel. The bottom through here is sand and the current has built up over a dozen or so shallow sand mounds (easily seen in good light) that lie perpendicular to your course and stretching from the jetty to the shallows of the eastern shore. These sand mounds, one or two of which only have about 4'-4 ½' of water over them at MLW, are not very wide and if you bump you will likely be able to power over them. Sometimes there are shallower spots on one side or the other of these mounds so you might be able zig-zag your way through. Depths between these mounds are generally 6'-7' at MLW. As I mentioned earlier, 6½' can enter here but if you don't choose a good tide to enter on you might have to power your way over these humps. I believe that in an emergency, a 7' draft could enter here on an extremely high tide if the skipper didn't mind powering over these humps. The only problem would be that this same skipper would then need another extremely high tide to get back out.

As you approach the end of the jetty by the remains of the huge barge and crane, don't get careless, you have one or two more obstacles to avoid. At the eastern end of the entrance channel, across from the end of the jetty, lies a huge piece of steel bar that once marked the eastern end of the entrance channel. Instead of being exactly vertical, this bar leans over and is awash at high water and only about 6" of it juts above the surface at low tide. This steel bar

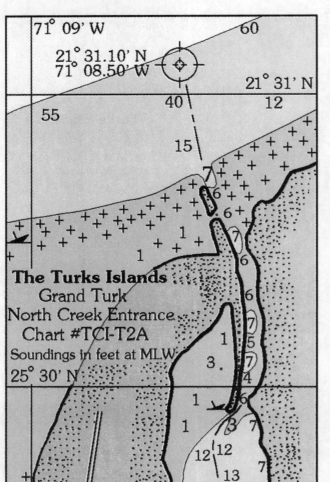

could do a lot of damage to your boat, so keep an eye out for it and don't stray too close to it. Just as you reach the end of the entrance channel at the barge you will come upon a grassy shoal that is not shown on other charts of the area. The reason for this is that it has just appeared over the last few years. The shoal, easily seen in good light, only has 3' of water over it in most places. If you have a high tide you can pass it on either side, but if the tide is low you can only pass between the shoal and the end of the jetty in 6'-7' at MLW close in to the jetty. Once around the grassy shoal area you will be in 8'-15' of water and you can anchor wherever your draft allows and you feel comfortable. The anchorage shallows west and northwest of the end of the jetty and south of the *Flamingo Cove Marina* dock on the eastern shore of the lake. You'll see several boats moored around the periphery of the anchorage and if you wish to explore the edges of North Creek, keep on the lookout for bits of floating line; these are mooring lines that no longer have floats on them.

About midway down the western shore is a government dock at North Wells where the police boat is kept. You are not allowed to tie to this dock, but you can dinghy in to the beach just north of the dock to leave your dinghy while you walk or hitchhike the mile or so into town. About 150 yards south/southeast of the police dock is a submerged wreck in 7' of water, so keep an eye out for it if you are in that vicinity. There is also a floating line next to the wreck with no float attached; you'll want to avoid it and keep that poly line out of your prop.

Over on the eastern shore of North Creek is the *Flamingo Cove Marina* dock. The marina caters primarily to small boats and will continue to do so until the entrance channel is dredged to 7'-8' say the owners. You can purchase diesel and water at the dock and the owners will move vessels around to accommodate a larger vessel that wishes to fuel up here. There is nobody on site at the marina and no infrastructure to speak of other than the dock and fuel pumps. The owners request that if you only need one or two jerry-jugs of diesel, please take them into town for filling as they must leave their shop (*MPL*) on Front Street in Cockburn Town to drive to the marina to pump your fuel. The marina will allow you to tie your dinghy up to their dock for the day for a fee. Contact *Flamingo Cove* or *MPL* on

VHF ch. 16 for more information. If you wish to rent a car for a few days you can park it inside the gate at the entrance overnight and it will be quite safe. But first make arrangements with the owners, Leah or Kirk.

If you take the road along the eastern shore of North Creek you will come to the ruins of the old U.S. Navy base and the Grand Turk Lighthouse. In the mid-19th century, at the height of the industrial revolution, this entire lighthouse was cast in iron in England and then shipped to Grand Turk. The light was reassembled on a bluff overlooking Northeast Reef in 1852-1854 and is credited with helping to sustain the lucrative salt industry in the Turks salt islands as well as saving countless ships. Today this one hundred and fifty-year-old lighthouse, the Silent Sentinel, awaits restoration. To get there by car, follow Lighthouse Road past the *Coral Reef Club* with its palm-tree shaded, hillside units, restaurant, swimming pool, and tennis court. Drive up The Ridge, Grand Turk's better residential area, past the entrance to *Flamingo Cove Marina* and you will come to the entrance to the abandoned U.S. base. Here you can take the dirt road to the left of the fence to reach the lighthouse. Watch out for the feral donkeys as you approach the old base. Divers on the nearby Northeast Reef might find the huge sections of railway that a sinking ship jettisoned on the reef in 1912.

High on the ridge at the southeastern end of North Creek is the red roofed *Island House*, a Mediterranean-style villa featuring air-conditioned units with a swimming pool and a great view of the anchorage. Just south of the *Island House* is a *Texaco* gas station where you can jerry jug fuel to your dinghy on the shore below it.

Just west of the northwestern shore of North Creek, Brian Riggs and other researchers found a Lucayan Indian site that was carbon-dated to 700 A.D., predating a site in Inagua that was estimated to be from around 900 A.D. A local dive instructor, Captain Bob Gascione, who lives aboard his R/V *Aquanaut* in the upper reaches of North Creek, recently found an ancient Lucayan paddle preserved under layers of mangrove leaves in the northwestern corner of North Creek. The paddle was dated to around 1100 A.D.; although off the island now for scientific evaluation and restoration, the paddle will soon be on exhibit at the *National Museum* in Grand Turk. This leaves Captain Bob once again up North Creek without a paddle (with apologies to Piers Xanthony).

A note for birdwatchers, there is a large flock of pink flamingos that are often seen in the area of the shallows around the entrance to North Creek. We were heading out early one morning and saw a flock of 40 in about a foot of water or less about 100 yards west of the entrance jetty.

THE FRONT STREET ANCHORAGE, COCKBURN TOWN, AND SOUTH BASE

The western shore of Grand Turk offers a fair lee anchorage just below the large *Cable and Wireless* tower. There are several breaks in the reef here and vessels with drafts to 8' can enter and anchor just off the heart of Front Street. The western shore of Grand Turk is a national park and vessels over 60' LOA are not allowed to anchor here except in two designated areas near the freighter dock by South Base as shown on Chart #TCI-T2. The western shore of Grand Turk is only tenable in winds from northeast to southeast. If a front threatens it is time to move around to the north side, to enter North Creek, or head south to anchor off the southeastern shore of Grand Turk at Hawksnest Anchorage, or in the lee of the island around South Creek. The anchorages along the western shore of Grand Turk near Front Street can be quite surgy at times, and that is one reason I recommend the North Creek anchorage so strongly. Another reason is the number of shallow bars and rocky shoals that lie between the reef and the shore. I much prefer to anchor in North Creek if at all possible

A GPS waypoint at 21° 28.13' N, 71° 09.13' W, will place you approximately ¼ mile west of the break in the reef at the Front Street anchorage. There are actually three breaks through the reef here. The waypoint will place you just off the northernmost one, the widest of the three. None of these reef entrances should be attempted early in the morning with the sun right in your eyes; good visibility is necessary anytime you attempt to pass through any break in any reef anywhere. The northernmost cut, the one most boaters use, is marked on its southern side by a white PVC marker at the time of this writing. If the marker is still there when you are, keep it to starboard when passing through this wide cut. If in doubt as to which side to take it on, check it out first by dinghy or call *MPL* on VHF ch. 16 or any of the dive shops on VHF ch. 68 for the latest in local knowledge. The cut itself has a minimum depth of 6' at MLW and is easily seen in good light. Any of these three cuts can be used to gain entry to the anchorage area inside the reef, but be warned that there are several shoals and rocky bars between the reef and the shoreline that you must avoid if you attempt to maneuver north or south along the shoreline.

About ½ mile north of the waypoint for the Front Street anchorage there used to be a nice anchorage just off Pillory Beach. The entrance is through a wide gap in the reef that is easily seen in good light and the holding good just off the resort. The Grant Turk landfall theory recognizes this as the place where Columbus first set foot in the New World and the area is now protected and no anchoring is permitted.

Photo courtesy of Nicolas Popov

Front Street from the water, Grand Turk.

Since 1766, the seat of Government for the Turks and Caicos Islands has been located in Cockburn Town on the western shore of Grand Turk. Although its legal name is Cockburn Town, everyone usually just says Grand Turk when referring to the island or the town. Cockburn Town, pronounced Co'burn Town, was first established by Bermudian Salt Rakers and the architecture hints of that heritage as well as others that influenced this British colony over the last 330-odd years. The houses on Grand Turk all reflect a lovely Old World charm; Duke and Front Streets are lined with historic 18th and 19th century landmarks that reflect the Bermudian architecture style of the salt era. The sidewalks of Cockburn Town are paved with cobblestones and the streetlamps are restored antiques, suitable for display in other places, but hard at work here. The town itself is well suited for a walking or bicycling tour (it's not unusual to find people bicycling around town going about their everyday business), and almost every building has a walled courtyard meant to keep wandering donkeys from munching on the foliage. Today the occasional donkey is a rarity. Most of the 100 plus donkeys were moved to the northeast end of the island in 1995 and some were spayed and neutered to control their rate of growth. These donkeys are the descendents of those that the Bermudian Salt Rakers brought with them to haul the salt carts around the island. At one time there were over 800 donkeys roaming the streets of Grand Turk. Some folks will gladly tell you tales about the infamous Buster. It seems that Buster had a reputation for having an aggressive sexual drive and was known to bite women on the rear. To be perfectly honest, Buster would bite just about anybody. Buster got to be such a pain (no pun intended), that he had to be put to sleep recently.

Front Street is the heart and soul of Cockburn Town, with several government offices and many businesses located along this seaside promenade. You may see a lot of folks riding bicycles, but not on narrow, one way, Front Street. The southern end of Front Street effectively starts at the southern end of Pond Street (and is called Duke Street at this point). Just southeast of the end is the *Building Materials* store, a large hardware store that also rents cars. Here you'll also find *K's Drugs* for over the counter medications. A block south of *Building Materials* is the *Diplomat Café*, home to fine native cuisine and a popular spot.

As you proceed up Duke Street the first place you will come to is the *Sitting Pretty Hotel* and the *Sea Eye Diving* operation. *Sitting Pretty,* which is located on both sides of Duke Street, offers nice economical accommodation and a good restaurant featuring island cooking as well as pizza. Cecil Ingram's *Sea Eye Diving* www.interlog.com/-reefnet/GTurk, is one of only three dive operations on the island and is wholly Turks and Caicos owned and operated.

As you proceed north you will notice a few private residences mixed in with the businesses along the Grand Turk waterfront.

Photo courtesy of Nicolas Popov

Front Street from the air, Grand Turk.

Next you'll come to *Captain Kirk's Guesthouse* (No relation to Captain James T. Kirk of the Starship *Enterprise*) and *MPL*, the local Yamaha distributor, Carolina Skiff dealer, and the only outlet for marine supplies on Grand Turk. If you need a diesel or outboard mechanic call *MPL* on VHF ch. 16 and ask for Kirk. Kirk and his wife Leah also run *Flamingo Cove Marina* on North Creek. Next door is the *Salt Raker Inn,* the 150-year-old home of a Bermudian shipwright that is now a wonderful 12-room hotel and restaurant. The *Salt Raker's* restaurant, the *Secret Garden*, offers excellent American and native cuisine and is open for breakfast, lunch and dinner in a courtyard setting. On Wednesdays and Sundays, owner Jenny Smith offers a barbecue with live entertainment. Next door is *Oasis Divers* - www.oasisdivers.com, where owners Everette Freites and Dale Barker love to pamper their guests on dives around Grand Turk and Salt Cay.

Traveling north you will soon come to Jan and Dave's *Conch Café* at the *Water's Edge Bistro*. Open everyday except Mondays for lunch and dinner in very informal surroundings, the *Water's Edge* is one of the most popular places to eat along the waterfront. Here you can have a seat and enjoy your meal listening to the waves breaking on the beach. Scooter rental is also available and the *Water's Edge Club* has three rooms available.

Your next stop is the recently restored *Turk's Head Inn*, originally built in 1840. All seven of the hotel's rooms are individually furnished with genuine antiques in keeping with the hotel's unique history as the original home of the island's salt overseer, then serving time as the British governor's guesthouse and also as the American Consulate. Many of the rooms have a private balcony with a sea view or a private garden patio as well as air-conditioning and cable TV. Guests of the hotel also have access to the governor's private golf course. The restaurant is highly rated by islanders and visitors alike, and serves up some of the best in international and local cuisine served in elegant surroundings. Alternatively, enjoy a relaxing drink in the pub style atmosphere of *Bonney & Read's Bar* which offers lighter bar snacks and live entertainment in the beautiful tree shaded garden that surrounds the hotel, an excellent spot to beat the heat with an ice cold drink. Just north of the Inn is *X's Place*, a unique art gallery with antiques and crafts available. Next door is *Sadler's Seaview Apartments* offering beautiful ocean views in a private garden setting.

At this point Duke Street curves to the sea and actually becomes Front Street; the seawall is all that separates you from the Turks Island Passage. On your right is the huge *Cable and Wireless* complex and to your left is the anchorage just off the town. The 260' tower is topped with a fixed red light at night. Here you can purchase phone cards, place a call, and even send or receive a fax. To receive a fax the fee is only $2.00, to send a fax *CAW* charges a three-minute minimum; this can amount to anywhere between $7.50 and $11.00 for a one page fax.

Northward you'll come to the *Arawak House*, *Barclay's Bank*, and the *Public Treasury* where you can purchase Turks and Caicos commemorative coin sets. Next door is the *Shell Shack* where owner Doug Gordon crafts some of the most unique shell jewelry you'll find anywhere, you must check out the *Shell Shac*k. Next door, the *Beachcomber Guest House*, is a charming bed and breakfast inn right on Front Street.

Next you will come to the government complex on Front Street. Here, in the center of the historic district, is the hub of some of the Turks and Caicos government though most offices have moved to the South Base complex. The bright blue West Indian flavored post office, the Bermudian accented *Legislative Council*, and several other government offices still open for business here everyday. In 1989, these buildings were renovated, a new brick forecourt was laid, and numerous trees and shrubs were planted along Front Street. Just behind the post office on Pond Street, the road that parallels Front Street and the town salinas, is the new Courthouse where you are welcome to sit in on court hearings as long as you are properly dressed (ladies no slacks, men no shorts, and no T-shirts on either of you).

Outside the government compound you will see some ceremonial cannons and the Turks and Caicos national flag. The flag consists of the Union Jack on a blue background along with the Turks and Caicos coat of arms depicting a flamingo, pelican, queen conch, turk's cap cactus, and a spiny lobster. A predecessor to the current flag showed the emblem of salt and sailing ships that was the official flag of the Turks and Caicos Islands during the salt days. The odd part is that one of the salt stacks on the emblem had an entrance resembling the entrance to an Eskimo igloo. The flagmaker commissioned for this job mistakenly thought the Turks and Caicos Islands were near the North Pole.

Further down Front Street you'll pass *St. Mary's Anglican Church* and its memorial to the Turks and Caicos islanders who died in World Wars I and II. The other Anglican Church on the island is *St. Thomas'* situated next to the Anglican cemetery. If you head east on Moxey Street by the Courthouse you will cross the pond and the pink building, on your right will be *City Market*, a pretty nice little grocery store. A note about shopping in Grand Turk. The plane comes in on Wednesdays and the fresh fruits, veggies, and meats that arrive then will show up on the shelves that afternoon and there is usually some left the next day also. In other words, Tuesday is not the day to shop for fresh goodies on Grand Turk. Passing *City Market*, take your second right at the two story yellow building on Frith Street and *Sarah's Shopping Center* will be on your right. *Sarah's* has fresh veggies, fruits, milk, ice cream, and frozen meats as well as some bulk goods. Grocery shopping on Grand Turk involves going to each of these stores as no one particular store is likely to have it all. If you head north on Pond Street from the Courthouse and take the next right at

Church Folly you will come to *Missick's Bakery*, *Neville's Auto Parts*, and the *Philatelic Bureau*. The Turks and Caicos Islands are known far and wide to stamp enthusiasts for their colorful postage stamps and a visit to the *Philatelic Bureau* is a must for anyone with an interest in the Turks and Caicos series of postage stamps.

Back on Front Street, your next stop on your northward journey is the *Victoria Public Library*. Here you can check out a book for a small deposit and they have quite a selection of reading material as well as reference books. If you have any books that you would care to donate, by all means please do. The nearby *Library Tennis Court* hosts several concerts and variety shows each year. You will now come to the intersection of Front Street and Prison Folly, the wide road that takes you one block east to the old prison and a new modern office development

Next is the *Harbour House* where you will find the offices of *Scotia Bank*, *Georgian Trust*, and the *Turks and Caicos Banking Company*. Garbage is a problem on Grand Turk. There used to be several dumpsters scattered about the island but they have all rusted. Today all garbage pickup is done on a door to door basis, though you might see the odd can bolted to a power pole but they won't hold much. For boaters, it has been suggested that you take your bagged garbage to a wooden walled outdoor receptacle next to *Scotia Bank*. This is where everybody in the *Harbour House* leaves their garbage and it must make do for the occasional cruiser too. Behind the Harbour House on Pond Street is *Caribe West Discount Liquors*, a *Fed-Ex* office, and *Cee's Grocery and Wholesale Supplies*. *Cee's* is a great place to stop to pick up bulk goods with excellent prices on cases of sodas. *Cee's* is also the island's *UPS* agent.

After *Harbour House* the one-way section of Front Street ends at the *Odd Fellow's Lodge*, a two-story building with a large eye painted on one side. The *Lodge* is one of Grand Turks several *Masonic Lodges* and it is said that the proclamation of the emancipation of slavery was read from the veranda of this building on August 1, 1838. Northward from here is the old *Customs Shed* which houses the *Turks and Caicos Islands Tourist Board* so if you need tourist related information, this will be a handy place to stop.

A great place to eat is next, the *Poop Deck*, a great local hangout serving some of the best native cuisine at affordable prices with an ever-changing daily special. Across the street is *TIMCO, Turks Islands Importers*, where you can get some fresh and frozen foods, as well as cases of sodas, and alcoholic beverages. Next door is *A-1 Business Machines*, a *Canon* dealer where you can pick up computer and office supplies and have minor repairs made.

A trip to Grand Turk is not complete without a stop at *Peanut's Pepper Pot Snack Shop,* run by Phylistiana "Peanuts" Butterfield, one of the most popular tourist stops on Front Street. Peanuts, an excellent cook and rake n' scrape musician, is known far and wide for her conch fritters, her "rhythm pills", which promise, with the help of a can of Dragon Stout beer, to put "it" back if "it" has gone away. Wonderful Peanuts is a friend and mother to all who enter her establishment and got her moniker from selling peanuts at the nearby airport. East of Peanut's place on Pond Street is *Dot's Food Fair, Dot's Liquor Store,* and *Dot's Gift Shop*. *Dot's Food Fair* is a very well stocked grocery and dry goods store with fresh produce, canned goods, ice cream, fresh meats, non-prescription drugs, and a selection of beers. *Dot's Boutique and General Merchandise* on Pond Street carries clothes, household furnishings, office supplies and books.

Heading north from *Peanut's Pepper Pot* you'll come to Mitch Rolling's *Blue Water Divers* www.microplan.com/ bluerake.htm Mitch also owns the *Eagle Ray Recording Studio* that he built in the basement of his home. Mitch, who is known as the singing divemaster, and his friend Dave, another singing divemaster, have released an album entitled *Grand Turk Blues*. Mitch performs at the nearby *Salt Raker Inn*'s Wednesday and Sunday night barbecues.

Next to *Blue Water Divers* is the *Guinep House*, one of the oldest stone buildings on the island and named after the large tree in the front yard. *The Guinep House*, situated on Front Street directly facing the sea and the *Columbus National Marine Park*, is the home of the *Turks and Caicos National Museum* and was constructed of ship's timbers in Bermudian seafarer's tradition. The building itself is fully air-conditioned and on those hot afternoons it's a perfect place to escape to and cool down. But relief from the climate is not the only reason one should pay a visit to the museum. The *Turks and Caicos National Museum*, opened in 1991, has recorded in its archives and displays, the cultural history of the Turks and Caicos Islands, their discovery, the impact of the early European settlers, and the role that the islands played in the great 20th century space race. Tools and pottery that date back to Lucayan times will give you an idea of how these peaceful people lived. The museum proudly displays an extremely well presented marine reef replica with many interesting facts on reefs and reef fish. But the museum's centerpiece is its fascinating collection of artifacts from the *Molasses Reef Wreck*, the oldest shipwreck in the Americas and the first shipwreck site in the Caribbean to be scientifically excavated.

Measuring just 19 meters long, the caravel, having safely crossed the treacherous Atlantic, ran aground on the reef and sank in about 15'-20' of water, laying undiscovered for some 400 years until it was found by treasure divers in 1976. An unscrupulous salvager tried to gain financially from the excavation by claiming the ship was the *Pinta*, one of Columbus' original three ships. The claim was soon proven to be false and the government of the Turks and Caicos

Islands took over the salvage and identification process. A government permit was issued to the Institute of Nautical Archaeology at Texas A &M's National Museum under the direction of Dr. Donald H. Keith. Irate treasure hunters then tried to dynamite the site but their efforts resulted in minimal damage. Dating of Lucayan pottery pieces found on the site placed the ship on the reef prior to 1513 (remember, all the Lucayans were forcibly removed from the Turks and Caicos islands by 1513) and researchers speculated that the ship was a slaver enroute to Hispaniola. The ship was armed with state-of-the-art weapons of the period, and the *National Museum* can boast to having the largest selection of 16th century wrought iron, breech-loading cannons in the world. Following the salvage, cataloguing and preservation of the 2,000-plus artifacts comprising selections of arms, tools, personal effects and pottery, the artifacts were returned to Grand Turk, where they are now exhibited at the museum with the ship's huge anchor hanging from the wall as the centerpiece of the exhibit. *The Turks and Caicos National Museum* has a new newsletter, the *Astrolabe*, and plans are afoot to build a complementary museum in Provo, not a duplicate, but one with different offerings oriented to the Caicos group of islands. Definitely stop in and visit the museum's Director Barry Dressel and Manager Brian Riggs and visit the gift shop, with its locally made crafts and selection of Caribbean books located on the second floor.

North of the museum, shoppers might want to visit one of the last fish processing plants in the Turks and Caicos Islands, the *Sea View Fish Market*. Owner Jonathon Missick has been fishing these waters since he was nine years old. Jonathon is an excellent source of fishing tales if you can find the time to listen. He can tell you how the fishing was big on Grand Turk before the "old people died away." Next door is Captain Sam Seymour's tiny but well stocked *Pilot House Store*. If you head east from here you will come to Pond Road. Take a left on Pond Road, which now becomes Hospital Road, and you'll find *The Regal Begal* a few blocks north. This is probably the best place on the island for local dishes johnny cake, boiled fish, peas and rice, and anything made with conch.

Just north of the Front Street area on the western shore of Grand Turk is the *Guanahani Beach Resort* on Pillory Beach, though by some to be the first place Columbus set foot in the New World. The resort has 16 spacious air-conditioned rooms and the popular *Shipwreck Restaurant and Lounge*.

If you were to drive south from Front Street towards the southern end of the island you will pass the airport and soon come to *Government House*, the governor's residence that is called simply *Waterloo*. *Waterloo* was built in

Photo Courtesy of Nicolas Popov

Peanut's Pepper Pot Snack Shop, run by Phylistiana "Peanuts" Butterfield.

1815 (the same year as the Battle of Waterloo) and is not open to the public except by special invitation. The cabinet, the *Executive Council*, meets every week at the governor's office, a small modern single-story building with it's own entrance marked *Governor's Office*. Just past the white wall that surrounds *Waterloo* and the governor's private golf course is the entrance to Governor's Beach, a beautiful sandy beach with a backdrop of shady casaurinas. As of winter 2002, a 72-room hotel/resort complex is still planned for construction on *Governor's Beach*. The plantation styled edifice is to have elements of Bermudian and Grand Turk architecture to retain the quaint character of Grand Turk while it caters to the upscale tourist clientele.

A little further south is the entrance to South Dock and the huge South Base government complex which houses *Immigration*, *Customs*, and several other prime governmental agencies. Your first sight of Grand Turk when approaching from South Caicos or points south will probably be the huge white bulbous FAA antenna that at first glance resembles a water tank high on the hill above *South Base*. The large FAA antenna there has a fixed red light at its top. The new concrete *South Dock*, just south of the older steel dock, is the place you'll need to tie up to clear in at Grand Turk. If you need fuel call *Texaco I* on VHF ch. 16 and they will deliver fuel to the dock for you.

A GPS waypoint at 21° 25.90'N, 71° 09.20'W will place you approximately ¼ mile west/southwest of the new *South Dock*. If your intent is to clear in call *Grand Turk Harbourmaster* on VHF ch. 16 for instructions. If you only need fuel and have already cleared in elsewhere call *Texaco I* for instructions. Vessels over 60' are allowed to anchor in the vicinity of the dock between latitude 21° 26.12' N and 25°25.85' N. The dock itself is designed for vessels to 275' with drafts of 12' at the bow and 15' at the stern.

Just to the east of *South Base*, along the road that leads southward around the complex, is a remarkable sight, especially for sailors who use wind generators aboard. Here is a 75' tall, red and white striped wind powered generator that was built with a grant from the Canadian government. The 5KW AC generator is a vertical tower with two blades that resemble an eggbeater. The top is buoyed by wires and the whole contraption revolves with an incredible amount of noise (and I thought my old wooden-bladed Windbugger was noisy!). It takes 17 knots of wind for the unit to create enough power to be efficient; less than 17 knots and the unit is not even turned on.

Just south of South Base is the *Arawak Inn and Beach Club* located at one of Grand Turk's best beach diving locations on a secluded stretch of white sandy beach on the southwest side of Grand Turk. The *Inn* features 14 air-conditioned units right on the beach, cable TV, a fresh water pool, a beach bar and restaurant, horseback riding and a daily shuttle service into Cockburn Town. Wade into the water and out a few hundred yards and you can dive on the pristine Grand Turk Wall that hosts a magnificent array of marine life.

Divers will also want to check out the old South Dock and the area called The Pits. The old steel South Dock was constructed in the mid-1950's to service the island's shipping and the U.S. Missile Tracking Station on Grand Turk. Over the years garbage, cargo, and all manner of flotsam and jetsam associated with the exchange of freight have settled in the surrounding waters. A variety of marine creatures have taken to calling this garbage dump home and can be viewed and photographed in their natural environment. Please exercise caution as some of the debris, such as monofilament fishing line left by careless fishermen, may entangle and trap the unwary diver.

While we're discussing the southern end of Grand Turk, I should mention that a huge multi-million dollar project by the *Beacon of Light Development Company*, a group of Christian investors, began construction on Grand Turk. The *White Sands/Hawksnest* project is designed to make the southernmost tip of Grand Turk the economic hub of the island. Scheduled plans include condominium construction around the harbor; more than 20 pastel colored, 3,000 square foot houses with concrete docks overlooking the harbor, which is also scheduled for dredging. A hurricane proof marina is also on the slate as well as a jetport, a "*Fisherman's Village*", hotels, luxury homes, restaurants, and bakeries. There is to be minimal auto traffic and golf carts will probably be used for transportation. One of the more beneficial aspects of this project is the building of a much-needed medical college.

Grand Turk celebrates a couple of unique holidays such as the *McCartney Day* celebrations on June 5th. James Alexander George Smith (JAGS) McCartney inspired Turks and Caicos Islanders to be proud of their heritage. McCartney witnessed a certain pride that Jamaicans had in their roots and endeavored to bring the same pride to his people in the Turks and Caicos Islands. The *Grand Turks Cactus Festival* has replaced the yearly carnival as one of the most popular events of the year. The *Cactus Festival* features sports, dancing, art, and costume contests as well as an island beauty pageant.

HAWKSNEST ANCHORAGE

Along the southeastern shoreline of Grand Turk is the historic Hawksnest Anchorage as shown on Chart #'s TCI-T2, TCI-T3 a good shelter from westerly winds. Hawksnest Anchorage offers good protection in winds from west/southwest through northwest to north, while safe anchorage can also be found in the lee of Gibbs Cay in northeast through southeast winds. Vessels can also seek shelter from westerly winds further north along the eastern shore of Grand Turk past the entrance to South Creek, as shown on Chart #TCI-T2. Although these anchorages can get very surgy at times, the holding is good. Entrance to these anchorages is through one of several cuts through the reef south of Grand Turk.

Hawksnest Anchorage, once called Reef Harbour, for all practical purposes lies off the southeastern shore of Grand Turk, but, is sometimes shown on some older charts as lying between Grand Turk and Cotton Cay, protected by a reef to the west, and Long Cay and a reef to the east. Turks Island Landfall theorists claim that this is the anchorage that Columbus claimed would hold "all the ships in Christendom." Entrance for larger vessels of 10' draft is south of the reef between Salt Cay and Cotton Cay from the west and south of Pinzon Cay (once called Breeches Island and sometimes still referred to as East Cay) in the east. The U.S. Navy surveyed Hawksnest Anchorage during World War II with an eye to establishing an anti-submarine tracking base for Catalina Flying Boats, but nothing came of it.

Today, entrance to the Hawksnest Anchorage for the average cruising boat is through one of several breaks in the reef south of Grand Turk. Just south of Boaby Rock Point on Grand Turk is Little Cut, sometimes called Small Cut on some charts. As well as being shallower and narrower than Big Cut, Little Cut is often hard to pick out, which is why I recommend Big Cut for someone not familiar with these waters. A GPS waypoint at 21° 24.60'N, 71° 09.25'W, will place you approximately ¼ mile northwest of Big Cut (sometimes called Great Cut) as shown on Chart #TCI-T3. From this waypoint look southeast and you will see three cays about a mile or two distant. Line up with the center of the southernmost cay and head in on it on an approximate heading of 135°. Once again, I must advise that this heading is

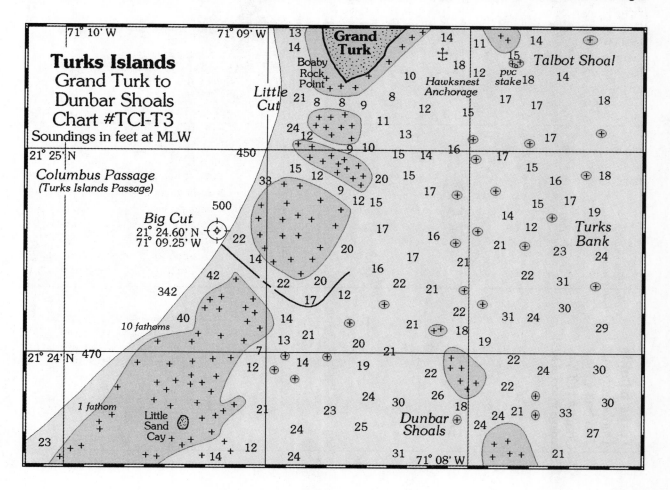

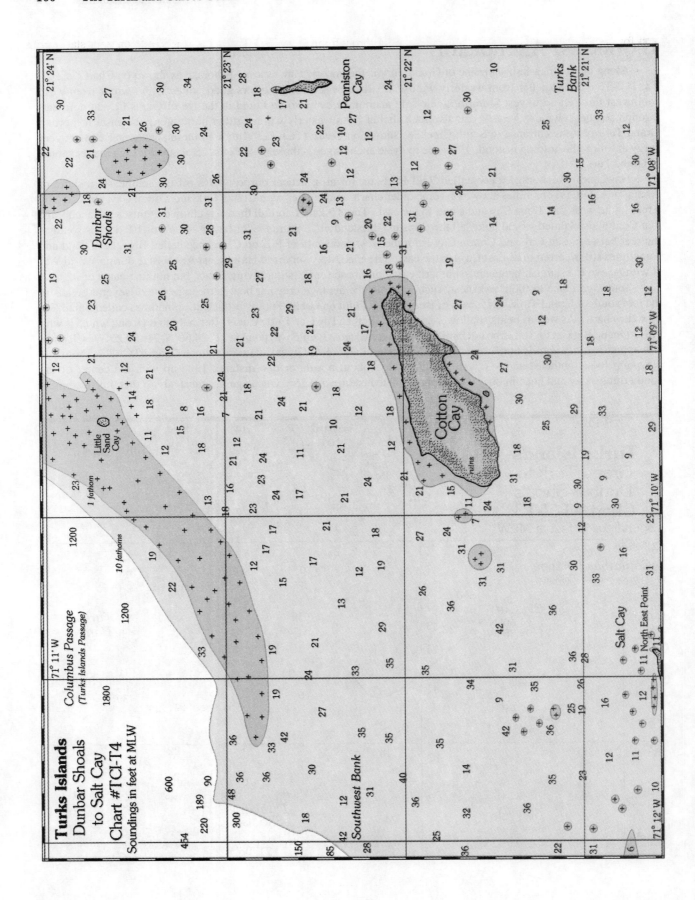

Turks Islands
Dunbar Shoals
to Salt Cay
Chart #TCI-T4
Soundings in feet at MLW

Columbus Passage
(Turks Islands Passage)

71° 11' W

Dunbar Shoals

Penniston Cay

Cotton Cay

ruins

Little Sand Cay

1 fathom

10 fathoms

1200

1200

1800

600

454   220   189   90

300

150

85

Southwest Bank

Turks Bank

Salt Cay

11 North East Point

21° 24' N

21° 23' N

21° 22' N

21° 21' N

71° 08' W

71° 09' W

71° 10' W

71° 11' W

71° 12' W

just for orientation; you must use your eyes to pilot through the reef here. The reef to the south, on your starboard side as you head southeast, is the shallowest and the easiest to see. Once inside, begin to steer north/northeast to anchor in Hawksnest Anchorage properly in northwest and northerly winds, taking care to avoid the eastern side of the reefs you just passed through. If the winds are southwest to west, continue northeast around Talbot Shoal and Gun Reef to anchor in the lee of Grand Turk just south of the entrance to South Creek (where Lucayan indians once kept their canoes) as shown on Chart #TCI-T2. As you pass Talbot Shoal keep an eye out for the buoy that marks the very shallow reef of its southern tip. You can actually pass between this reef and Talbot Shoal but it is so much easier and safer just to round the buoy in deeper water and be done with it. Bear in mind that the buoy may be long gone by the time you cruise these waters; use extreme caution through here.

The only problem with the anchorage south of South Creek, other than the surge, is that you are right in the flight path to the airstrip and you will be buzzed all day long by plane after plane, including a few large jets. The well-lit building with the huge fence west of the mouth of South Creek is the new prison. If you seek a lee in moderate northeast to southeast winds you can anchor in the lee of Gibbs Cay with good protection but watch out for a few scattered heads in the vicinity. A word of warning: these anchorages along the southeastern shore of Grand Turk can get quite rolly when there is no wind to keep you perpendicular to the ever-present surge.

The small islands of Gibbs Cay and Round Cay were once called The Twins and later The Sisters on a French chart that dates to the mid-18th century and are today protected under the national park ordinance as a bird sanctuary. During the early summer months, sooty and noddy terns nest here and raise their young. These islands once played a small part in the defense of Grand Turk. At the summit of Gibbs Cay you will find the ruins of a lookout post which, with the cannon placement on Gun Hill on the mainland of Grand Turk, served as a line of defense for Grand Turk. Gibbs Cay was the location of a French gun emplacement in 1780 called Ft. Castries and was later used as a fort by Turks islanders in fear of a French invasion of Hispaniola in 1791. The offshore elkhorn coral reefs offer some excellent shallow water snorkeling and even some small tunnels for the more experienced diver.

Long Cay, once called Pelican Island, lies about 1½ miles southeast of Grand Turk, as shown on Chart #TIC-T2. This uninhabited island is a sanctuary for the Turks and Caicos rock iguana, the same creature that is also found on Little Water Cay northeast of Provo at Leeward Going Through. Visitors to this 1½ miles long narrow cay must apply for a permit from the *DECR*, in Grand Turk. A little further south is Pear Cay, once called Bird Island, whose rocky shoreline has little to offer save for some excellent snorkeling and diving on the reefs off its western shore. In settled weather you can anchor in the small reef-encircled harbor between Long Cay and Round Cay, but you may need to set a bridle to keep from rolling with the surge.

At 65' in elevation, Martin Alonzo Pinzon Cay, usually just called Pinzon Cay and formerly known as East Cay, is the highest of the Turks Island group. The island is named after the pilot of the *Pinta* on Columbus' first voyage to the New World. The only inhabitants of this cay were those who manned a lookout post here and treasure hunters that based here in 1970 while searching for treasure on the Silver Banks. The ruins of their base camp are still visible on the southwestern shore of the island. There is somewhat of a surgy lee anchorage along the northwestern shore. There is a small blow hole on the eastern side surrounded by several small rocky pools that are perfect for bathing. Pinzon Cay is home to a magnificent growth of the native turk's head cactus, one of the only remaining places in the islands where they are still found in the wild.

Cotton Cay, as shown on Chart #TCI-T4, is the largest and lushest of the uninhabited Turks Islands. The island is privately owned, but access is allowed as of this writing. The cay was once owned by the Harriot Family of Salt Cay fame and as such was used as a retreat and for cattle grazing. Ashore you will find the ruins of their support buildings and many pasture walls. A beautiful subterranean grotto leads to rock enclosed cove near the ruins of the old house on the western shore of the island. Recently two Lucayan sites were found on Cotton Cay as well as two sites on nearby Long Cay. Just to the east of Cotton Cay lies Penniston Cay, whose rocky shores offer little to the cruising skipper. Tropicbirds frequent the southern shore in spring and early summer.

Salt Cay

Seven miles southeast of Grand Turk lies what some tourist brochures refer to as "the land that time forgot." Salt Cay was originally called *Caiceman* or *Canamani* by the ancient Lucayans and later known as *Petite Saline* by the French. Little on the cay has changed since 1900 when the salt industry flourished. The large inland salt pond that still dominates Salt Cay's land area was the attraction and the focus for commerce on Salt Cay for hundreds of years from the time of the Lucayan traders, to the Bermudian Salt Rakers who first arrived in 1645, to even more modern times when Salt Cay was still a busy port well into the 1960's. The skeletons of old windmills that pumped brine into the flats still stand in the salt ponds while nearby giant salt piles sit unused and untouched for years. In 1845 Salt Cay was the home of the Turks Island Whaling Company. The remains of the *Taylor House*, the old whale watching outpost, still sits on the highest spot on Salt Cay on Taylor Hill along the eastern shore, and is easily seen from anywhere on the cay. Captured whales were taken ashore at Whale House Bay on the eastern shore for processing of their meat, oil, and ambergris of which a 150-lb. chunk sold for $20,000 in New York in 1955. But that was then and this is now; and nowadays an estimated 3,000 humpback whales pass by unmolested between January and March on their way to their winter breeding grounds on the Mouchoir and Silver Banks that lie east and southeast of the Turks Islands.

Recently some local residents and a couple of American investors began an attempt to resume salt production on Salt Cay. A company called *Sun Crystals Trading Company* has leased 250 acres of Salt Cay and plans to employ modern technology in the salt production process, while employing 40 local residents. Four salinas and most of the windmills will remain as mementos of the past. Donkeys, vital to salt production in the early years on Salt Cay, will not be used - to avoid contamination. The finer grades of salt produced is intended for use in water treatment and cattle feed, while the lower grades of salt will be used for snow and ice removal in northern climes.

Today a few dozen cars wander the roads, and the streets are used as much by cows and donkeys as people (it wasn't until 1989 that a fence was built around the airport to keep donkeys off the runway). Beautiful beaches border much of the Salt Cay shoreline, while herons and other birds feed in the salinas and in the marshlands to the south. The distinctively Bermudian style homes, all with dusty but neatly swept dirt yards, set a unique tone and style. Salt Cay is a vestige of the old Turks and Caicos, a window to a simpler and slower time. It has been said that Salt Cay is "...what the Caribbean used to be." Salt Cay, often regarded as a living museum of industrial archaeology of the Salt Raker era, has been designated a *UNESCO World Heritage Site* to preserve the history and culture of this tiny island. This ensures that all future development on Salt Cay must be in absolute harmony with its historic past

You will probably notice that the island is primarily inhabited by the very old and the very young; those in the middle, for the most part, are off on the other islands seeking their fortunes. The 200 or so residents that remain are all very friendly and quick with a bit of conversation for the passing stranger. The sign at the airport says it all: Bon Voyage! Return by any means! Salt Cay is one of those islands that, no matter how long you stay, you find that you really did not stay long enough. I am certainly guilty of that.

A GPS waypoint at 21° 19.90'N, 71° 13.25'W, will place you approximately ¼ mile west of *Deane's Dock* as shown on Chart #TCI-T5. If approaching from the south or east your first sight will probably be of the huge *White House* that absolutely dominates the Salt Cay shoreline. The holding along the eastern shore of Salt Cay can only be rated as poor

Turks Islands
Salt Cay
Chart #TCI-T5
Soundings in feet at MLW

Salt Cay.

to fair with a light layer of sand mixed with rocks and other rubble over a rock bottom. You can anchor anywhere along Salt Cay's western shore between *Deane's Dock* and the *White House*; the holding is about the same. The entire western shore of Salt Cay is quite rocky as you get closer in to shore. The southern third of the western shore has a few more sandy patches to set your anchor in but I never feel comfortable anchoring off Salt Cay's western shore.

My favorite anchorage, and one that is rarely taken advantage of by visiting cruisers, is in North Bay just off beautiful North Beach on the northern shore of Salt Cay. The entrance is gained by going north of the reef at North West Point and working your way in towards the beach, dodging the few coral heads and small patch reefs that are easily seen in good light. Don't try this route early in the morning with the sun in your eyes. The holding is good in sand, but the anchorage is only good in southeast to southwest winds and a little surge might work its way in during periods of stronger winds. This anchorage is not recommended with winds from west through north to east or with the threat of a windshift to those directions during the night, as you won't find your way out in the dark.

Deane's Dock is well protected but open to the southwest. The entrance is over a rocky bottom with only 4' at low water at the entrance, with anywhere between 2'-4' at MLW along the walls where you could tie up once you get around the shallow spot in the center. If you should tie up inside during a frontal passage, expect a strong surge to move you about quite a bit. For information on how to enter the dock call *Salt Cay Divers* on VHF ch. 16. If you need gas, diesel, or groceries, you can get all three at Nathan Smith's place just southeast of *Deane's Dock* by the large fuel tanks. If you need a diesel mechanic ask for Perry Tolbert.

The anchorage on Salt Cay's western shore is just off the only settlement on Salt Cay, Balfour Town. Balfour Town is divided into two sections, the north side and the south side. On the north side you can find Leon Wilson's *One Down One To Go Restaurant*, also known as the *Big W*. Leon, former chairman of the Turks and Caicos Tourist Board and the unofficial "Ambassador of Good Will" for Salt Cay, serves great chicken, conch and hamburgers. In town you'll also find the government clinic, well staffed by Murial and her assistant Coralene, with a government doctor visiting about every three weeks. Right in the middle of Balfour Town is Irene Been-Legget's *Halfway House*. The tourist brochures boast that Irene's hospitality and excellent cooking has convinced more than one of her guests to retire to Salt Cay.

On the western shore of Salt Cay you will find the impressive *White House*, the ancestral home of the Harriots, Bermudian salt merchants. When the hurricane of September 1813 destroyed the old Harriot home with a 15' tidal surge, the Harriot clan decided to build a structure that would withstand whatever nature threw its way. The two-story house, the oldest standing building on the cay, was constructed between 1834 and 1840. The house was built of stone with the seaward edge in the shape of a ship's prow to protect it from heavy waves on the side-walls and possible flooding. The entire first floor was used for salt storage and even today, salt can still be seen in the interior of the first floor. The pointed roof was fashioned by shipwrights with massive wooden beams reinforced with stout knees. She appears able to withstand quite a lot of torture and has over the last 150 years. In 1940 and 1941, *Paramount Pictures* filmed *Bahama Passage* starring Madeleine Carroll and Sterling Hayden on Salt Cay with the *White House* starring in several scenes. Also in town you can find *the Brown House*, an old wooden hotel. *The Brown House* has a beautiful veranda and currently has caretakers who rent out smaller, private homes nearby.

Salt Cay's North Beach is one of the most beautiful beaches in the entire Turks and Caicos archipelago. The *Windmills Plantation*, a small but luxurious resort and now a growing condo concern, sits on the beach, just a short walk from the airport. Good food and accommodations can also be found at Bryan Sheedy's *Mt. Pleasant Guest House* (more about Bryan in a moment), and at the *Castaway's Beach House* with a half-dozen getaway cottages right on the beach.

Salt Cay is an almost virgin diving area. The island is blessed with a wall drop-off running the length of its western shore. Local residents Ollie Been and Debbie Manos run the very relaxed *Salt Cay Divers* http:// www.saltcaydivers.com and they will be happy to be your guides to Salt Cay's wealth of dive sites, including the much acclaimed wreck of the *H.M.S. Endymion*. Lying about 15 miles southwest of Salt Cay near Endymion Rock as shown on Chart #TCI-T1, the *H.M.S. Endymion*, a 140', wooden-hulled British Man-of-War lies in only 25' of water near Endymion Rock, sometimes called Endymion Reef. She was carrying reinforcements for the islands during a war with France when she went down in 1790 after hitting the reef and was only recently discovered. Divers can explore her 18 nine-foot long cannons, her four 15' anchors, her huge bronze keel bolts that can testify as to the size of the warship, and all sorts of other debris lying scattered about the nearby seabed. Needless to say, settled weather is necessary to visit this site. Military personnel from the bases on Grand Turk used to dive on the wreck site in the 1950's, but over the next few decades it was all but forgotten. Bryan Sheedy, an American who owns and operates the *Mount Pleasant Guest House* on Salt Cay, rediscovered the wreck in 1991. The *Mount Pleasant Guest House* was built in 1830 and is simply chock-full of fine furniture, pewter artifacts, original paintings, and bicycles that you can rent to tour the island. The *Mt. Pleasant Guest House* also offers horseback riding. Bryan, a rodeo rider in his youth, used to run *Porpoise Divers* before turning over the operation to Ollie and Debbie, who renamed it *Salt Cay Divers*.

The eastern shore of Salt Cay is very rocky and is best explored by dinghy on a calm day. In the salinas along the eastern shore are two blue holes lying almost side by side. The blue holes are only about 20'-30' in diameter and who knows how deep. One diver has reportedly entered the holes to a depth of 250' without seeing bottom.

On Southwest Beach the *Sunset Reef* has two air-conditioned units with TV, CD, complimentary bicycles, whale watching deck and golf cart rentals available.

Those skippers bound for the Dominican Republic can head south of Salt Cay to a GPS waypoint at 21° 17.60 N, 71° 14.10'W, approximately ¾ mile southwest of the reef south of Salt Cay. From this position you can take up a course of 178° for the 83-mile run to Luperón or a course of 170° for approximately 92 miles to Puerto Plata. This route will carry you over part of the Turks Bank that lies east of Great Sand Cay; you should have water at or near 10 fathoms in its vicinity. If you begin to get into water much less than this you have perhaps drifted to far to the west, nearer the eastern shore of Great Sand Cay. If this happens simply head a little more east until in deeper water.

GREAT SAND CAY

Great Sand Cay, commonly called Big Sand Cay and shown on some older charts as Seal Cay, was once a habitat for the West Indian monk seal and the manatee, the former hunted to extinction and the latter well on its way. Legend has it that Spanish treasure is buried on the cay and it is claimed that a British Captain Delaney recovered $130,000 in pirate treasure from a cave on Great Sand Cay in 1850.

Great Sand Cay is a desert paradise. Iguanas and curly-tailed lizards roam the prickly pear cactus-decorated landscape. Twice a year green and hawksbill turtles nest on the beautiful western beach south of the light and nurse sharks gather in the shallow lagoon during their season. On the eastern shore of the island a great stone arch called

71° 17' W

71° 16' W

71° 15' W   46   21° 14' N

10 fathoms

33

18   30   1 fathom

36   14   North Rock

12   32   18

9   Middle Rock
(White Island)

8   16   8

42   22   12   7   South Rock

14   7   9

28   12

28   28   7   21° 13' N

30

*Columbus
Passage*

31   29

10

49   25   Tucker Rock

15   7   *Sand Cay
Sanctuary*

34   12   22

Nor'   *numerous scattered
heads and small
patch reefs*

15   West
Point

23   14   *The
Creek*   21° 12' N

12

45   35

22

*Beacon
Hill*   light
Fl W ev 2 sec
85', 10M

21° 11.65' N
71° 15.50' W   15

*West
Bay*   9   32

12

31   24   9   *numerous scattered
heads and small
patch reefs*

**Great
Sand
Cay**   22   15

15   13   21° 11' N

48   27

12

21° 10.80' N
71° 15.50' W   20

54   13   22

33

33

Turks Islands   40   *Three
Marys*

Great Sand Cay

Chart #TCI-T6   *To
Dominican
Republic
(see text)*   *rock
awash
at HW*

Soundings in feet at MLW   47   32   21° 10' N

The Looking Glass, carved from the limestone by the flow of the ocean's waters, stands in mute testimony to the sea's power. The dangerous reefs southwest of Sand Cay took their toll on so many passing ships that a light was finally established on the cay in 1848. Nonetheless ships still continued to pile up on nearby Endymion Reef. The eastern shore offers excellent beachcombing; there is all manner of flotsam and jetsam that has washed ashore on the cay from the open Atlantic. As with so many of the land parks in the island chain, visitors are supposed to have a permit from the *DECR* in Grand Turk to walk ashore.

If heading south from Salt Cay, be sure to keep west a bit to avoid the reefs north of Great Sand Cay as shown on Chart #TCI-T6. The large light tower (Fl W ev 2 sec, 85' 10M, usually not working) on Beacon Hill just north of the beach is easily seen from seaward and makes a great landmark from any direction. A GPS waypoint 21° 11.65'N, 71° 15.50'W, at will place you approximately ½ mile west of the anchorage off the beach in West Bay, as shown on Chart #TCI-T6. From this waypoint, head in towards the beach and anchor wherever your draft allows. This is a great anchorage in winds from northeast to southeast, though some surge can make it a bit rolly at times. The holding is good in sand and there are plenty of reefs, heads, and ledges to snorkel north and east of Big Sand Cay.

Those skippers bound for the Dominican Republic can head south of Great Sand Cay to a GPS waypoint at 21° 10.80'N, 71° 15.50'W, approximately ¾ mile southwest of the reef at the southern end of Great Sand Cay. From this position you can take up a course of 176° for the 77-mile run to Luperón or a course of 167° for approximately 86 miles to Puerto Plata. Be sure to keep the small trio of rocks shown on Chart #TCI-C6 as the Three Marys well to port when heading southeastward towards the DR. Also, don't stray near the vicinity of the Endymion Reef (or Endymion Rock as it is sometimes shown) as shown on Chart #TCI-T1. The water over the reef is between 4' and 8' in places. It's best to give it a wide berth to the west or pass between it and Great Sand Cay.

Part III

THE DOMINICAN REPUBLIC

This section is not intended to be a cruising guide to the Dominican Republic - far from it. Rather, I offer the two most popular destinations that cruisers visit before or after their Turks and Caicos cruise. First we will discuss Luperón, by far the most popular stopover in the Dominican Republic and arguably the best hurricane hole in the Caribbean. We will then cover Puerto Plata, the commercial center of the northern coast of the Dominican Republic (usually just called the DR). I urge all mariners plying these waters to carry adequate charts of the Dominican Republic aboard. As for routing information along the northern coast of the DR between Luperón and Samaná, I will not even attempt to offer any. Instead, I suggest you get a copy of Bruce Van Sant's *The Gentleman's Guide to Passages South* and follow the excellent advice contained therein that is gleaned from Bruce's years of experience.

Located on the northern edge of the Caribbean Sea, the Dominican Republic (Republica Dominicana) occupies the eastern two-thirds of the island of Hispaniola, the second largest island of the Antilles. Although it shares a border with Haiti, the two vastly different countries and cultures have little in common. While the inhabitants of Haiti have French and African cultural roots, the population of the Dominican Republic have a mixture of African, Amerindian and Caucasian roots and the culture and language is Hispanic. Economically the DR is far more developed than Haiti, with a much higher standard of living and quite free of the unrest that plagues Haiti. The principal religion is Roman Catholic and the Church is very influential on several issues such as education, divorce and birth control; but its overall influence however has diminished over the years.

The Dominican Republic has three major metropolitan areas. Santo Domingo, the capital, with a population of over two million, is the capital and lies on the southern coast. On the northern coast lies Puerto Plata, one of the DR's main tourist resorts, with some 60,000 year-round residents. Santiago, located in the central highlands, is the country's leading industrial center, with a population of over 250,000. Sosúa, near Puerto Plata and La Romana and Punta Cana, at the eastern end of the island, all have growing resort populations. The rest of the DR's seven-million-plus population lives in or around a dozen or so smaller towns and villages.

The economy of the DR is dominated by agriculture, with 56% of the country used for crops or pasture. Small farmers produce staple foods such as plantains, beans and sweet potatoes. Agricultural products account for two thirds of export earnings. The rest comes largely from minerals, like bauxite, nickel and gold. The DR is among the top ten gold-producing countries of the world and has the largest single gold mine in the Western Hemisphere. The income from the export of these metals is about equal to the amount spent on imported petroleum. Most of the remaining imports are manufactured goods such as machinery, chemicals and foodstuffs. In recent years the government has made great efforts to improve the economy by stimulating the tourist industry. The new Presidente is opening doors every year with the intent of increasing tourism. More than 500,000 tourists visit the country each year to enjoy the climate and the beautiful beaches. The DR has a little bit of everything for everyone. Its main cities offer all kinds of attractions, from its breathtaking landscapes and pristine beaches, to its modern shopping malls and exciting nightlife. But by far, the most attractive feature of the DR is the friendliness of its people.

Visitors will probably want to visit some of the better known historical sites in the DR. In Santo Domingo you can check out *Columbus' Castle (Alcazar)*, the *St. Francis Monastery*, the *Cathedral of Santo Domingo*, the *Museum of Royal Houses, Columbus Square*, the *Ozama Fortress, El Faro a Colón* (the *Columbus Lighthouse*) and the first street ever built in the new world, Calle Las Damas. The Autonomous University of Santo Domingo (UASD), is the oldest university in the Americas dating back to 1538. In Puerto Plata, Fort San Felipe bears witness to Nicolás de Ovando's founding of that city in 1502.

There are 16 national parks, 9 natural monuments and 7 reserves in the Dominican Republic, all under the control of the *Dirección Nacional de Parques*. Among the most popular is Bermudez National Park at Duarte Peak. A word of warning here; the strenuous hike up and down Duarte, the highest mountain in the Caribbean at 10,417 feet, takes at least two days. Los Haitises National Park, located on the southern shore of Samaná Bay (Bahía de San Lorenzo), is a protected coastal region known for its mangrove swamps, its caves with Taino rock paintings and strange rock formations called mogotes that emerge from the sea and are unmatched for their eerie beauty. The National Park of the East, southeast of La Romana, is of great interest to those who want to explore prehistoric caves, some of which have pre-Columbian petroglyphs. Not far off its beautiful beaches lies Isla Saona, which has several excellent hiking trails. The Reserva Antropológica de las Cuevas de Borbén was extended in 1996 to protect the El Pomier caves, in San Cristóbal, under threat from limestone quarrying. The caves are of enormous archaeological value, with over 4,000 wall paintings and 5,000 rock drawings. Cave #1 contains 590 pictograms, making it superior to any other cave painting site in the Caribbean. Other places of interest are the Los Tres Ojos National Park, the Marine Mammals Sanctuary, the National Botanical Garden and the Parque Zoológico Nacional. The Reservas Científicas, the Scientific Reserves, include lakes, patches of forest and the Banco de la Plata, the enormous Silver Banks where hump-backed whales migrate from the Arctic every year to mate and give birth. About 50 boats conduct trips to the Silver Bank and work out of Samaná.

Since the Dominican Republic is located just south of the Tropic of Cancer, the temperature varies little from season to season. Average temperatures range from 80°-95° F during the day to the low 70's at night. Although the DR is in the tropics, the trade winds, the surrounding ocean and high elevations combine in some areas to produce a climate that is far from typical of the tropics. In fact, frost is common on the highest peaks of the Cordillera Central. In most areas, however, temperatures are moderately high and vary little from season to season. Rainfall is normally greatest on the mountain slopes over which the easterly trade winds blow and decreases on the opposite slopes and in the major valleys. Annual precipitation averages about 60 inches, but the mountainous areas receive considerably more moisture. The rainy season is from June to November.

Citizens of the United States and Canada may enter the DR with a passport or with an original birth certificate and a photo-bearing official document (such as voter's registration or driver's license). Minors may enter with only an original birth certificate. Cuban residents of the United States may enter with their U.S. residency card and additional official photo-bearing document. American and Canadian visitors are required to purchase a tourist card for U.S. $10.00 upon entry. If you're heading to the DR from the Turks and Caicos or The Bahamas, remember to get a departure clearance when leaving those waters. Visitors leaving by air are required to pay a U.S. $10.00 departure tax. Personal electronics are admitted into the Dominican Republic, although professional video equipment, television cameras and other related items may need special clearance. Guns will need to be checked in when entering.

After clearing into the DR you will probably want to exchange your dollars for pesos. Don't change very much more money than you plan to spend. Only 30% of Dominican currency exchanged by visitors can be changed back into dollars upon departure (a tip - save your currency exchange receipts). Although it's extremely tempting, one should avoid changing money on the black market. Absolutely no more than U.S. $5,000 may be taken out of the country when you leave. Arrests have been made for even small currency-law violations. Foreign currency can be changed into Dominican pesos at *Banco de Reservas* booths at the airports, major hotels, or at commercial banks. Banking hours are 8:30 A.M to 3:00 P.M., M-F. Airport booths remain open to service all incoming flights, up to 24 hours if necessary. Traveler's checks and major credit cards are widely accepted. Cash advances are available at some commercial banks. The rate of exchange fluctuates around RD $14.00=U.S. $1.00. When tipping, a 10% gratuity (as well as an 8% sales tax) is often included in the bill. Please note that the practice of tipping taxi drivers is not the custom in the DR but it is widely practiced. As for provisioning, you'll want to check out the excellent deals on wine, rum, cigars and *El Presidenté* beers. Bear in mind that the DR practices the Latin tradition of the siesta. Many shops close for long lunches from 12:30 P.M. to 2:30 P.M. However, major shopping centers, supermarkets and stores frequented by visitors usually remain open from 9:00 A.M. to 7:00 P.M. In the DR, daylight-savings time is in effect year-round, so the time is one hour ahead of EST in the fall and winter and the same as EDT in the spring and summer. Electricity is the same as in the U.S., 110 volt, 60 cycle.

Baseball is a passion in the DR; there are more baseball players from the Dominican Republic playing in the North American major leagues than from any other Caribbean nation. Most major league clubs maintain small baseball camps in the Dominican Republic and the DR's professional winter league draws many U.S. players.

The DR celebrates all the normal holidays such as New Year, Good Friday, Easter (Monday), Columbus Cay (October 12) and Christmas. Holidays unique to the DR include Our Lady of Altagracia Day (January 21), Independence Day (February 27), Ascension Day (varies) and Our Lady of Mercedes Day (September 24). The feast of the Epiphany (January 6) is usually celebrated on the closest Monday or Friday as is Juan Pablo Duarte's birthday (January 26), Restoration of the Republic Day (August 16), Labor Day (May 1) and Constitution Day (November 6). The feast of Corpus Christi is celebrated in either May or June depending on the year; check locally to be certain. Dominicans love festivals and the calendar year has several for you to enjoy. Carnival in Santo Domingo takes place along the Santo Domingo Malecón the week of February 27 during the Independence Day celebrations. The famous Merengue Festival is a lively celebration of the country's national music, with Merengue bands performing at most major hotels and along the Santo Domingo Malecón. This huge party takes place from the last week in July through the first week of August. The term "Merengue" refers both to the music and the dance, which evolved in the Dominican countryside among the happy people of a divided island. The history of the Merengue is woven into the fabric of Dominican history itself. This Afro-Caribbean dance became part of country life and is still danced today around the squares of small villages, next to bonfires on secluded beaches, in ballrooms and in nightclubs throughout the world. In the traditional countryside settings, the music is provided by a *Perico Ripiao*, a small band made up of an accordion, a drum, a guira and a box bass. Puerto Plata's Merengue Festival is held during the second week of October. Christmas celebrations begin in early December and end on Epiphany Day on January 6.

Americans needing the assistance of the U.S Embassy in Santo Domingo can telephone 809-541-2171 or fax the embassy at 809-686-7437. The mailing address is: Ambassador Donna Jean Hrinak, Unit 5500, Santo Domingo, APO AA 34041. In Santo Domingo the Embassy sits at the corner of Calle Cesar Nicolas Penson and Calle Leopoldo Navarro.

The DR's phone communications are handled by the privately owned telephone company *Codetel*, a *GTE* subsidiary and *Tricom*, a *Motorola* joint venture. Direct dialing to and from the DR is quick and easy using the 809 area code. The DR's phone system is one of the most sophisticated telecommunications systems in Latin America with capabilities such as international direct dialing, faxing, teleconferencing, electronic mail and now videoconferencing. *All America Cable and Radio, ITT* and *RCA Global Communications* also provide cable, fax, telex services and long distance calling services. Check out Internet service by *Codetel* on the web at http://www.codetel.net.do. The Dominican Republic postal service boasts over 190 branches and is the least expensive (although slowest) way of sending and receiving international mail. The postal service also has a higher priced express mail service similar to the U.S Priority Mail. Private couriers include *DHL, Fed Ex, UPS* and several local P.O. Box courier services such as *Express Parcel Service*. There are 120 AM radio stations on the island, no FM stations, 6 HF stations and 18 television stations scattered about. Amateur radio operators can get a 30-day reciprocal (HI) for no charge upon clearing in.

Divers will be happy to know that the waters surrounding the island of Hispaniola hold some 400 shipwrecks that have produced many valuable artifacts over the years. The DR is a great place for beginner divers as well as for serious underwater explorers. Although the North coast near Puerto Plata and Sosua might prove disappointing for the experienced diver due to the extensive damage the reefs there have suffered. The Southern shore and the eastern side of the island offer dive sites to satisfy the most demanding diver. *La Caleta Underwater Park* is located just a short boat ride from Boca Chica. There divers will enjoy good vizabliity and a fertile underwater life. Divers may also visit the wreck of the *Hickory*, an old treasure hunting ship. Catalina Island is a good spot for wall diving and large fish. The island of Saona is also a great spot for the larger marine creatures. As tourism develops on the island, diving in the Dominican Republic might soon become very popular and the dive sites more crowded.

A BRIEF HISTORY OF THE DOMINICAN REPUBLIC

The island that we know as Hispaniola was first inhabited by Ciboney Indians and later by Taino Indians who still occupied the island when Christopher Columbus discovered it on December 5, 1492. The native Indians had named the island *Quisqueya* but Columbus changed its name to *Hispaniola* (from *Isla Espanola,* the "Spanish Island"). Columbus lived here for many years prior to his death and his remains are said to be buried in the *Cathedral of Santo Domingo* in Santo Domingo. Christopher Columbus' brother Bartholomew founded Santo Domingo in 1496, making the city the oldest permanently occupied settlement in the Americas. At that time there were more than a million native Taino Indians on the island but within 50 years most had died of starvation, overwork in the gold mines and epidemics of European diseases. The gold that could be obtained using the 16th century mining techniques was exhausted by 1530. Spain lost interest in Santo Domingo soon after the discoveries of Mexico and Peru. The Spaniards who remained on the island turned to cultivating sugar cane, using black slaves imported from Africa.

In 1697, Spain ceded the western third of Hispaniola to France. By the end of the 1700's, the new French possession known as St. Domingue was one of the world's richest colonies, producing vast quantities of sugar and cotton. By 1795, France had gained control of the entire island but slave uprisings in the western section in 1804 led to the creation of Haiti, the world's first black republic. In 1814, Spain regained control of the eastern part of the island, but the Dominicans declared their independence in 1821. In 1822, the Haitians invaded the Dominican Republic and ruled it by force for almost 22 years, but the Dominicans did not lie down and accept this intervention. They launched the Trinitary secret society founded by Juan Pablo Duarte and under the leadership of Ramon Matias Mella and Francisco del Rosario Sanchez, the Spanish-speaking inhabitants of the east rebelled against the Haitians and proclaimed their independence on February 27, 1844, calling their nation the Dominican Republic. This period of occupation is often considered the cause of an antagonism that still separates Dominicans from Haitians. One favorable consequence of Haitian rule, however, was the freeing of slaves in the DR.

Unhappily, liberation from the Haitians did little to bring peace and economic progress to the DR. During the rest of the 19th century, the Dominican Republic suffered severe economic difficulties, scores of revolutions, armed invasions from Haiti and another period of Spanish domination from 1861 to 1865. Money was borrowed and spent recklessly by corrupt governments and by 1916 the country was in political and economic chaos. In 1905, the United States established partial control of the Dominican economy to protect American investors. Increasing debts and internal disorders resulted in the occupation of the DR by U.S. Marines in 1916 in order to restore order and protect the approaches to the Panama Canal. This occupation lasted for eight years and, though there was opposition to it, the enforced political stability permitted major social and economic advances.

In 1924, the U.S. occupation ended; in 1930 there was another revolution and the DR fell into the hands of a dictator, Gen. Rafael Leonidas Trujillo Molina. For nearly 31 years, until his assassination in 1961, Trujillo headed a ruthless police state. At the cost of political freedom, the DR had another period of imposed stability that, combined with favorable sugar prices, stimulated impressive economic growth. In December 1962, the first free elections in nearly 40 years brought the leftist Juan Bosch to the presidency. His reform program led to his overthrow by the military in September 1963. Five years of political turmoil after Trujillo's death led to another intervention by the United States. When Bosch's supporters attempted to restore him to power in 1965, civil war broke out and U.S. troops were sent in to restore order and the status quo and ease U.S. concerns about the possibility of a Cuban-style Communist takeover. Since then the political scene has been relatively orderly, with freely elected presidents. In 1966, Joaquin Balaguer was elected president. His right wing authoritarian rule continued until the election of 1978, when Antonio Guzman defeated Balaguer in a very controversial election. Guzman was in turn defeated by Salvador Jorge Blanco in 1982. Balaguer, elderly and blind, was narrowly reelected in 1986 and 1990. In 1988 Blanco was convicted of corruption in absentia and in 1992 was sentenced to 20 years in prison.

Much wealth has been generated, but it has always been unequally distributed. The bulk of the population remains poor and undernourished. In the 1980's, the low price of sugar in the world market brought on a series of economic crises. Under Salvador Jorge Blanco, who was president from 1982 to 1986, the government instituted an austerity program. Wage controls and the removal of food subsidies led to rioting in 1984. Economic difficulties persisted in the debt-ridden nation through the 1990 election, in which Balaguer defeated his long-time opponent, Juan Bosch. Austerity measures dictated by the International Monetary Fund were still in force in 1992. The 1991 deportation of illegal Haitian immigrants worsened relations with Haiti.

Today, with a new leader, President Fernandez and a huge influx of European tourist money, the DR's future is looking rosy. The older establishment is slowly opening up and the Dominican Republic is moving forward now with increasing speed towards a brighter economic future.

LUPERÓN

By far, the nearest, most popular destination when heading to the Caribbean from the Turks and Caicos, is Luperón. In years past we would have to give that honor to Puerto Plata; but since Luperón became an official port of entry, Puerto Plata's yacht traffic has dropped off considerably. Luperón was named after General Luperón, who was one of the Dominican Republic's greatest heroes. In 1879, under his leadership, the country was reorganized and set on the road to economic recovery. Luperón, which is sometimes shown as Puerto Blanco on some charts, is usually the name given to this entire area, but most insist that Puerto Blanco is the bay and Luperón is the town. Either way, it is a favorite stop for cruisers bound north from the DR and Puerto Rico. This tiny harbor is one of the best hurricane holes in the Caribbean and many cruisers tend to call it home for the season staying months at a time. I know a couple who might just spend the rest of their lives there. They love the cheap rum, wine and dining as well as the secure protection that Luperón has to offer. The people love boaters in Luperón; boaters really help the economy here and the locals appreciate it and go out of their way to be accommodating. There is a boater's net every Sunday and Wednesday on VHF. Ch. 68 where you can pick up the latest info about what's going locally.

From Great Sand Cay in the Turks and Caicos Islands, the waypoint off Luperón bears approximately 176° at a distance of 77 nautical miles. If approaching from the waypoint just south of Great Sand Cay you can head directly for this waypoint with no dangers. Your first sign of impending landfall may well be while you are still 20 miles north of the Dominican Republic. Cabo Isabella is clearly seen as the highest spot around. As you approach the entrance to the bay at Luperón, keep Cabo Isabella to starboard. There are some hills to both the right and left of the entrance channel

Photo by Star Droshine

Fruit and Vegetable Vendor, Luperón.

but the very conspicuous hotel makes another good landmark. Keep the hotel well to starboard; the entrance to Luperón lies approximately ½ - ¾ mile to the east of the hotel.

Your sense of smell may also alert you to your impending landfall. Very often, from far offshore, the air will suddenly be filled with the aroma of dirt, trees and farm animals. Quite a refreshing change if you've gotten used to the dry, desert-like islands of the Turks and Caicos. You might find yourself sniffing the air much as a dog would.

As shown on Chart #DR-1, the entrance to Luperón lies between a large shoal area on the western side of the entrance and another area to the eastern side of the entrance. Caution is called for when entering the channel to Luperón, in poor light the shoals are difficult to make out, though they are marked much better these days. Approaching the entrance slowly in the morning light, you may be able to make out the shoal fairly easily, as the water may still be clear then. Later during the day, as the winds pick up (about 9:00A.M. the breeze fills in and blows all day till just after dark), it gets a little harder to discern the shoal from offshore, even when it is breaking slightly. From the GPS waypoint at 19° 55.50'N, 70° 56.50'W (approximately one mile north of the entrance channel), a good course is to keep the eastern cliff close on your port bow until you can make out the red, 55-gallon drum buoy that now marks the shoal. Bear in mind that the drum is in shallow water and that it may have moved or it may not be there when you are. Keep and eye out for the breaking shoal off the eastern shore and take the red buoy to starboard (red-right-returning). The entrance to the anchorage is hard to make out until you get fairly close and it opens up before you.

As you approach the entrance, keep the red marker well to starboard and keep close in to the eastern shoreline where the deeper water lies. Do not put the red stake close to starboard, you'll run aground on the very shoal you are trying to avoid. As the entrance to the inner harbor opens up to starboard you'll spot some colored stakes leading you in, remember, red-right-returning here. These markers are 8" diameter wooden poles that were just installed in the summer of 1998. They stand 5' or less out of the water and are painted red and green (red, right, returning). Pass between the two outer poles and follow the line well into the harbour; be sure to stay between the poles. You'll pass between four red poles and five green poles before the large harbour and town dock opens up before you. There is one last green marker just east of the end of the town dock. Boats can anchor anywhere in the harbor, near the marina, or in the seldom used eastern harbor. The water in the harbor is muddy brown. The bottom here is basically mud and the holding is great, but it takes a few days for your anchor to set here. Boats drag frequently as people often forget that they are anchoring in 20' of water and fail to put out enough scope. But if you do drag, unless you run into another boat or the dock, it's all mud and mangroves around you to act as a cushion. The town dock is marked with a red light (GP Fl R, ev 10 sec.) that works well although it is not visible outside the harbour.

If you need to clear in, anchor nearer the town dock part of the harbor at the southwestern end of the anchorage and hoist your "Q" flag. Sometime during the day the Commandancia's offical will come out to your boat to clear you in. This person will likely say he is with the "Navy" and may have a translator with him. A lot of boats simply take their papers into town to clear in and save the Commandancia's men a trip out (you know how impatient we cruisers can be). All crew may come into town while you do this. Walk to the end of the dock and the first building you come to is a small blue trailer-like structure on your right, this is *Immigracion*. Check in here first. You will have to pay $10.00 per person aboard and $10.00 for the boat. Then go across the street, over the small bridge and up the hill to the Commandancia's office and check in there. If they ask for money tell them "No, Senor." Immigration tells me that they often try to get money from cruisers which only goes directly into their pockets. The only other fee you will have to pay is a $5-$10 fee for usage of the harbour, although as of 2002 an Agriculture representative began charging $5.00 to ask you if you had a pet aboard. Any other fee or fees should not be paid.

Now let's discuss what we'll find in this lovely harbor. In a small cove that lies just to starboard off the entrance channel is the *Puerto Blanco Marina*. If

Photo by Star Droshine

Kiwi John's, Luperón.

you wish to head to the marina from the channel, head west between the third and fourth red poles and watch out for the shoals between the channel and the deeper water closer to the marina. There are several small mud shoals in this area that you must weave between. The shoals rise up from 20' depths to lie about 1'-2' under the surface; use caution, lots of folks run aground here. The marina has a small boat dock with room for about seven or eight boats and it usually stays full; the bar at the marina is a popular hangout for cruisers with Monday night pot lucks, daily happy hours from 5-7 P.M. and other events during the week such as the Sunday nautical swap meet where cruisers buy and sell their no longer needed charts and courtesy flags. There is electricity and water dockside, but be prepared for frequent power outages. There is also a dinghy dock where you can get water for washing (1-2 pesos per gallon depending on who's charging you). Some folks will drink this water but I don't recommend it; bottled water is also sold here as well as throughout town at 18 pesos for a 5 gallon bottle. There is a refundable deposit of U.S. $10.00 required for the bottles. You can also have your laundry done for you at 35 pesos to wash (includes soap) and 35 pesos to dry. When here you must check out Rosa's *Dominican Treasures Gift Shop*.

A short walk north of the marina is the *Caribbean Village Luperón*, the beachfront resort that you used as a landmark when approaching Luperón. The resort is spread over 16 lush, landscaped acres, with gorgeous views of the Atlantic Ocean. The large resort boasts 441 beautifully appointed air-conditioned rooms. The resort offers SCUBA lessons in their pool, bicycles, windsurfing, snorkeling, sailing, tennis, a gym with sauna and Jacuzzi, aerobics, table tennis, billiards and horseback riding on the beach. Also on site are several boutiques, a buffet-type restaurant, a beach restaurant and a disco. There is some nice snorkeling along the jetties by the hotel, but be forewarned: if you walk the beaches in the DR you will sometimes find vendors hawking their wares. They're usually very friendly and understand a firm no. This is not much of a problem in Luperón, as the vendors are not allowed on the beach. It tends to be more of a problem from Puerto Plata eastward.

Just inland from the large town dock is the town of Luperón. Not much bigger than South Caicos, Luperón is quite a bit busier and much more alive. Everywhere you go you'll find people talking, music playing and cars and motorcycles roaring by. Many people live in homes that also house their business where they might sell veggies, rum, water, or sodas. Prices are great in the DR and Luperón is no exception. You can easily find rum at $3-$4 a bottle, wine for $2-$3 a bottle and a carton of DR produced cigarettes for half of what an equivalent brand would cost in the States (and I'm told they taste as good as U.S. brands). You can eat out for next to nothing; a lunch in one of the more inexpensive places will run you in the neighborhood of $2-$4. I love *Laisa's* just in from *Codatel* on the same side of the street. Almost directly across from *Codatel* is a great little restaurant on the corner that serves excellent food (lunch for four costs under $25.00 there).

To start our tour of th town of Luperón, let's begin with the first stop you will have to make; you must change your American dollars into pesos. The first rule is do not change very much more money than you plan to spend. Only 30% of Dominican currency exchanged by visitors can be changed back into dollars upon departure (a tip - save your currency exchange receipts). Although it's extremely tempting, one should avoid changing money on the black market; not to worry though, there is little if any black market activity in Luperón. In early 2002, the exchange rate was 16.5

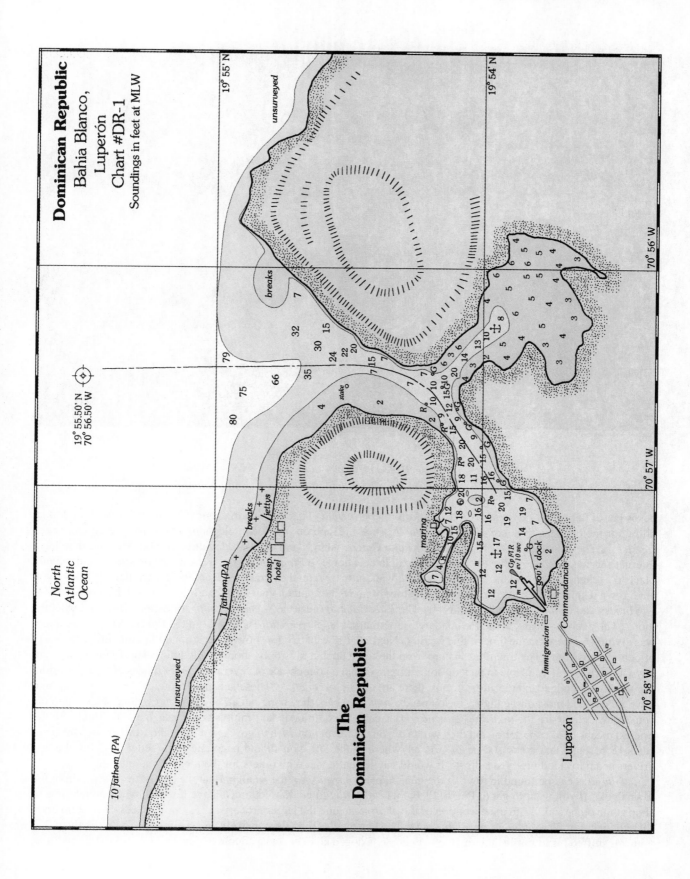

Dominican Republic
Bahia Blanco,
Luperón
Chart #DR-1
Soundings in feet at MLW

19° 55' N

19° 54' N

unsurveyed

breaks

19° 55.50' N
70° 56.50' W

North
Atlantic
Ocean

unsurveyed

10 fathom (PA)

1 fathom (PA)

breaks

jettys

consp.
hotel

stake

marina

Gp Fl R
ev 10 sec

gov't. dock

Immigracion

Commandancia

**The
Dominican Republic**

Luperón

70° 56' W

70° 57' W

70° 58' W

Photo by Andy Lowe

Bahia Blanco, the harbor at Luperón.

pesos per dollar at *Codatel* and 16.0 at *Puerto Blanco Marina*. This may again change by the time this is printed so allow for the changes time creates. The *Codatel* office in Luperón, the local telephone company (the equivalent of *Batelco* in The Bahamas or *CAW* in the Turks and Caicos Islands and open all day until 10:00 P.M., yes, they have internet service, also, the yellow house behind Codatel is home to *Punta Internet*), is the most convenient and reliable place to exchange your dollars. To find *Codatel*, walk into town on the main road from the government dock. As you enter town it splits and Duarte Street forks off straight in front of you on your right hand side. Follow Duarte Street for two blocks and *Codatel* will be on your left. The *Pink Cambio* (near the *Supermercado*) sometimes offers a few tenths more. The exchange bank at the *Pola*, a large supermarket (*supermercado*) across from the *Burger King* in Santiago, was giving 16.5 pesos at the time of this writing. Next, you'll want to know how to get around Luperón; the easiest way of course is by foot. The town lies just up from the town dock and is only about a mile long. But if you want to get anywhere else, of if you have to pick up something, you have your choice of several different modes of transportation. For those on a budget and the adventurous, there are the *motorconchos*. These are small motorcycles that roar around town all day and most of the night. If you need a *motorconcho*, they hang out all day long at *Codatel*. Next up in the conveyance chain are the taxis and *guaguas*. Basically cars are taxis and minivans are guaguas. The taxis are the priciest means of transportation but they will take you wherever you wish to go. A motorconcho from town to the hotel costs 15 pesos; a taxi costs 100 pesos. As anywhere in the DR, you should negotiate for a better deal, but the taxi drivers seem to stand pretty steadfast. It would pay to rent a van with others for the most economical method.

*Guagua*s can be found in town at the guagua park, *parquecito*, the small park at the end of town away from the town dock. If you want to get to Puerto Plata this is the way to go, but you must leave Luperón with enough time to shop at the other end. With the exception of the *pharmacia* and the larger grocery stores, most places close from noon till two for siesta. The *guaguas* run all day but only when they're full; they are truly an experience. You're likely to find yourself stuffed into a minivan with 16 other people, a dog, a chicken and a couple of goats. If headed to Puerto Plata, take a guagua to Imbert (home of the closest bank and *ATM* machine though you can draw pesos at *Codatel* on your *Visa* card) for about 18 pesos. From Imbert to Puerto Plata it is about 10 pesos by bus. If headed to Santo Domingo, there are daily buses available from Luperón. One final note: if you are planning on doing major provisioning, you should consider renting a van for the day; you won't be able to carry a lot on a *guagua*.

You can rent a car in Puerto Plata for around 500-1000 pesos a day. You can rent a car in Luperón from Estelvina Felipe (the local dentist), or you can speak to José, one of the local tour guides. As you approach town from the dinghy dock, the first house on the left is José's.

Now that you have your pesos and a way to get around, if you're like most cruisers you're ready to search out a place to eat. The typical Dominican meal consists of a meat, rice and beans and plantains and can be had for about 35-85 pesos at the many *comedors* around town. *Café Luperón* serves a very filling Dominican lunch and there are usually two meats to choose from. You also get rice and beans and salad for 30 pesos, about U.S. $2.00. Theresa, the owner, speaks a little English and loves cruisers, as do most folks here. *La Yola* has a great atmosphere, cool breezes and a two for one happy hour. The menu has reasonable prices for lunch and dinner and offers pizza with a good variety of toppings. Another great stop is *Los Almendros*, at the intersection by *Codatel* while across the street from *Codatel* is my favorite little place. Just past *Codatel* is *Aqui Luis*, a popular hangout for cruisers with a disco upstairs.

Now that you've filled your cruising tummy, you'll probably want to check out the shopping. But we'll discuss shopping in Luperón in a moment. First, let's start with some basic needs. There is a medical clinic in Luperón where two of the three doctors in residence speak passable English. The clinic is located at the end of Calle Luperón, two blocks south of *Codatel* and then three blocks southwest. While the clinic can deal with most basic health problems, for testing you will be referred to the *Laboratory Luperón*, just across from the guagua park. If you have your samples in before 1200 you can usually get the results by 1700. The prices are right here. A blood and fecal test is U.S. $6.00 and

Photo by Star Droshine

The dinghy dock in Luperón.

the office visit is free. All the clinics are free to residents of the Dominican Republic and cruisers, but the more serious medical problems, such as those that require a visit or a stay at one of the hospitals in Puerto Plata or Santiago can cost quite a bit. Most medical insurance is accepted throughout the DR and drugs that can only be acquired by prescription in the U.S., are available without a prescription in the DR, and most are very inexpensive. It helps to know the Spanish translation of the drug when you head for the *pharmacia. Farmicia Danessa* on Parque Central are very knowledgeable and even have photo developing available.

There are no local diesel or outboard mechanics but Persio Núñez at *Núñez & Núñez* in Santiago has a nice machine shop and rebuilds gasoline as well as diesel engines. His number is 809-522-8202, or 809-522-2200. There is a small welding shop on the right as you approach Luperón from the town dock. If you need a good refrigeration man, look up Mariano in town. There is a new marine supply outlet in Luperón called, aptly enough, *Luperón Marine Supply*, and it lies just around the corner from *Codatel*.

Gasoline and diesel are usually both easily available in town, though if Luperón is out, you may have to get a taxi to El Estrecho to visit the station there. You can haul your own jerry cans, but the gas station is on the road to Imbert, all the way on the other side of town, about a mile from the dinghy dock. You'll find several Dominicans hanging around the dock that will take your cans and fill them for you, usually for about a $.25 a gallon more. These very innovative young men will bring 55-gallon drums of fuel out to your boat and siphon the diesel into your tank. It's usually easiest to ask José and he'll have somebody deliver fuel and/or water to your boat shortly. Another option is to hire a *motorconcho* for 10 pesos. The only problem with that is that you must hang on to the bike and the gas cans while enroute.

If you need propane, the propane fill station is past the cockfight arena (a busy place on a Friday afternoon), about ½ mile past the gas station. You'll notice it by the conspicuous white propane tank. The normal way to get propane is get to hire a motorconcho for 10-25 pesos. Propane is cheap in the DR; 2-4 pesos a pound. A 20lb propane tank costs about U.S. $2.60 to fill up (compare that with $7-$8 in the U.S. and $15-$22 in parts of Exuma and $15.00 in Provo). A word of warning about the safety valves that they are putting on propane tanks in the U.S. (the kind that do not open unless the fitting is connected). You cannot get these filled in Luperón at this time. If you have one of these tanks you'll have to go to the hardware store (ferreteria) and pick up an older style valve for about U.S. $6.00 and install it on your tank.

You can have your mail sent to you care of Ana Lopez's. Make sure it is addressed to Ana Lopez, Casa Lopez, your boat name, Juan Pablo Duarte #36, Luperón, Dominican Republic. Ana is the *UPS* representative here and her phone number is 809-571-8175. If you wish to send or receive faxes you can handle that at *Codatel*. The fax number there is 809-571-8052. Be sure that your boat's name is at the top of each page of any fax you receive, they get a lot of faxes in at *Codatel*.

Now let's talk about the shopping in Luperón. To begin with, the produce trucks that regularly run to the marina have some of the best deals. Listen for their call on VHF ch. 68. If they don't have what you want tell them and they'll bring it next time. As you walk around town you'll notice fruit and vegetable stands (and small gift shops) everywhere and everyone is willing to deal. You'll have no problem finding mangoes, avocados, cucumbers, tomatoes, yucca, plantains, potatoes, carrots, onions and large, fresh pineapples that go for about 10 pesos. Broccoli and lettuce are hard to find in Luperón. In town, the *Supermercado del Sur* will take special orders and deliver to the marina or town dock and, they habla inglais!

Cigar smokers will want to sample the DR's great cigars. Cigarette smokers will appreciate the fact that Dominican *Marlboros* go for about 125 pesos (about U.S. $9.00) a carton; I am told that they taste the same as U.S. *Marlboros*. *Nacionals* go for about 90 pesos (U.S. $6.00) a carton and are a great deal. Rum is cheap, about 100 pesos for a half-gallon. For cheaper wines and spirits not available in Luperón, a trip to Puerto Plata is called for, especially a visit to the rum factory. Certain items such as bacon, cheese, broccoli, lettuce, powdered drinks (not milk), butter (not canned margarine), packaged meats, deli meats, cake mixes, canned cream and yeast are difficult to find in Luperón. A once a month trip to Puerto Plata or Santiago will be all you need to stock up on these items if you are planning to stay a while.

We've all heard about the provisioning in Puerto Plata. You can also get anything you need in Santiago, though it is farther away. The *ferreterias* (hardware stores) and *supermercados* are literally brimming with all kinds of goodies for the cruiser with big eyes and pockets full of pesos. *Pola* and *Nacionale* are the two largest stores and are stocked like *Super WalMarts* back in the states. You can even have lunch there while you do your shopping; both have nice cafeterias. *Nacionale* even has a *Baskin Robin* for those who crave their 53 flavors. One final note: it's cheaper to buy local brands whenever possible, especially locally manufactured toilet paper that goes for about a third of the cost of U.S. toilet paper.

If you like horseback riding you must visit *Mario's Ranch*. Mario will pick you up and take you on ½ day and full day horseback riding trips.

To the west of Luperón, reachable by a new road, is the town of La Isabella. Here, on his second voyage to the New World in 1493, Columbus founded the first European town in the Americas with the first court and where the first Mass was said in the New World. Today, only the layout of the town is visible, but there is a small hotel by the ruins. Currently, the Dirección Nacional de Parques is undertaking the restoration and archaeological excavation of La Isabella. To get to La Isabella from Puerto Plata you can either take a tour from Puerto Plata, or take a carro público from Villanueva y Kundhard in Puerto Plata to the village of La Isabella. To get to La Isabella from Luperón, either make local arrangements with a taxi or rental car, or travel to Puerto Plata to hook up with a tour group. Between La Isabella and Montecristi are the lovely beaches of Punta Rucia at Estero Honda.

PUERTO PLATA

Puerto Plata, once the primary destination of cruisers southbound from the Turks and Caicos, is visited far less frequently today since Luperón has become a port of entry. Puerto Plata, with population of about 60,000, is now primarily a commercial harbor and it shows. On land, Puerto Plata and almost the entire Atlantic coast of the DR is a very popular tourist haven, especially among Europeans. Perhaps the finest beaches in the Dominican Republic can be found along the superb Atlantic Coast, sometimes called the Amber Coast, a 75-mile strand of unspoiled beaches on the north side of the island, where Puerto Plata is the principal city. The town itself was founded in 1502 and was named *Port of Silver* by Columbus after being inspired by its shimmering waters.

A GPS waypoint at 19° 49.10'N, 70° 41.55'W, will place you almost ½ mile north of the outer buoy (LR "2", Fl R) as shown on Chart #DR-2. From Great Sand Cay in the Turks and Caicos, this waypoint bears approximately 167° at a distance of approximately 86 nautical miles. If approaching from the Turks and Caicos Islands you can head directly for this waypoint, but, if you're approaching from Luperón, don't just punch in the waypoint and head for it. Stay offshore a bit and round the small rock that Bruce Van Sant shows as Owen Rock, keeping it well to starboard. You can pass between Owen Rock and the mainland of the DR, although there are several shallow areas of less than one fathom in depth at MLW. Also, there are numerous shallow heads and rocks that are awash at high water and lay almost a quarter mile offshore in places near the harbor entrance. A great landmark is Mt. Torres, Loma Isabel de Torres, with its huge statue of Christ at its 2600' summit. From the waypoint, head south until you can enter between the outer buoys, red-right-returning here. In the daytime you can make out the range at the southwestern end of the harbor consisting of two large orange-capped white columns. At night this range is lit with flashing red lights that are hard to make out unless you are lined up correctly, just off to one side or the other a few degrees. The entry range is approximately 225° magnetic but the channel is deep, wide and fairly well marked; but like all aids to navigation, they might not be there when you, are so keep an eye on the range. Don't stray east of the green markers, the water shallows rapidly in their area. The yacht anchorage area is shown on Chart #DR-2 and lies just west of the large commercial dock. Expect a surge through here and a lot of roll from local traffic. The water can also be very sludge-like at times; once you leave Puerto Plata you might want to clean your waterline. You'll also find yourself cleaning your decks quite often due to the soot from the nearby power plant. If you need to clear in you can anchor and row in to meet with the Commandante or you med-moor at the old concrete dock; use caution, the bottom is similar to that in Luperón. Allow a day or two for your anchor to set. There is no security at the dock, so be forewarned. I cannot advise you to visit or not to visit Puerto Plata, but I do not understand why so many cruisers stop here when nearby Luperón is a far more comfortable and safer anchorage. Besides, it is fairly easy to gain access to Puerto Plata by road from Luperón.

Puerto Plata itself is a small city, but its downtown area features what is called the "old" Puerto Plata, full of old wooden houses, some new buildings and much local color. In this sector you will find structures characterized by the strong influence of late Victorian styles. Here you'll find quaint gingerbread houses, their white fences simply aflame with bougainvillea and the recently restored gazebo in the central square of Independence Park.

Before we take a mini-tour of what you can expect to find in Puerto Plata, remember that if you are led into a shop by a local boy, tour guide or taxi driver, you will more than likely be paying a hidden commission on the price of your purchase, even after you have bargained the merchant down to his rock bottom price. If you want an approved guide, call the *Association of Official Tour Guides* at 586-2866. There is also a tourist train, the *Amber Tour Train* (not on rails!) that runs from Playa Dorada Plaza to Fort San Felipe, the *Amber Museum*, the *Rum Factory*, Parque Central, and several gift shops three times daily. The 2½ hour trip costs approximately U.S. $11.50 and you can pick up tickets at the Discount Plaza. By all means visit the *Rum Factory*. On their tours they used to offer all the rum you could drink (not

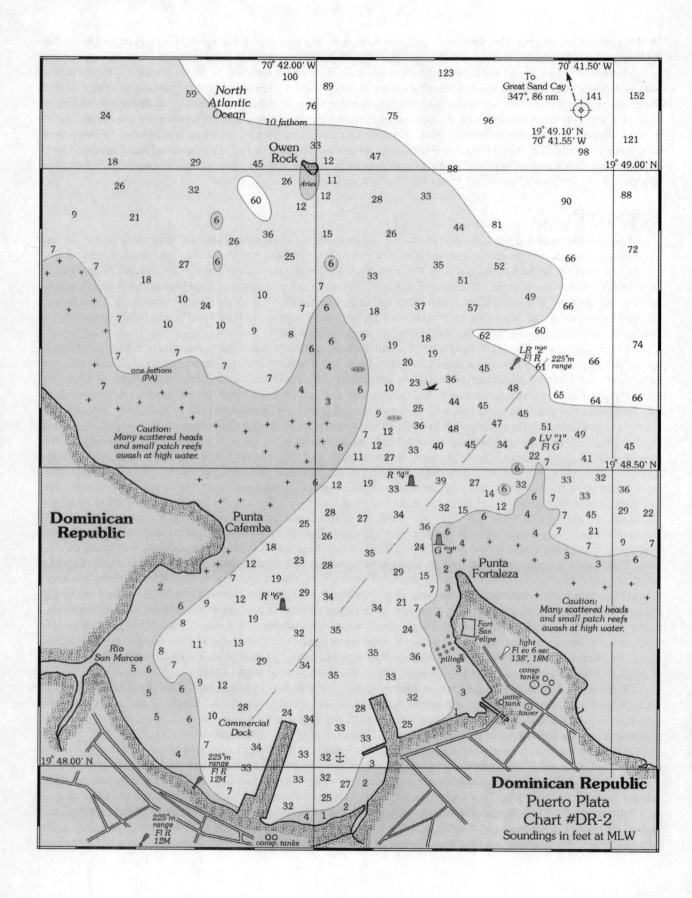

70° 42.00' W
100

70° 41.50' W

123

To
Great Sand Cay
347°, 86 nm   141   152

59   North
Atlantic
Ocean

89

76

75

96

19° 49.10' N
70° 41.55' W

121

24

10 fathom

33

98

Owen
Rock

12

47

88

19° 49.00' N

18   29   45   26   dries   11

26   32   12   28   33   90   88

60   26   15   26   44   81

9   21   6   36   25   35   52   72

7   6   18   33   51   66

7   7   27   6   7   6   37   57   49   66

18   10   10   6   18   62   60

7   10   10   9   8   19   19   LR "2"   74
                                    Fl R   225°m range
7   7   7   6   6   20   45   61   66

one fathom
(PA)   4   10   23   36   48   65   64   66

7   3   6   10   44   45   45

9   25   48   47   51   45
                                LV "1"
Caution: 6   7   12   36   34   40   Fl G   49
Many scattered heads   12   33   45   22   41   45
and small patch reefs   11   27   40   45   7
awash at high water.   6   6   19° 48.50' N

12   19   R "4"   39   27   6   33   32

28   33   34   32   14   6   33   36

Punta   25   26   27   34   32   15   12   7   45   29   22
Cafemba   18   28   35   36   24   6   4   3   21   7   7

12   23   29   24   G "3"   4   3   3   6
Dominican
Republic   7   19   15   2   Punta   3
                            Fortaleza
2   R "6"   29   34   7   3

6   9   12   19   34   24   4   Fort
                                    San   Caution:
8   35   21   7   Felipe   Many scattered heads
                                    and small patch reefs
11   13   32   35   36   3   pilings   light   awash at high water.
Rio   35   33   Fl ev 6 sec.
San Marcos   9   12   34   35   3   138', 18M   consp.
5   6   28   33   32   tanks

5   6   10   24   34   28   32   3   water
                                            tank
5   6   Commercial   33   33   tower
            Dock
28   24   34   32   27   2   1

4   34   33   25   2

19° 48.00' N   225°m   33   32
                range   7   25
                Fl R
                12M

225°m   4   1   Dominican Republic
range   Puerto Plata
Fl R   Chart #DR-2
12M   consp. tanks   Soundings in feet at MLW

the same today), and they used to have only three rules for those who partook of these tours. One, you had to wear a shirt. Two, you had to wear shoes. And three, you could not fall asleep while on the tour!

In the center of town you can find the *Amber Museum* (Duarte St.) with some of the most remarkable specimens of this gemstone, the designated national gem. The mountains behind Puerto Plata contain the world's richest deposits of amber, a fossilized tree resin. Parts of these same mountains appeared in the movie "Jurassic Park."

A visit to Fort San Felipe, the oldest such structure in the New World will give you a good insight into the history of Puerto Plata. This 16th century fortress was built to resist attack from French and English pirates and was later used as a prison. Today the fortress is a museum filled with interesting memorabilia of the city's past. If you like the Fort in the daylight, wait until you see it all lit up at night. Just past Fort San Felipe is the General Gregorio Luperón Monument.

At nearby Mt. Torres, Loma Isabel de Torres, you might be able to catch a cable car to the 2,600' summit. The cable car closed in 1997 and is scheduled to reopen soon. Atop Isabel de Torres is a statue of "Christ the Redeemer" that looks down on Puerto Plata. At the base of the statue is a gift shop/arcade, a café, botanical gardens, and some fantastic views of the coastline. You can even try to tackle the mountain by horseback, bicycle, and car but be forewarned: the road is next to impassable in spots.

To the west of Puerto Plata is the Costambar resort area, which has not been quite the success that it was originally planned to be. A 9-hole golf course closed in 1997 because of the noise and soot from the power plant. At the eastern end of Puerto Plata is Long Beach, a popular spot with the local crowd but not the tourists who are steered elsewhere for obvious reasons.

Most of the major hotels are located in the Playa Dorada area that lies east of Puerto Plata, about three miles from the airport. This is an impressive beachfront, thoroughly protected by coral reefs, with lovely beaches and great snorkeling. The *Playa Dorada Resort* is the umbrella name for the complex of 14 large hotels with over 3300 rooms, an exceptional golf course designed by Robert Trent Jones, and many other sporting facilities. Many of the resorts in Playa Dorada will not allow a Dominican on the premises, even if you are single and they are in your company. However, many Dominicans go there every weekend anyway to eat, dance, and catch a movie. The resort tends to give a poor review of the surrounding area with the intent of keeping their customers and their money inside the complex. This practice seems to be changing with the help of President Fernandez's tourism policy.

Montellano lies to the east of Playa Dorada, about halfway to Sosúa. Montellano is not a tourist spot so to speak, but it does process most of the sugar cane for the northern coast of the DR and offers tours of its processing plant. For a bit of local flavor you might want to visit Las Brisas on the river, the local bar and disco. A bottle of rum, a bucket of ice, and two sodas will only set you back about U.S. $4.00 and a good time is known to be had by all. Sunday afternoons are their busiest.

If you are not interested in the "all inclusive" attitude at Playa Dorada you might want to try Cofresi Beach, a small, pretty, palm shaded cove that offers a beautiful panoramic view of the rest of Puerto Plata and offers several hotels and cabanas. Most of the hotels offer windsurfing, sailing, water skiing, snorkeling, scuba diving and deep-sea fishing.

About 16 miles east of Puerto Plata, nestled on a hillside above a sheltered cove, is the enchanting village of Sosúa. If you want to get away from the fast paced and touristy Playa Dorada scene, Sosúa is the place for you. Although I have not sounded the harbor for this guide, Bruce Van Sant has a nice sketch chart of it in his Passage's South. Sosúa is actually two villages straddling the bay: Los Charamicos to the west and El Batey to the east. They are not far apart and a walk through and between the two doesn't take long. Los Charamicos, where years ago the plantation workers lived, has a typical Dominican village atmosphere complete with lively restaurants and bars, street vendors, loud music, and screeching chickens. El Batey, the part of town where the plantation owners live, is the hub of tourist activity in Sosúa. Here you'll find upscale restaurants, bars, boutiques, and luxurious resort hotels and villas along with a large ex-pat community. Sosúa is popular with tourists from both North America and Europe because of its lovely beaches and dives sites; the snorkeling here is great. You can even take a taxi here from Puerto Plata and rent snorkel gear if you prefer.

German Jewish refugees founded Sosúa after World War II (then dictator Rafael Trujillo, hoping to gain favor with the U.S., let them in), who started up sausage production and a dairy. Today the town, which has a lively nightlife and an arts community, has become a center for immigrants from North America and Europe. During the Holocaust many European Jews sought refuge as a respite from the atrocities. As history's most infamous massacre was being perpetrated, a small Caribbean nation was to provide a respite from the atrocities. While the world turned its back and remained immersed in apathy, the Dominican Republic bestowed mercy on the oppressed by offering asylum. They settled on tiny Sosúa and the colony became official on January 30, 1940, when the Dominican government and a private philanthropic organization, the *Joint Distribution Committee of New York*, signed the *DORSA* (Dominican Republic Settlement Association) agreement and some 600 settlers moved in. The atmosphere of warm hospitality found in this beautiful yet unfamiliar land was conducive to the flourishing of Jewish-owned businesses. So cordial were the natives that, over the years, the Jews assimilated their culture and co-mingled with them to create genuinely Dominican families where the Jewish traditions were still preserved and respected. What is most remarkable is the fact that after five decades, and despite the changes of government, the passing of generations and the advent of tourism, the spirit of the decree whereby the Jewish were given political asylum has remained untouched. Today, the few remaining Jews enjoy the same consideration, respect and freedom of religion as in the first days of the colony.

Just east of Sosúa is Cabarete, one of the world's top windsurfing spots. In the mid-1980's Cabarete was only an empty beach and a handful of old wooden houses. Then it was discovered to be the best windsurfing location in the Caribbean, and one of the best in the world. Today Cabarete hosts the annual *Windsurfing World Cup*. For music lovers, Cabarete also hosts the *Jazz-Blues Merengue Festival*. On its mile-long main street, you will find a wide selection of windsurfing centers, hotels, restaurants, discos, and gift shops. Further east you'll find even more exotic, secluded beaches such as La Preciosa and Diamante.

A LITTLE BASIC SPANISH

(Just enough to get you into trouble!)

While command of the Spanish language is not a prerequisite for happy cruising in Puerto Rico, knowing a little will certainly help you get by better and everybody will love you for at least trying.

Buenos Dias. Good morning.
Buenas tardes. Good afternoon.
Buenas noches. Good night.
¿Cómo está usted? How are you?
¿Muy bien gracias, y usted? I am fine thank you, and you?
¿Cómo se llama? What is your name?
Me llamo es . . . My name is. . .
¿Habla usted inglés? Do you speak English?
¿Habla usted Español? Do you speak Spanish?
¿Hay alquien aqui que hable inglés? Is there anybody here who speaks English?
No muy bien. Not very well.
Muy poco. Very little.
¿Cómo se dice. . . ? How do you say. . .?
¿Cómo? What did you say?
No entiendo. I don't understand.
Escríbamela, por favor. Please write it down for me.
¿Donde está el. . .? Where is . . .?

anclaje-anchorage	*embarcadero*-wharf, quay
arrecife-reef	*ferretería*-hardware store
bahia-bay	*Immigración*-Immigration
bano- bathroom	*lavandería*-laundry
bajo-shoal	*mecánico*-mechanic
banco-bank	*médico*-doctor
Capitán de Puerto-Harbormaster	*pasaje*-passage
caleta-cove	*punta*-point
canal-channel	*rada*-roadstead
desembarcadero-landing	*supermercado*-supermarket
ducha-shower	*telefono*-telephone

¿Donde puedo comprar . . . ? Where can I buy . . .?
Necesito. . . I need. . .?
¿Tiene usted . . . ? Do you have. . . ?

    agua-water
    agua potable-drinking water
    arroz-rice
    azúcar-sugar
    café-coffee
    camarones-shrimp
    carne-meat
    cebolla-onions
    cerveza-beer
    chillo-snapper
    cigarillos-cigarettes
    ensalada-salad
    fosforos-matches
    fuego-a light
    gasoil-diesel
    gasolina-gasoline
    helado- ice cream
    hielo-ice
    huevos-eggs

jamón-ham
jugo-juice
jugo de naranjas-orange juice
langosta-lobster
leche-milk
limones-limes
mantequilla-butter
mero-sea bass
narnaja-orange
pan-bread
patatas-potatoes
pavo-turkey
pina-pineapple
plátanos-bananas
pollo-chicken
propano-propane
queso-cheese
setas-mushrooms
sopa-soup
té-tea
Tomate-tomato
vino-wine

Colors, Numbers, Directions and Days:

blanco-white	*negro*-black	*azul*-blue	*rojo*-red	*verde*-green
amarillo-yellow	*aquí*-here	*allí*-there	*la derecha*-right	*la izquierda*-left
uno-1	*dos*-2	*tres*-3	*quatro*-4	*cinco*-5
seis-6	*seite*-7	*ocho*-8	*nueve*-9	*diez*-10
once-11	*doce*-12	*trece*-13	*catorce*-14	*quince*-15
diéz y seis-16	*diéz y seite*-17	*diéz y ocho*-18	*diéz y nuevo*-19	*veinte*-20
veinte y uno-21	*treinta*-30	*cuarenta*-40	*cincuenta*-50	*sesenta*-60
setenta-70	*ochenta*-80	*noventa*-90	*cien*-100	*ciento y uno*-101
mil-1,000	*mil uno*-1,001	*lunes*-Monday	*martes*-Tuesday	*miércoles*-Wednesday
juevos-Thursday	*viernos*-Friday	*sábado*-Saturday	*domingo*-Sunday	*ahora*-now
manana- tomorrow				

¿Quién? Who?
¿Qué? What?
¿Cuando? When?
¿Donde? Where?
¿Por qué? Why?
¿Cómo? How?
¿Qué lejos? How far is it?
Está lejos. It's far.
Está cerca. It's near.
¿Qué hora es? What time is it?
¿A qué hora? At what time?
Tengo hambre. I'm hungry.
Perdóneme. Excuse me.

¿Puede ayudarme? Can you help me?
¿Qué es eso? What is this (that)?
¿Cuánto cuesta? What does it cost?
Por favor. Please.
Quisiera... I would like...
Quiero... I want...
comer-to eat
lo mejor-the best
un habitacion a room
Dame éste. Give me this one.
Dame eso. Give me that one.
No tengo dinero. I have no money.
¡No se mueva! Don't move!
¡Manos arriba! Put your hands up!

REFERENCES
AND
SUGGESTED READING

Blake, Julia. *Turks and Caicos Pocket Guide*: Domy Graphix Ltd., 1997

Botting, Douglas. *The Pirates*: Time-Life Books, Alexandria, VA, 1978

Boultbee, Paul G. *Turks and Caicos Islands*: World Bibliographical Series, Vol. 137, Clio Press, Oxford U.K./ABC Clio, Santa Barbara, CA, U.S.A.

Bowditch, Nathaniel. *The American Practical Navigator*: LL.D., DMA Hydrographic Center, 1977

Campbell, David G. *The Ephemeral Islands, A Natural History of the Bahamas*: Macmillan Education, 1990

Craton, Michael. *A History of the Bahamas*: San Salvador Press, Ontario, Canada, 1986

Defoe, Daniel (Capt. Charles Johnson). *A General History of the Robberies and Murders of the Most Notorious Pirates*: Routledge and Kegan Paul, Ltd., London, 1955

Ellms, Charles. *The Pirates Own Book*: A. & C. B. Edwards, New York, and Thomas Cowperthwait & Co., Philadelphia, 1842

Esquemelin, A.O. *The Buccaneers of the Americas*: George Rutledge & Sons, London, 1893

Fields, Meredith. *The Yachtsman's Guide to the Bahamas*: Tropic Isle Publishing, annual

Fuson, Robert H. *The Log of Christopher Columbus*: Tab Books, Blue Ridge Summit, PA, 1987

Gascoine, Capt. Bob. *Diving, Snorkeling, & Visitors Guide to the Turks and Caicos Islands*: Graphic Reproductions, Miami, FL, 1991

Gosse, Phillip. *The Pirates Who's Who*: Rio Grande Press, 1988

Hart, Jerrems C. and William T. Stone. *A Cruising Guide to the Caribbean and the Bahamas*: Dodd, Mead and Company, New York, 1982

Hendrickson, Robert. *The Ocean Almanac*: Robert Hendrickson, Doubleday, New York, 1984

Hutchings, C.D. *The Story of the Turks and Caicos Islands*: 1977

Innes, Brian. *The Book of Pirates*: Bancroft and Co., Ltd., 1966

Jaggers, Tony. *A Shipwreck Guide to the Bahamas and the Turks and Caicos, Vol. I*: American Southern Printing, Sarasota, FL, 1994

Las Casas, Fray Bartolomé de. *The Diario of Christopher Columbus' First Voyage to the Americas, 1492-1493*: Translated by Oliver Dunn and James E. Kelley Jr., Norman: University of Oklahoma Press, 1989

Lee, Robert E. and John Blair. *Blackbeard the Pirate*: Winston-Salem, NC, 1974

Marvel, Josiah. *A History of the Turks and Caicos:* unpublished monograph

Marvel, Josiah and Leonora Harvey Missick. *An Essay on the Constitutional History of the Turks & Caicos Islands*: unpublished monograph

Marx, Jennifer. *Pirates and Privateers of the Caribbean*: Krieger Publishing Company, Malabar, FL, 1992

Pavlidis, Stephen J. *On and Off the Beaten Path, The Central and Southern Bahamas Guide*: Seaworthy Publications, Inc., Port Washington, WI, 2002

Pavlidis, Stephen J. *The Exuma Guide, A Cruising Guide to the Exuma Cays, 2nd Edition*: Seaworthy Publications, Inc., Port Washington, Inc. WI, 2002

Pavlidis, Stephen J. *The Abaco Guide*: Seaworthy Publications, Port Washington, WI, 2002

Pavlidis, Stephen J. with Ray Darville. *A Cruising Guide to the Exumas Cays Land and Sea Park*: Night Flyer Enterprises, U.S.A., 1994

Popov, Nicolas and Dragan. *Island Expedition, The Central and Southern Bahamas*: Graphic Media, Miami, FL, 1988

Popov, Nicolas and Dragan. *The Bahamas Rediscovered*: Macmillan Press, London, 1992

Rigg, J. Linton. *Bahama Islands: A Boatman's Guide to the Land and Water*: Scribner, NY, 1949

Sadler, Herbert E. *Turks Islands Landfall, Vol. 1-7*: Grand Turk

Sailing Directions For the Caribbean Sea: Pub. #147, Defense Mapping Agency, #SDPUB147

Seyfarth, Fritz. *Pirates of the Virgin Islands*: Spanish Main Press, St. Thomas, USVI, 1988

Smithers, Amelia. *The Turks and Caicos Islands, Lands of Discovery*: Macmillan Education, London, Second Edition, 1995

Van Sant, Bruce. *The Gentleman's Guide to Passages South, 6th Ed.*: Cruising Guide Publications, 1998

Whipple, Addison B.C. *Pirate Rascals of the Spanish Main*: Doubleday and Co., New York, 1957

Woodbury, George. *The Great Days of Piracy in the West Indies*: W.W. Norton and Co.

APPENDICES

APPENDIX A: Navigational Aids

A-1: Lights

Navigational lights in The Turks and Caicos Islands should be considered unreliable at best. Their characteristics may differ from those published here and are subject to change without notice. It is not unusual for a light to be out of commission for long periods of time; for example. Latitude is North and longitude is West. Positions are approximate. Listing of lights is from north to south. Please note that due to the efforts of Beryl Nelson of Providenciales, North West Point Light on Providenciales is now working after years of disrepair. Also note that the light at the eastern end of Providenciales as moved from Crist Point to Bird Cay.

LIGHT	CHARACTERISTIC	HT.	RNG.
THE CAICOS ISLANDS			
North West Point, Provo	Gp Fl (3) W ev 15 sec		14M
Providenciales, Bird Cay	Fl W ev 10 sec		12M
Cape Comete, E. Caicos	Gp Fl (2) W ev 20 sec		12M
West Caicos, SW Point	Q R	52'	
French Cay	Fl R	10'	
South Caicos*	Fxd W	50'	9M
Long Cay, east end	Fl R ev 2.5 sec		5M
Dove Cay, west end	Fl G ev 2.5 sec		5M
Bush Cay	Gp Fl (2) W ev 10 sec		14M
THE TURKS ISLANDS			
Grand Turk Lighthouse***	Fl W ev 7.5 sec	108'	6M
Head of S. Dock-front***	2Fl W & R ev 3 sec	20'	3M
Head of S. Dock-rear	Fl ev 3 sec	30'	3M
Salt Cay, NW Point	Gp Fl (4) W ev 20 sec		8M
Great Sand Cay	Fl W ev 2 sec	85'	10M
DOMINICAN REPUBLIC			
Luperón-head of dock	Gp. Fl R ev 10 sec ****	30'	3M
Puerto Plata-sea buoy	Fl R		
Puerto Plata "LV-1"	Fl G		
Punta Fortaleza	Fl W, ev 6 sec	138'	8M
Puerto Plata Range	Fl R, 12M *****		

* Visible 180° - 90°
** There is also a Fl R, 3M S, and a Fl W 1.1M S.
*** This is a synchronized range light on a bearing of 084°.
**** Not seen from outside the harbour.
***** This is a synchronized range light on a bearing of 084°.

A-2: Towers

LOCATION	LIGHT	HT.
Providenciales: CAW*	Fxd R	260'
Providenciales: CAW	Fxd R	70'
Middle Caicos: CAW	Fxd R	260'
South Caicos: N end	Fl R	480'
South Caicos: CAW	Fxd R	260'
Grand Turk: NE Point	Fxd R	
Grand Turk: CAW	Fxd R	260'
Grand Turk: S end, FAA	Fxd R	
Grand Turk: S end twins	Fxd R	

* Cable and wireless antenna towers: all are red and white striped and have a cut-off, stumpy appearance, they do not end in a needle-like spire.

APPENDIX B: MARINAS

Some of the marinas listed below may be untenable in certain winds. Dockside depths listed may not reflect entrance channel depths at low water. Check with the dockmaster prior to arrival. All the marinas can handle your garbage disposal problems, however some may levy a charge per bag for those who are not guests at their docks. For cruisers seeking services 'Nearby' may mean either a walk or short taxi ride away.

MARINA	FUEL	SLIPS	DEPTH	GROCERIES	DINING
TURKS AND CAICOS					
Providenciales					
Caicos Marina & Boatyard	D & G	24	6'-8'	No	No
Leeward Marina	D & G	1	8'	Nearby	Yes
South Side Basin Marina	D & G	10	7'	No	No
Turtle Cove Marina	D & G	40	6'	Nearby	Yes
South Caicos					
Sea View Marina	D & G	3	7'	Yes	Nearby
Grand Turk					
Flamingo Cove	D	*	5'	No	No
Salt Cay					
Deane's Dock	**	***	4'	Nearby	Nearby
DOMINICAN REPUBLIC					
Luperón					
Puerto Blanco Marina	None	7-8	7'	Nearby	Yes

* Small boats and dinghies only
** Diesel and gas is available from Nathan Smith's next to dock.
*** Deane's Dock has walls to tie to and draft is restricted to less than 4' inside at MLW, check with Salt Cay Divers on VHF ch. 16 before entry.

APPENDIX C: SERVICE FACILITIES

As with any place, businesses come and go, sometimes seemingly overnight. Certain entries on this list may no longer exist by the time this is published. Listings in the Dominican Republic are listed by city and then "DR". All listings in the Turks and Caicos are area code (649) while locations in the DR are area code (809).

FACILITY	LOCATION	TEL. #	E-MAIL ADDRESS
CAR RENTALS			
Avis	Providenciales	946-4705	*avis@provo.net*
Avis: airport	Puerto Plata, DR	586-0285	
Avis: Ave. Luperón	Puerto Plata, DR	586-1366	
Budget	Providenciales	946-4079	*budget@tciway.tc*
Dutchie's Car Rental	Grand Turk	946-2244	
Estelvina Felipe (Dentist)	Luperón, DR		
Hertz-airport	Puerto Plata, DR	586-0200	
Island Rent a Car	Providenciales	946-4475	
Kalola's Car Rentals	Puerto Plata, Sosúa, DR		
Lucke Car/Jeep Rental-airport	Puerto Plata, DR	568-0217	
Middle Caicos Rentals	Middle Caicos	946-6185	
National: airport	Puerto Plata, DR	586-0285	
National: Ave. Luperón	Puerto Plata, DR	586-1366	
Nelly Rent a Car: airport	Puerto Plata, DR	586-0505	
Old Nick Rental Cars	North Caicos	946-7284	
Pat Hamilton	North Caicos	946-7141	
Payless Car Rental	Puerto Plata, DR	729-5377*	
Preferred Car Rental	Providenciales	941-3782	*PreferredCar@tciway.tc*
Provo Rent a Car	Providenciales	946-4404	*RentACar@provo.net*
Rent a Buggy	Providenciales	946-4158	*reservations@tciway.tc*
Scooter Bob's (Turtle Cove)	Providenciales	946-4684	

Sea View Marina	South Caicos		
Sierra Rent a Car	Bottle Creek, North Caicos	946-7317	
Sunrise Auto Rental	Providenciales	946-4705	
Sunshine Auto Leasing	Airport, Grand Turk	946-1588	
T&C National Car Rental	Providenciales	946-4701	
Thrifty Car Rental	Puerto Plata	586-3418	
Thrifty Car Rental	Sosúa, DR	571-2215	
Tropical Auto Rental	Grand Turk	946-2095	
Tropical Auto Rental	Providenciales	946-5300	*Tropical@provo.net*

DIESEL REPAIR

Caicos Marina & Boatyard	Providenciales	946-5600	*caicosmarinashp@tciway.tc*
Caribbean Marine Diesel	South Side Basin, Provo	941-5903	
George Nixon	Providenciales	946-5763	
MPL Enterprises	Grand Turk	946-2227	
Percy Tolbert	Salt Cay		
Persio Núñez-Núñez & Núñez	Santiago, DR	582-8202	
Sea View Marina	South Caicos		

ELECTRONICS-MARINE

Walkin Marine	Providenciales

HAULOUT

Caicos Marina & Boatyard	Providenciales	946-5600	*caicosmarinashp@tciway.tc*

HULL REPAIR/PAINTING

Caicos Marina & Boatyard	Providenciales	946-5600	*caicosmarinashp@tciway.tc*

INTERNET ACCESS

Banana Boat (Turtle Cove)	Providenciales		
Cable & Wireless	Providenciales		
Provocom, Ltd. (Ports of Call)	Providenciales	946-5624	*provcom@tciway.tc*
Tcionline (Ports of Call)	Providenciales	941-4711	

MACHINE SHOPS

Núñez & Núñez	Santiago, DR	582-2200
Tibor's	Providenciales	941-5802

MARINE SUPPLIES

Luperón Marine Supplies	Luperón, DR	
MPL Enterprises	Grand Turk	946-2227
Walkin Marine	Providenciales	946-4411

OUTBOARD REPAIR

MPL Enterprises	Grand Turk	946-2227
Sea View Marina	South Caicos	
Walkin Marine	Providenciales	946-4411

SAIL REPAIR

Gil's Island Craft	Providenciales	941-5851

TAXIS AND BUSES

Cardinal Arthur	Conch Bar, Middle Caicos	946-6107
Carlin Forbes	Bambarra, Middle Caicos	946-6115
Ernest Forbes	Bambarra, Middle Caicos	946-6140
Gardiner's Taxi	North Caicos	
Glinton's Taxi	South Caicos	
Headly Forbes	Bambarra, Middle Caicos	946-6109
Henley's Cab Service	Grand Turk	946-2331
Hillside Taxi	South Caicos	946-3284
Hormel Harvey	Conch Bar, Middle Caicos	946-6101
Jack Williams Taxi	Grand Turk	946-2239
Lightbourne Taxi	South Caicos	

Morris Bus	Providenciales	
Nell's Taxi Service	Providenciales	941-3228
Paradise Taxi	Providenciales	941-3555
Provo Taxi U Bus Group	Providenciales	946-5481
Rosemary's Taxi	Grand Turk	941-0704
Sand Dollar Tours	Grand Turk	946-2018
Teddy "Nathan" Smith	Salt Cay	946-6928
Wee 10 Base	South Caicos	

* *This is an 800 number and can be dialed from the U.S.*

APPENDIX D: GPS WAYPOINTS

Caution: GPS Waypoints are not to be used for navigational purposes. GPS waypoints are intended to place you in the general area of the described position. All routes, cuts, and anchorages must be negotiated by eyeball navigation. The author and publisher take no responsibility for the misuse of the following GPS waypoints. Waypoints along any tight passage offer a false sense of security and any navigator who uses waypoints to negotiate a tricky passage instead of piloting by eye is, to be blunt, a fool and deserving of whatever fate befalls him or her.

Waypoints are listed from north to south. Latitude is 'North' and longitude is 'West.'

#	DESCRIPTION	Latitude	Longitude
	THE BAHAMAS		
1.	Northwest Point - 1½ nm W of light	22° 27.10'	73° 09.90'
2.	Abraham's Bay - eastern entrance between the reefs	22° 21.07'	72° 58.45'
3.	Start Bay - ½ nm SW of best holding	22° 20.30'	73° 05.30'
4.	Abraham's Bay - ¼ nm SSE of eastern entrance	22° 20.80'	72° 58.30'
5.	Abraham's Bay - ¼ nm SW of western entrance	22° 19.25'	73° 03.40'
6.	Southeast Point - 1 nm WSW of anchorage	22° 16.70'	72° 48.40'
	THE CAICOS ISLANDS		
7.	Ft. George Cut - ½ nm NW of cut	21° 53.70'	72° 07.90'
8.	North West Point, Providenciales - ½ nm N of reef in deep water	21° 53.10'	72° 19.90'
9.	Wheeland Cut - ½ NNE of cut	21° 52.65'	72° 17.65'
10.	Leeward Cut - ½ nm NW of cut	21° 50.40'	72° 10.40'
11.	Malcolm Roadstead - ½ nm W of Tiki Huts	21° 49.85'	72° 20.80'
12.	Stubb's Cut - ¼ nm NW of cut	21° 48.93'	72° 11.30'
13.	Wiley Cut - ¼ nm NNW of cut	21° 48.85'	72° 21.35'
14.	Leeward Going Through - S entrance, ¼ nm ESE of Bird Rock	21° 48.60'	72° 07.30'
15.	Sellar's Cut - ½ nm N of cut	21° 48.40'	72° 12.40'
16.	Jacksonville Cut, East Caicos	21° 47.10'	71° 34.90'
17.	Deep water on Banks for shortcut to Leeward	21° 45.50'	72° 07.00'
18.	Cooper Jack Bight - ½ nm SW of entrance to Discovery Bay	21° 45.05'	72° 14.00'
19.	Turning point to Boatyard - 1 mile SSE of entrance channel	21° 44.80'	72° 10.30'
20.	Sandbore Channel - ¾ nm W of entrance	21° 44.50'	72° 27.25'
21.	Sapodilla Bay - ¼ nm S of anchorage	21° 44.25'	72° 17.40'
22.	Bay Cay - 1 nm ESE of, beginning of route to Boatyard	21° 43.75'	72° 14.00'
23.	West Caicos, Clear Sand Road - ¾ nm S of Southwest Point	21° 36.75'	72° 29.00'
24.	Freighter Channel - SW waypoint	21° 35.75'	72° 23.25'
25.	French Cay - ½ nm W of anchorage	21° 30.60'	72° 12.70'
26.	Starfish Channel	21° 30.25'	72° 06.75'
27.	French Cay - ¾ SW of anchorage on edge of Caicos Bank	21° 29.75'	72° 12.65'
28.	South Caicos, Cockburn Harbour - ¼ nm SE of entrance	21° 28.70'	71° 31.70'
29.	Long Cay Cut - ½ nm NW of cut and anchorage area	21° 27.40'	71° 34.75'
30.	Long Cay Cut - ½ nm SE of cut in Columbus Passage	21° 26.55'	71° 34.15'
31.	Fish Cays - ¾ nm N of	21° 23.50'	71° 37.25'

#	DESCRIPTION	Latitude	Longitude
32.	West Sand Spit - 2 nm SW of	21° 20.50'	72° 10. 05'
33.	Big Ambergris Cay - 1 nm NW of anchorage	21° 19.75'	71° 39.75'
	THE TURKS ISLANDS		
34.	Grand Turk, North Creek - ¼ nm N of entrance channel at jetty	21° 31.10'	71 ° 08.50'
35.	Grand Turk, Front Street anchorage - ¼ nm W of break in reef	21° 28.13'	71° 09. 13'
36.	Grand Turk, South Dock - ¼ nm WSW of end of dock	21° 25.90'	71° 09.20'
37.	Big Cut - ¼ nm NW of	21° 24.60'	71° 09.25'
38.	Salt Cay - ¼ nm W of Deane's Dock	21° 19.90'	71° 13.25'
39.	Salt Cay - ¾ SW of S end, waypoint to take up course to DR	21° 17.60'	71° 14. 10'
40.	Great Sand Cay - ½ nm W of anchorage in West Bay	21° 11.65'	71° 15. 50'
41.	Great Sand Cay - ¾ SW of S end, waypoint to take up course to DR	21° 10.80'	71° 15. 50'
	THE DOMINICAN REPUBLIC	**Latitude**	**Longitude**
42.	Luperón - 1 nm N of entrance channel	19° 55.50'	70° 56.50'
43.	Puerto Plata - ¾ nm N of sea buoy	19° 49.10'	70° 41.55'

APPENDIX E: LISTING OF PROTECTED AREAS IN THE TURKS AND CAICOS

HISTORICAL SITES:
Caicos Islands: Boiling Hole on South Caicos; Cheshire Hall ruins on Providenciales; Fort George Cay; Molasses Reef Wreck; Sapodilla Hill and West Harbour Bluff Rock Carvings on Providenciales.
Turks Islands: Salt Cay; the wreck of *H.M.S. Endymion* south of Big Sand Cay.

NATIONAL PARKS:
Caicos Islands: Admiral Cockburn Land and Sea Park at South Caicos; the Conch Bar Caves on Middle Caicos; the East Bay Islands off North Caicos; Fort George Land and Sea Park at Fort George Cay; Princess Alexandra on Providenciales; Chalk Sound on Providenciales; North West Point Marine Park on Providenciales; West Caicos Marine Park on West Caicos.
Turks Islands: Grand Turk Cays Land and Sea Park; Columbus Landfall on Grand Turk; South Creek on Grand Turk.

NATURE RESERVES:
Caicos Islands: Belle Sound and Admiral Cockburn Cays at South Caicos; Vine Point (Man O' War Bush) and Ocean Hole at Middle Caicos; Cottage Pond on North Caicos; Pumpkin Bluff Pond on North Caicos; Dick Hill Creek and Bellefield Landing Pond on North Caicos; the Princess Alexandra Nature Reserve consisting of Little Water Cay, Mangrove Cay, and Donna Cay; North West Point Pond on Providenciales; Pigeon Pond and Frenchman's Creek on Providenciales; Lake Catherine on West Caicos.

PROTECTED BUILDINGS:
North Caicos: The ruins of Wade's Green and the Bellefield Plantation.
East Caicos: The ruins of the Jacksonville Plantation.
West Caicos: The ruins at Yankee Town.
South Caicos: DC's House and the Salt Sheds and Salt Works.
Grand Turk: Guinep Tree Lodge (The National Museum); Police Station; Turk's Head Inn; Miss Wood's House; the Government House and the Governor's Mansion (Waterloo House); the Prison.

RAMSAR SITE:
The wetlands on the southern side of North, Middle and East Caicos are of international importance and is afforded protection under the RAMSAR Convention, an international treaty.

SANCTUARIES:
Caicos Islands: Three Mary's Cays; French Cay; Seal Cays; Bush Cay.
Turks Islands: Big Sand Cay; Long Cay.

UNESCO HERITAGE SITE:
Salt Cay.

APPENDIX F: LOGARITHMIC SPEED SCALE

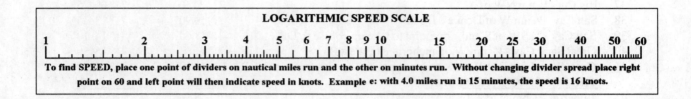

APPENDIX G: DEPTH CONVERSION SCALE

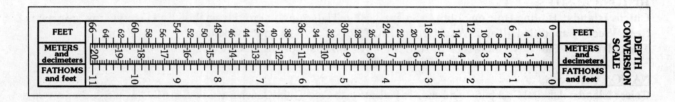

APPENDIX H: METRIC CONVERSION TABLE

Visitors to the Turks and Caicos Islands will find the metric system in use and many grocery items and fuel measured in liters and kilograms. As a rule of thumb, a meter is just a little longer than a yard and a liter is very close to a quart. If in doubt use the following table.

1 centimeter (cm) = 0.4 inch	1 inch = 2.54 cm
1 meter (m) = 3.28 feet	1 foot = 0.31 m
1 m = 0.55 fathoms	1 fathom = 1.83 m
1 kilometer (km) = 0.62 nm	1 yard = 0.93 m
1 km = 0.54 nautical nm	1 nautical mile = 1.852 km
1 liter (l) = 0.26 gallons	1 gallon = 3.75 l
1 gram (g) = 0.035 ounce	1 ounce = 28.4 g
1 metric ton (t) = 1.1 tons U.S.	1 pound = 454 g

About the Author

Stephen J. Pavlidis has been cruising and living in The Bahamas aboard his 40' sloop *IV Play* since the winter of 1989. In January of 1990, he began cruising and living in the Exumas where he met Ray Darville, the new Warden of the Exuma Cays Land and Sea Park in February of 1993. Ray soon drew him into a working relationship with the Park as a volunteer Deputy Warden. In this role he quickly gained an intimate knowledge of the waters of the Exumas.

Realizing that The Exuma Cays Land and Sea Park deserved a bit more recognition than is given in even the best guides to the area, he and Ray produced *A Cruising Guide to the Exuma Cays Land and Sea Park.* The favorable response to that publication in turn led to *The Exuma Guide*. The excellent response to that work has in turn led to the complete coverage of the remainder of the Bahamas in *On and Off the Beaten Path, A Guide to the Central and Southern Bahamas*, and *The Abaco Guide* which covers the Abacos and Grand Bahama. While cruising the Southern Bahamas, Steve began to frequent the Turks and Caicos Islands. Steve fell in love with South Caicos and through exploration, discovered that the entire island group offered much more to the visiting boater than the sparse coverage given by other publications would lead one to believe.

Dwight Outten

Dwight Outten was born on May 21, 1972 on Middle Caicos and started painting with acrylics on canvas while attending high school on the island of Grand Turk. It was here that Dwight was encouraged to continue by his art teacher, Ianthe Williams, herself a well known Turks and Caicos artist. In early 1990, Dwight moved to Providenciales and began working for the local telephone company. He soon made his first contact with the Bamboo Gallery and had his first solo show in December of 1990. Since that time Dwight Outten has participated in several group and solo shows throughout the U.S. and the Caribbean. In 1992, Dwight won the first prize at "Carib Art," in an *All-Caribbean Art* contest sponsored by *UNESCO*. Dwight's work has been featured in galleries in the West Indies, the United States, and Europe and he has been written up several international publications such as *Islands Magazine*. Dwight's themes are mostly Turks and Caicos landscapes as well as compositions inspired by the animal world of the Turks and Caicos Islands. His Caicos flamingos are his trademark.

Phillip Outten

Phillip Outten, no relation to Dwight but also a young artist at 33, hails from Grand Turk though he now lives on Provo. During his early 20's Phillip spent several years travelling the Turks and Caicos Islands and the U.S. He returned and formed a dance group and then realized his ambition to paint. He received support from several friends in the Turks and Caicos Islands and later refined his technique under the direction of Nina Chandler at the *Alliance of Arts* in Ft. Meyers, Florida. Phillip had his first solo show at the *Bamboo Gallery* in Provo in 1994 and has since exhibited his works in shows throughout the Turks and Caicos and Florida.

Phillip works with acrylics on canvas and his early works reflected his dreams and the unconscious. They displayed a rhythmic line and color palette that has been said to be reminiscent of Gaugin. Phillip often used water scenes in these early works as he considered it an essential life force symbolic of wealth and good fortune. Phillip, a Rastafarian, looks to his faith for inspiration and says his art reflects his meditation and places he wants to be. Over the years Phillip's style has matured and his current works are based on realism and the colors are more subtle.

Today Phillip has expanded his artistic output with carvings and he shares his time, knowledge, and experience with students at Leeward's *Ashcroft School.*

INDEX